IMPERMANENT BLACKNESS

Impermanent Blackness

THE MAKING AND UNMAKING OF
INTERRACIAL LITERARY CULTURE
IN MODERN AMERICA

KOREY GARIBALDI

PRINCETON UNIVERSITY PRESS

PRINCETON & OXFORD

Published by Princeton University Press
41 William Street, Princeton, New Jersey 08540
99 Banbury Road, Oxford OX2 6JX

press.princeton.edu

All Rights Reserved

ISBN 978-0-691-21190-9
ISBN (e-book) 978-0-691-24512-6

British Library Cataloging-in-Publication Data is available

Editorial: Anne Savarese and James Collier
Production Editorial: Kathleen Cioffi
Jacket Design: Katie Osborne
Production: Erin Suydam
Publicity: Jodi Price and Carmen Jimenez
Copyeditor: Elisabeth A. Graves

Jacket image: Macro of folded book signatures by Keira McKee / Alamy Stock Photo

This book has been composed in Arno

Printed on acid-free paper. ∞

Printed in the United States of America

10 9 8 7 6 5 4 3 2 1

For my mom

Students, to you 'tis giv'n to scan the heights
Above, to traverse the ethereal space,
And mark the systems of revolving worlds.

—PHILLIS WHEATLEY, "TO THE
UNIVERSITY OF CAMBRIDGE,
IN NEW-ENGLAND" (1773)

Not wholly this or that,
But wrought
Of alien bloods am I,
A product of the interplay
Of traveled hearts.
Estranged, yet not estranged, I stand
All comprehending;
From my estate
I view earth's frail dilemma;
Scion of fused strength am I,
All understanding,
Nor this nor that
Contains me.

—GEORGIA DOUGLAS JOHNSON,
"COSMOPOLITE" (1922)

CONTENTS

IMPERMANENT BLACKNESS

Introduction

FEW PEOPLE REMEMBER the best-selling Black author of the twentieth century: Frank Yerby. Six months after the publication of Yerby's *The Foxes of Harrow* (1946), a historical romance set on an antebellum plantation near New Orleans, the novel became the first book written by a Black author to sell more than a million copies. In early 1947, the Associated Negro Press reported that a nationwide poll, administered by Harlem's Schomburg Collection of Negro Literature of the New York Public Library, had named Yerby as one of a dozen African Americans who had "done the most for the improvement of race relations 'in terms of real democracy'" in the previous year.[1] A few months later, *Foxes* became the first Black-authored book adapted into a film by a major Hollywood studio, after 20th Century Fox paid Yerby $150,000 for the story, or nearly $2 million in today's dollars.[2] By 1949, the *Chicago Defender* predicted that the zeitgeist in Hollywood films heralded many more empowered, dynamic portrayals of Black Americans. The *Defender's* estimates for the future also pointed to the adaptation of Yerby's *Foxes* as "the first of the current movie wave" to initiate the trend.[3]

The Washington Post praised Yerby as a "gifted Negro writer," albeit one who had written "two propaganda novels which were turned down by publishers." This journalist affirmed that instead of giving up, Yerby found a way to revisit "his original serious intention of bolstering the Negro cause" through melodramatic historical novels, "which book buyers will read, liberally laced with a message."[4] On the eve of the Cold War, Yerby was considered a prominent example of an African American who advanced "interracial understanding, mutual respect and co-operation between the colored and white races."[5] Although Yerby became an exceptionally visible and successful Black author in mid-century America, today he is virtually unknown. How could this be?

Yerby's career, cultural inspirations, and professional relationships represent a forgotten era of interracial literary culture that is the focus of this book.[6] While the term *interracial* is not as familiar as it once was, this was how contemporaries often described cross-racial collaborations and cultural influences for much of the twentieth century.

During and after the 1960s Civil Rights Movement, *interracial* typically referred to sex or romance across racial lines. In the preceding decades, however, racially progressive authors and critics used the term *interracial* to describe a broad range of cultural interactions and literary texts. Books, plays, and other works by Black authors that enjoyed critical and commercial success with readers and audiences across the color line were also perceived as interracial and were credited for promoting cross-racial thinking and habits.

Yerby's success was exceptional, but his absence from literary and cultural history is emblematic of broader elisions in American—rather than exclusively African American—letters. Dozens of Black writers and literary professionals were once at the forefront of America's publishing business, carving out new ways to fit into the literary field. These Black authors were highly accomplished editors and publishers, in addition to maintaining other roles that frequently intersected, and they forged innumerable forgotten partnerships with white peers.

Led by Black writers and publishers, the best writing and collaborations of this understudied tradition challenged inequitable, separatist, and exclusionary conventions in the mainstream publishing trade. But as calls and demands for racial integration in American society competed with rallying cries and action plans for Black Power during the 1960s, positive assessments of the term *interracial* and interracialism declined. Changes were made possible by interracialism, but they often appeared small, and working across racial lines in the twentieth century was frequently tense. In 1959, W.E.B. Du Bois remarked: "If one were not careful, an interracial meeting would be an interracial fight."[7] Around the same time, James Baldwin, in a letter to Lorraine Hansberry, divulged that his novel in progress, which was later published as *Another Country* (1962), was a "grim interracial drama."[8] In another example, in 1967, a typical Black commentary on race riots in Detroit posited: "The phrase 'black power' which cropped up early and disappeared of its own inappropriateness, really had no emotional force in an atmosphere of interracial looting, interracial vandalism, interracial incendiarism and interracial sniping."[9] Without question, this is a grim conception of interracialism. Yet negative and fraught uses of the term in the 1960s were by no means new.

FIGURE 0.1. *Strange Barriers* (New York: Lion Library, 1955), an anthology of short stories by Thomas Wolfe, Frank Yerby, William Faulkner, Richard Wright, Ann Petry, and other writers, edited by J. Vernon Shea, was one of numerous attempts at mid-century to challenge the "strange barriers" that segregated Americans of different races from one another. Cover art by Clark Hulings.

Fear of social and cultural interracialism in American life contributed to the rise of anti-Black rhetoric after the Civil War. The most well-known examples of interracial print culture before, during, and after the Civil War included auto-biographies by the formerly enslaved, including prolific Black authors such as Frederick Douglass and a host of others.[10] From the 1860s onward, however, the widespread belief, especially among white people, that humans could and should be classified into separate "races" based on immutable traits passed on through generations was used to justify eugenics, racial separatism, and many other forms of prejudice and exclusion. In short, racial mixing was perceived as a threat to the alleged superiority of the white race and the prospect of white nationalism.

Between the turn of the century and the mid-1960s, a growing number of Black authors and cultural professionals responded to these biases with bold proclamations that the United States was their country as well. It was the norm for ambitious Black writers and publications to attack cultural barriers between races and ethnicities, and many intellectuals, artists, media firms, reading communities, and cultural professionals refused to see American literary culture in racially discrete terms.

Impermanent Blackness traces a long history of challenges to racist standards in the predominantly white publishing business throughout the twentieth century, facilitated by Americans of all races at the top of their fields. I focus on the many Black writers, editors, and others who contributed to these efforts but who have been forgotten, overlooked, or simply taken for granted. Once perceived or labeled as "interracial" or "integrationists," they pushed the boundaries of what Black writing was and what counted as "American" and "African American" literature.

Before the late 1910s, supporters and enemies alike considered the Black poet, editor, and critic W. S. Braithwaite (1878–1962) the finest and most influential anthologist in the United States. As Jessie Fauset, the novelist and literary editor of the NAACP's *Crisis* magazine, wrote in 1920: "Every person in this country who is interested in poetry has the latest Braithwaite Anthology in his library, and many poets who scorned the early efforts of [this] Negro lad are now standing on tip-toe to know whether he will include their work in his book."[11] Fauset was not exaggerating. When *The Crisis* noted Braithwaite's death decades later, the obituary stated that "most of his readers know that the compiler of the annual *Anthology of Magazine Verse* (1913–1929) was a Negro" and that he "was one of the few American Negro artists who realized that art knows no color line."[12] Braithwaite's loyal readers would have known him as one of the most acclaimed interracialists of his generation.

National Association for the Advancement of Colored People

WILLIAM STANLEY BEAUMONT BRAITHWAITE, Fourth Spingarn Medalist; born in Boston, Mass., December 6, 1878. He is the author of two volumes of verse, three anthologies of English poetry and five anthologies of American magazine verse. He is the most prominent critic of poetry in America.

73

FIGURE 0.2. W. S. Braithwaite was awarded the NAACP's fourth Spingarn Medal for outstanding achievement by an African American, as announced in *The Crisis*, July 1918.

Discussing this unifying vision that launched his career in an essay on "contemporary" Black poets written for *The Crisis* back in 1919, Braithwaite proclaimed: "All great artists are interracial and international in rendering in the medium of any particular art the fundamental passions and the primary instincts of humanity."[13] Skeptics and rivals such as Claude McKay scoffed: "In Braithwaite's writings there was not the slightest indication of what sort of

American he might be. And I was surprised one day to read in the Negro magazine, *The Crisis*, that he was a colored man."[14] When McKay asserted that Braithwaite's literary work was not Black enough for his tastes (or intuition), he failed to note, or chose to ignore, that this "colored man" had mentored, promoted, and published scores of aspiring Black writers in an era when others refused to. Decades later, countless African Americans took McKay's criticism at face value, further calling into question Braithwaite's insistence years earlier that he was building support for cultural unity across the United States.[15]

In the twenty-first century, interracial print culture and networks are primarily associated with the Harlem Renaissance of the 1920s far more than any other decade or period. George Hutchinson's landmark book *The Harlem Renaissance in Black and White* (1995) was the first major study of the Harlem Renaissance to make a case for the cultural power of interracialism between the 1910s and mid-1930s.[16] More recently, several major historiographies and literary studies have shed new light on the remarkably complex racial, transnational, and chronological dimensions of the Harlem Renaissance.[17]

Despite an impressive corpus of scholarship on the first quarter of the twentieth century, however, histories of Black and interracial authorship, literary work, and institutional support before—and after—the 1920s are less well known.[18] As the literary scholar Daylanne K. English has observed, the enormous influence of this period demands an awareness of how it has been constructed: "I do not wish to argue that there was no cultural flowering during the 1920s. But I do want to suggest that there is a contemporary academic selection process at work whereby the Harlem Renaissance often emerges as the most compelling moment in the history of African American culture."[19] Rethinking and traversing commonly accepted literary categories and chronologies helps clarify the ambitions of scores of published Black authors who defied racial assumptions and expectations in their published work. *Impermanent Blackness* interrogates how cultural labels (e.g., the Harlem Renaissance) are established, by looking critically at the writers and editors who wanted to create an equitable print culture, unbound by the limits and constraints of Jim Crow.

In the first issue of the Chicago-based magazine *The Champion* (1916–1917), for example, the editor, Black poet Fenton Johnson, wrote, "We realize that it is not possible to bring about a literary Renaissance by holding ourselves aloof from those aspiring, nor can we gain results by publishing [material] which does not measure up to [this] standard."[20] A few months later, Johnson boasted: "America is at her highest poetic level, a renaissance due to both the Great War

FIGURE 0.3. *The Favorite Magazine* (Autumn 1920) was edited and published by Fenton Johnson.

and her social growth, but the world would not be aware of this condition if it were not for these [annual] Braithwaite anthologies."[21] In *The Champion* and other short-lived publications, Johnson enthusiastically encouraged "the reconciliation of the races."

Even during the Great Depression, Black authors employed by Chicago's Federal Writers' Project published a popular, meticulously produced pamphlet entitled *Cavalcade of the American Negro* (1940), assuring their diverse readership that cultural segregation was waning: "A co-operative program of interracial action is in process of realization through the furtherance of mutual acquaintanceship and mutual understanding of the common interests."[22] As the literary historian Liesl Olson writes: "Interracial collaborations in Chicago, often difficult but not unusual, occurred through projects sponsored by the Works Progress Administration, through leftist circles, and through the individual daring of artists and writers."[23] Praising Braithwaite's contributions to this work, the chapter "Literature and Art" in the Works Progress Administration's *Cavalcade* outlined how he had challenged white readers' assumptions about Black poetry: "The influence of [Paul Laurence] Dunbar made it difficult for a Negro poet to find readers unless he wrote Negro dialect. Nevertheless there was a group of Negro poets who clung to the ideal of conventional language. Most notable of these were William Stanley Braithwaite of Boston, [who is] best known as an anthologist and critic."[24] Braithwaite indeed strongly opposed the perpetuation of cultural stereotypes used to denigrate African Americans. His stance on this matter in the years after Dunbar's death in 1906 heralded the game-changing potential of twentieth-century literary interracialism at its best.

African American support for these publishing achievements remained fairly steady until the late 1950s. As the literary historian Werner Sollors has explained, cultural emphases on Black and white solidarities shifted "as interracialism became decriminalized, more commonplace, and so widespread as to become an accepted part of the commercial culture, and, indeed, so much a part of ordinary and socially sanctioned human life that the emotions some of the earlier writers brought to this theme seem almost beyond comprehension today."[25] In the decades prior to the 1960s, facing challenges that ranged from lackluster white liberalism to downright hostile white supremacists, Black interracialists romanticized rather than repudiated the feasibility of a robust, multiracial democracy.

During the first six decades of the twentieth century, African American readers and critics recognized publishing clout and financial success as civil rights achievements. When the *Pittsburgh Courier* "saluted" Frank Yerby for his commercial successes in 1948, it explained: "For [a] Negro author to make the list of best-sellers in the highly competitive field of writing is still a rarity. For a Negro author to make a best-seller's list in books not dealing primarily with Negroes, is still more a rarity if not unprecedented."[26] At the time, it was subversive for African Americans to publish anything that was not distinctively Black. The previous year, when other Black newspapers outlined why Yerby merited a mention on the "Race Relations Honor Roll" for 1946, they all reported that sales of *Foxes* had "exceeded those of any book ever written by a Negro American." While many readers knew Yerby was African American,

The CRISIS

Vol. 12—No. 4   AUGUST, 1916   Whole No. 70

ONE DOLLAR A YEAR   TEN CENTS A COPY

FIGURE 0.4. From the turn of the twentieth century, popular photographs of Black children wrapped in or holding American flags signaled the power, value, and necessity of fighting for an inclusive democracy. This photograph, credited to "Turner," appeared in *The Crisis*, August 1916.

critics and booksellers on both sides of the color line were confident that white Southern readers "probably do not know the author is a Negro."[27] In 1947, one Black critic, reporting on a well-received talk Yerby gave at the University of Pennsylvania, joked about how surprised white Southerners would be if they knew how "scholarly" and "colored" this novelist was: "Incidentally, Yerby has numerous profitable invitations from Dixie to address ladies' literary groups. [Yerby] chuckled to think what would happen if he accepted and showed up to address the aristocracy of Natchez, Mobile, Savannah, or Charleston," in the era of Jim Crow.[28]

The same year, a Harvard-trained Black chemist asserted in the *Afro-American*, "Except for 'Uncle Tom's Cabin,' [1852] Yerby's novel [*Foxes*] is the only important one which has condemned the entire social system of the antebellum South, by showing not only how completely unmoral and immoral it was, but also how futile!"[29] Yet two decades later, as the Civil Rights Movement became more militant, Yerby's cultural prominence and breakthroughs had become far less important, as perceptions of writing across racial lines and foregrounding white protagonists changed. Langston Hughes remarked, possibly with some jealousy, in another nationally distributed African American newspaper: "Although Mr. Yerby is not white, his writing is. And no Negro writer has made as much money as he has, ever."[30] Nonetheless, Hughes included Yerby's work in *The Best Short Stories by Negro Writers* (1967).[31] Only in recent years have scholars investigated how varied and contradictory African American readers and critics' responses were to Yerby. This book shows how a broader set of prominent Black writers preceded him in fashioning and refashioning American and African American cultural standards, including Braithwaite, Charles Chesnutt, Alice Dunbar Nelson, Jessie Fauset, Jean Toomer, Juanita Harrison, Ellen Tarry, and Richard Wright, among others. These Black authors—and several white interlocutors—cultivated networks that paved the way for Willard Motley, Alice Childress, Julian Mayfield, Lorraine Hansberry, and many others at the center of the story that follows.

During and after the 1960s, debates among African Americans about the role and impact of popular Black writing and criticism became more heated and more public. It became popular to accuse authors such as Braithwaite, Yerby, Hansberry, Ralph Ellison, and scores of others of not being Black enough. A poem by Amiri Baraka published in 1973 declared: "In the midst of chaos, and near injury / we survive, because we are still young and correct / and black enough to be tough."[32] Disavowals and sharper critiques of older generations of Black writers who were widely associated with interracialism—Baraka was a figurehead for this turn—paralleled a radical shift in how demands for a biracial democracy were framed and sold to the literate public. In short, the difference between the Black-organized, racially inclusive calls by Fenton Johnson and his colleagues "For A Bigger and Better America" in a representative issue of *The Champion* published in 1917 and the title of Julius Lester's *Look Out Whitey! Black Power's Gon' Get Your Mama!* (1968) couldn't be starker.

Cartoon by E. C. Shefton

"THE RECONCILIATION OF THE RACES"

FIGURE 0.5. "The Reconciliation of the Races," a cartoon by E. C. Shefton, appeared in *The Champion Magazine*, January 1917.

This study is not intended, and should not be misconstrued, as a criticism of Black-authored books that were unapologetic in emphasizing racial conflict during and after the 1960s. Without question, Lester's *Look Out Whitey!* championed African American pride and autonomy. At the same time, many books in this genre also reified racial differences between "Blacks" and "whites," thus refuting common definitions of "interracialism" altogether. Or as Black author and filmmaker Kathleen Collins asked in the title as well as the last line of her most famous short story: "It's 1963. Whatever happened to interracial love?"[33] After the 1950s, interracialism was on life support.

Revealing the complexities of this multiracial world of literary production would have been impossible without consulting dozens of excellent biographical studies and revisionist narrative accounts of this period.[34] Archive-based research has never been more prominent in Black literary studies. I build on overlapping but distinct layers of scholarship by revisiting personal diaries, letters, and other firsthand accounts preserved in manuscript collections; popular commentary and literary criticism; and archived book contracts, historical advertisements, and high-profile endorsements.[35]

Though relatively small in number, cross-racial collaborations in the decades up to the 1960s helped affirm and legitimate Black lives in an epoch when white supremacists casually denied the shared humanity of people of color. Interest in soliciting Black authors capable of connecting people irrespective of their race or ethnicity signaled for others that the reform and advancement of both American and African American writing mattered. In a draft of his own philosophy of literature at mid-century, Chester Himes, one of the most popular Black authors of the post–World War II era, noted: "Theoretically, I believe that the problem of humanity is humanity, itself; that the hunger of an Italian child can not be divided by color from the hunger of an American Negro child."[36] Drawing from carefully preserved materials like these, in conjunction with dozens of exchanges between authors and readers, this study brings to life a rich sense of the personal relationships and intellectual influences that reaffirmed interracialism—and those that, at various moments, reified demands that Black and white communities remain "divided by color," even in print.

Chapter 1, "How to Segregate a Renaissance," examines the first three decades of the twentieth century, a period when an unprecedented number of African Americans united with white counterparts to begin dismantling racial imbalances in the publishing world. W. S. Braithwaite was hailed by readers, writers, and critics of all races for inaugurating a "poetic renaissance" in America prior to World War I. Or as one influential white editor stated after this global conflict, "William Stanley Braithwaite, the anthologist, lent his strongest encouragement to the *renaissance*."[37] Braithwaite was far from alone in promoting this loose-knit cultural movement, which ultimately extended well beyond poetry. During the 1910s, scores of commercially oriented literary professionals created space in various domains for Black authors. The interracial print culture that emerged included periodicals, plays, novels, anthologies, poetry volumes, sociological studies, literary criticism, short story collections, travel memoirs, and autobiographies. Black writers and literary themes were better represented than ever while Braithwaite held power. Yet by the mid-1920s, roughly the apex of the Harlem Renaissance, a growing number of Black intellectuals were criticizing white contemporaries for popularizing an offensive mix of exotic and stereotypical images of Black people. Several of these white authors had already launched racist attacks on Braithwaite, actively denigrating his contributions to modernizing and advancing American literature and criticism.

Chapter 2, "Integration and Its Discontents," illuminates the depth and breadth of Black writing in the 1930s and 1940s, when Black intellectuals such as Braithwaite, Grace Nail Johnson, and James Weldon Johnson mentored a new generation (post–Harlem Renaissance) of Black writers to keep advocating for literary desegregation—in short, for antiracist narratives about Black life and critical recognition of Black art that blurred racial distinctions and categories. When W.E.B. Du Bois resigned as editor of *The Crisis*, after calling for a segregated economy for African Americans, Braithwaite assured him in 1934: "Your stand is a triumphant call to the youth of a new generation."[38] In these years, a diverse cohort of Black artists, intellectuals, and aspiring professionals gained more opportunities and assumed more prominence in organizations on both sides of the color line. Their achievements and professional prospects were precarious, transient, and often exploitative. Sharing much in common with Braithwaite's reputation a generation earlier, Frank Yerby and Willard Motley's best-selling novels published in the 1940s were described by several of their contemporaries as "raceless." Yet this was an inadequate characterization of their multiracial, multiethnic books, as important scholarship on "white-life" novels and novelists has pointed out.[39] Another Black writer, Juanita Harrison, the author of one of Macmillan's best-selling travelogues, *My Great, Wide, Beautiful World* (1936), was also an important

JUANITA HARRISON
author of "My Great, Wide, Beautiful World"
(Macmillan)

FIGURE 0.6. Promotional photograph of Juanita Harrison, author of
My Great, Wide, Beautiful World (New York: Macmillan, 1936).

precursor to Motley, Yerby, and Richard Wright's commercial successes. Harrison
and Yerby, in particular, chafed at, rejected, and defied political affiliations. But it
was virtually impossible for Black authors such as Yerby to evade either racism or
politics in the United States in the early Cold War years, even when they tried.[40]

Chapter 3, "Challenging Little Black Sambo," highlights an overlapping
group of Black writers and cultural interracialists, from different backgrounds,

who wrote and illustrated an impressive range of books for children and young adults. Since the first decade of the twentieth century, numerous authors, artists, and editors devoted time and energy to bringing Black and white characters together in the same juvenile texts—but on much fairer terms than those popularized by Helen Bannerman's *Little Black Sambo* (1899). Shedding new light on the ubiquitous resistance to the racial reform of children's books within the corporate publishing trade, which was dominated by white female editors by the 1940s, affirms how groundbreaking improvements and achievements in this sector were. Muriel Fuller, Frank Yerby's first literary agent, was also a leading children's book editor at mid-century. Her commentaries, correspondence, and notes on juvenile literature form the core of this insider's portrait of the children's book business that flourished at mid-century.

Chapter 4, "What Was Postwar American Culture?" explores the tumultuous Cold War years of the late 1940s and 1950s, when scores of Black cultural professionals fought for and wooed broader audiences of readers and media consumers than ever before. New and increased capacities for inexpensive paperback printing supported larger and larger print runs of cheaper and cheaper books by Black writers. Biracial networks of entrepreneurial authors and booksellers diversified popular reading for generations of Americans, elevating African American writing to new heights. A fast-growing segment of editors were deeply supportive of interracial books and a host of other collaborations between people of different races and ethnicities. As debilitating as the anti-Communist Red Scare was, African Americans refused to give up on the potentially liberating power of Black-authored books and Black cultural representation. Optimism and deliberate efforts to work across the color line to attract white as well as Black audiences were hallmarks of an era when interracialism became a cultural standard.

The final chapter, "Toward Division," documents how Black and cross-racial books, meetings, and exchanges became fractious in the 1960s. In the end, literary and artistic interracialism, promoted by Braithwaite and numerous other Americans of all backgrounds, faltered during and after the Civil Rights Movement.[41] As race relations deteriorated, demand for vitriolic mass media rose sharply. In this chapter I argue that sensationalized Black print and cultural programming—sponsored, and often written, by white authors, editors, and cultural professionals—stood in stark contrast to the aims of an established cohort of African American artists, writers, and intellectuals in the 1960s. While the broad-based Black Arts Movement that emerged in this era established magazines, publishing houses, and other institutions to elevate Afrodiasporic

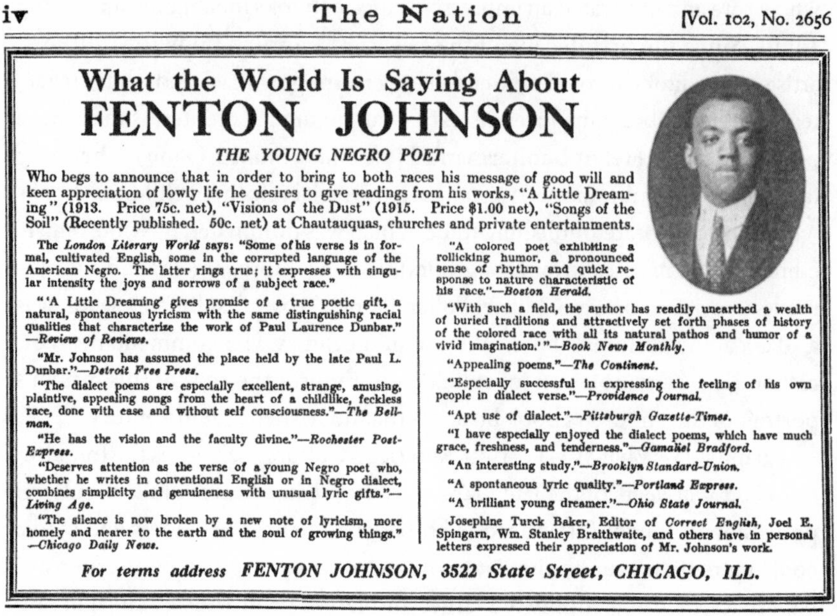

iv The Nation [Vol. 102, No. 2656

What the World Is Saying About

FENTON JOHNSON

THE YOUNG NEGRO POET

Who begs to announce that in order to bring to both races his message of good will and keen appreciation of lowly life he desires to give readings from his works, "A Little Dreaming" (1913. Price 75c. net), "Visions of the Dust" (1915. Price $1.00 net), "Songs of the Soil" (Recently published. 50c. net) at Chautauquas, churches and private entertainments.

The *London Literary World* says: "Some of his verse is in formal, cultivated English, some in the corrupted language of the American Negro. The latter rings true; it expresses with singular intensity the joys and sorrows of a subject race."

"'A Little Dreaming' gives promise of a true poetic gift, a natural, spontaneous lyricism with the same distinguishing racial qualities that characterize the work of Paul Laurence Dunbar." —*Review of Reviews.*

"Mr. Johnson has assumed the place held by the late Paul L. Dunbar."—*Detroit Free Press.*

"The dialect poems are especially excellent, strange, amusing, plaintive, appealing songs from the heart of a childlike, feckless race, done with ease and without self consciousness."—*The Bellman.*

"He has the vision and the faculty divine."—*Rochester Post-Express.*

"Deserves attention as the verse of a young Negro poet who, whether he writes in conventional English or in Negro dialect, combines simplicity and genuineness with unusual lyric gifts."—*Living Age.*

"The silence is now broken by a new note of lyricism, more homely and nearer to the earth and the soul of growing things." —*Chicago Daily News.*

"A colored poet exhibiting a rollicking humor, a pronounced sense of rhythm and quick response to nature characteristic of his race."—*Boston Herald.*

"With such a field, the author has readily unearthed a wealth of buried traditions and attractively set forth phases of history of the colored race with all its natural pathos and 'humor of a vivid imagination.'"—*Book News Monthly.*

"Appealing poems."—*The Continent.*

"Especially successful in expressing the feeling of his own people in dialect verse."—*Providence Journal.*

"Apt use of dialect."—*Pittsburgh Gazette-Times.*

"I have especially enjoyed the dialect poems, which have much grace, freshness, and tenderness."—*Gamaliel Bradford.*

"An interesting study."—*Brooklyn Standard-Union.*

"A spontaneous lyric quality."—*Portland Express.*

"A brilliant young dreamer."—*Ohio State Journal.*

Josephine Turck Baker, Editor of *Correct English,* Joel E. Spingarn, Wm. Stanley Braithwaite, and others have in personal letters expressed their appreciation of Mr. Johnson's work.

***For terms address* FENTON JOHNSON, *3522 State Street,* CHICAGO, ILL.**

FIGURE 0.7. Advertisement for Fenton Johnson's books in *The Nation* (May 25, 1916).

culture, a parallel nexus of white writers and publishers frequently exaggerated and embellished Black anger and racial tensions for profit. In 1969, one white publishing executive instructed publishers who sought to diversify their book lists that they "should not rely on consultants and researchers or even members of the black middle class, with whom publishers can talk comfortably." Instead, he advised them to "go into the ghetto," to establish connections with "the 'tough, angry' Negro who won't pull any punches," to capture "a tremendous black and Puerto Rican market."[42] In the 1960s, James Baldwin and Lorraine Hansberry rebuked white Americans who arbitrarily exacerbated racial divisions. The famous question Baldwin posed to the predominantly white readership of the *New Yorker* in 1962, "Do I really want to be integrated into a burning house?" encapsulates these tensions.[43]

Each chapter of *Impermanent Blackness* centers on Black and white authors who relied on a mix of romanticism and realism to convey African American perspectives against racist opposition. Since the 1910s, critics have accused some of the nation's most prominent Black writers of publishing texts that were too white to be fully appreciated by Black readers. Yet authors such as Fenton Johnson and the prizewinning essayist Isaac Fisher, who did not write

ISAAC FISHER

WINNER OF THE FIRST PRIZE

in

EVERYBODY'S "RUM" CONTEST

A Letter from

BOOKER·T· WASHINGTON

ISAAC FISHER

To the Editor of
Everybody's Magazine,
MY DEAR SIR:

As I have already written you, I was very much pleased to note, in the September issue of EVERYBODY'S MAGAZINE, that your First Prize of Five Hundred Dollars for the best essay on the subject, "What We Know About Rum, etc.," had been awarded to Isaac Fisher, a graduate of this institution.

I was not at all surprised to learn that he had won this prize, for in one way and another he has been winning prizes almost ever since his graduation from Tuskegee Institute. Counting large and small, he has won more than thirty prizes in essay contests with the best brains of this country.

From the time when I sat in one of the students' prayer-meetings here at Tuskegee some years ago, and saw a very small and rather poorly dressed boy stand up, and with diction that was almost perfect, manner intensely earnest, and ringing voice, declare: "I can not ever hope to match the logic of the gallant· Colonel Ingersoll; but poor in reasoning power as I am, I can not accept his philosophy because he takes away my Bible, on which I have been taught to lean for guidance, and gives me nothing

better in its place; and in spite of my ardent longing for life after death, tells me that the grave ends all, giving me nothing to quiet my soul's unrest"—ever since that night, I have known that Isaac Fisher was no ordinary student, and that under proper guidance he would become an unusually strong man. I backed my judgment by sending out on the farm for him the next morning, telling him that· his future was to be along literary lines, and offering him my personal interest to help him through the school.

Remembering his powerful speech in the prayer-meeting, I was astounded to find that he was in one of the lowest classes in the school.

The boy was having an unusually hard time to pay for his board and clothing, not having any money and being dependent entirely upon himself for support. But he did not complain and did not call on me for aid, as I intended that he should do. His doggedness and determination, together with rather unusual ability as a student and power as a speaker, made him many friends among the teachers, including Mrs. Washington, who saw to it that he had all the books he craved; and when I made him special news correspondent for the school,

523

FIGURE 0.8. Booker T. Washington wrote a letter in praise of the prize-winning essayist Isaac Fisher in *Everybody's Magazine*, April 1915.

primarily or exclusively about African American life, broadened the white public's awareness of how expansive Black creative and intellectual pursuits could be. Black authors who challenged racial conventions wanted to be in conversation with other creatives, intellectuals, and writers who reflected and meditated on the human condition. Forward-looking Black and white interlocutors (authors, critics, publishers, editors, and audiences to some degree) welcomed their literary contributions.

In the course of the twentieth century, the methods and motivations behind cultural interracialism were neither uniform nor inevitable. Some authors used, pitched, or became poster children for blurring racial lines in American literary culture to make a living. Others reached across the nation's tenacious social divisions to illuminate, interrogate, and rebel against Jim Crow or simply to enjoy what the historian Allyson Hobbs has termed "racial indeterminacy."[44] Whatever their reasons, these men and women were keen to undermine the cultural legitimacy of structural hierarchies in the United States and other white-majority nation-states. Proponents of distinctively Black and white literary standards maligned these efforts as conservative and inauthentic. But in many ways, their passion for artistic freedom and conviction to working across and moving beyond racial boundaries was radical.

These artists and intellectuals have much to teach us about the opportunities and challenges that underpin present-day commitments to building an inclusive American society. Attending to the elusive character of progressive interracial literary culture helps explain the reversals and discontinuities that still hinder racial pluralism. These men and women lived like dreamers and pragmatists at once. And this delicate interracial milieu is no less fragile, contentious, or urgent today.

1

How to Segregate a Renaissance

IN 1914, Caroline Giltinan, a white, thirty-one-year-old second-generation Irish American from Philadelphia, initiated a correspondence with W. S. Braithwaite, a Black poet, editor, and literary critic who lived in Cambridge, Massachusetts. At the time, many white readers and publishing insiders considered Braithwaite the most influential voice in American poetry and creative writing, proclaiming him among "those most responsible for the poetic renaissance in the United States."[1] Highly respected Black commentators such as historian Carter G. Woodson, the second African American to earn a doctorate from Harvard, described Braithwaite as "one of the foremost literary critics of our day."[2] Even skeptics conceded that Braithwaite was a "[m]aker of great audiences."[3]

Giltinan, a novice poet who had recently contributed to *Lippincott's*, was nervous about sending a letter in 1914 to someone as influential as Braithwaite: "All because I knew you are completely in touch with modern poetry, and your study and experience make your opinion the one to be valued most in all [of] America. I have lost my fear!"[4] Braithwaite's generosity and encouragement prompted similar enthusiastic responses from countless aspiring authors, simultaneously experimenting with poetry and other literary genres. In 1959, W.E.B. Du Bois praised "Braithwaite's compilation of all American poetry[,] which kept verse living when it tried to die," in his novel published that year.[5] Between 1906 and his retirement in 1945 from Atlanta University, a historically Black college, Braithwaite mentored and published hundreds of other men and women like Giltinan from similarly humble backgrounds—regardless of their race. This support was largely due to Braithwaite's exceptional commitment to professional courtesy. But it was also a key strategy in building popular support for a much grander design Braithwaite attributed his own successes to: expanding an inclusive artistic and intellectual milieu that modeled the

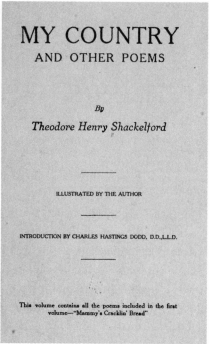

MY COUNTRY
AND OTHER POEMS

By

Theodore Henry Shackelford

ILLUSTRATED BY THE AUTHOR

INTRODUCTION BY CHARLES HASTINGS DODD, D.D.,L.L.D.

This volume contains all the poems included in the first
volume—"Mammy's Cracklin' Bread"

FIGURE 1.1. Theodore Henry Shackelford's *My Country and Other Poems* (Philadelphia: I. W. Klopp, 1916) included the author's photo opposite the title page, which notes: "This volume contains all the poems included in the first volume—'Mammy's Cracklin' Bread.'"

possibilities, and tremendous power, of egalitarian print. Books that are now obscure, such as Theodore Henry Shackelford's *My Country and Other Poems* (1916), asserted that America belonged as much to African Americans as to any other group.

Although little known in the twenty-first century, Braithwaite was once considered the foremost example of a synergy between Black authors and the white-dominated publishing business, which was frequently characterized as an American literary renaissance during and after the mid-1910s. In 1925, the "dean" of the Harlem Renaissance, Alain Locke, noted in Braithwaite's *Anthology of Magazine Verse for 1926* that loyal readers of the annual anthology, "and of the general and special magazines," would "know and concede that Negro genius has shared liberally in the renaissance of American poetry and made a substantial and distinctive contribution to it."[6] The multiracial "renaissance" in American letters Locke was referring to preceded the Harlem Renaissance.

But in our time, few readers either "know or concede that" Black "genius" played a "substantial and distinctive" role in reinvigorating the broader fields of American fiction and nonfiction in the decade and a half leading up to the 1920s.

White and Black cultural professionals continued working across racial lines, albeit under increasingly unequal terms, as the Harlem Renaissance gained momentum after World War I. By the mid-1920s, the white publishing establishment welcomed a host of new Black artists, writers, literary techniques, and cultural representations. But working across racial lines during the Harlem Renaissance often required Black authors to accentuate and exoticize their racial heritage. After lauding Braithwaite for establishing demand for "the long list of anthologies" of American and African American poetry years earlier, Du Bois reflected in 1959: "This Harlem Renaissance was an abnormal development with abnormal results. It was not a nation bursting with self-expression and applauding those who told its story and feelings best, but rather a group oppressed and despised within a larger group, whose chance for expression depended in large part on what the dominant group wanted to hear and were willing to support." According to Du Bois, it was during the Harlem Renaissance that "prizes" were offered "to those willing to distort truth and play court fool to American culture."[7] During the same period, new and established African American authors such as Braithwaite, Fenton Johnson, Charles Chesnutt, and Jean Toomer foundered as expectations and assumptions about Black arts and letters fluctuated in the years leading up to the Great Depression. More so than any member of this cohort, Braithwaite, in his success and eventual fall from grace, embodies the transformation of cultural interracialism between the early 1910s and the late 1920s.[8]

Braithwaite was born in Boston in 1878. His British Guyanese father hailed from a mixed-race, professionally distinguished, aristocratic family that immigrated to South America from Barbados in the 1860s. Yet Braithwaite's early life was much more closely tied to his mother's African American family, "whose origin," he later summarized, "was in the dark and tragic house of bondage."[9] Before fleeing to Boston after the Civil War, his mother and two sisters had been enslaved in North Carolina. The untimely death of Braithwaite's exceptionally well-connected father in the mid-1880s severed cross-border ties to his West Indian relatives and forced him into Boston's competitive, racially prejudiced job market at the age of twelve.[10]

Braithwaite's sand-brown complexion and his unwillingness to deny his identity as "an American Negro" made it virtually impossible for him to secure either an apprenticeship or steady work on the east coast until his mid-twenties.

Braithwaite later explained that these "racial conditions which closed the doors to the opportunities for employment of the kind I sought" had "convinced [him] that whatever may be the quality and distinctions of achievement in literature, if that literature was confined to racial materials and experiences, it would be appraised and judged by a different standard than the literature of American writers in general."[11] Once he gained a toehold in America's racially fragmented literary scene, Braithwaite was adamant that future generations of Black authors not be denied similar opportunities to shape their own artistic, intellectual, and professional identities. As Du Bois later noted in a letter to the president of Atlanta University, where Braithwaite taught, his friend and colleague was "an artist in life and habit, acquainted with the world and the best of the world. There is no one on our campus and indeed few in any institution, white or colored in the South, who has had such cultural contacts as he has had."[12]

In the first two decades of the twentieth century, Braithwaite's abiding commitment to building common cultural standards helped amplify a growing awareness that Black artistic and intellectual perspectives were diverse yet woefully underrepresented in American print culture. Black intellectuals like Braithwaite who aggressively sought the "distinction" of "achievement in literature" neither expected nor desired to pass as white Americans. The most ambitious writers in this generational cohort wanted to be regarded first and foremost as fellow humans and American citizens, and they positioned themselves as eager and equipped to bridge racial divisions in the literary field. Doing this work required a delicate balance between emphasizing that "all great artists are interracial" (as Braithwaite claimed in 1919) and cultivating networks and outlets for a larger number of Black cultural professionals.

The rise of inclusionary impulses among publishers in this era was driven in part by robust growth in the publishing sector prior to World War I. In 1906, the number of books generated in the United States was an estimated 7,139 distinct titles; by 1910, this figure had nearly doubled, reaching an estimated 13,470 books.[13] At the beginning of 1913, a *Publishers' Weekly* (*PW*) editorial cheered this bullish commercial market for books: "For the first time in many years we may venture to point out signs of a literary renascence." Sales figures were not the only reason the world of literary production seemed to be undergoing a seismic change. In the genres of poetry and essays, *PW*'s editors estimated that in 1912 alone, there were "more and better offerings than in any year of the past decade."[14] Public attitudes toward the "signs of a literary renascence" taking root in the United States prior to World War I remain ambiguous. What is clearer is that in some rarefied circles, writers and editors continued to characterize this epoch as a renaissance for several years, if not decades. In 1929, when avant-garde literary publisher Jane Heap titled her valediction in the final issue of the literary magazine *The Little Review* (est. 1914) "Lost: A Renaissance," she similarly attributed the cultural momentum supporting her work to the early years of the twentieth century.

According to Heap, "The revolution in the arts, begun before the war, herald[ing] a renaissance" had fragmented by the late 1920s.[15] Before the United States entered World War I, Braithwaite promoted more than a half dozen poems first published by the *Little Review* in his "12ᵗʰ Annual Review" of poetry in the *Boston Transcript*.[16] As the historian Lisa Szefel has observed, Braithwaite "single-handedly promoted the cause of American poetry" during the early years of this period.[17] Poetry boomed in the United States in large part due to Braithwaite's efforts: He carried the banner for a nascent literary tradition that, between 1904 and the late 1910s, connected Black and white figures within a burgeoning, multiracial cultural program. After the war, Braithwaite was still doing this work. Black author Georgia Douglas Johnson, whose first book of poetry Braithwaite penned an introduction for, informed Du Bois in 1924: "The New Anthology of Mr. Braithwaite's has many mentions of Crisis [magazine] writers therein. Five times is your specially presented young [Jean] Toomer named."[18] Unfortunately, sharing much in common with Heap (who published Toomer), by the mid- to late 1920s, Braithwaite saw that the racially and ethnically cosmopolitan literary renaissance of the 1910s was losing momentum.

Braithwaite was an important contributor to Alain Locke's canonical 1925 anthology *The New Negro* and remained heavily invested in cultivating African American writing following the decline of the broader renaissance.[19] And yet he does not fit neatly into the canonical circle of artists and intellectuals commonly associated with the Harlem Renaissance, and some of his Black successors accused him of writing "out of a Euro-American tradition" that "obliterated" his racial identity.[20] Others regarded his essays, expertise, journalism, popular anthologies, and accessible historical surveys such as *The Story of the Great War* (1919) as decisive challenges to patterns of racial segregation and exclusion across the literary field. How Braithwaite navigated these opposing positions and pressures as cultural leadership and sensibilities began to shift during and after World War I remains poorly understood. His attempts to transcend racial divisions in the 1910s were not wholly successful—but they were powerful nonetheless.

In 1917, echoing the optimistic view on the publishing trade outlined by
PW's editors four years earlier, Braithwaite emphasized the unifying features,
enthusiasm, and momentum he associated with America's literary renaissance:
"This renascence, now firmly accepted by everybody as a definite movement
in American life and literature, was fully a decade coming to maturity." Braithwaite's widely discussed essay estimated that the public's newfound interest
in poetry at the heart of this civic and cultural rebirth had "established an
audience, and the audience quickened the creative impulse," which ensured
that "[t]he Renaissance became a fact."[21] Braithwaite's summation of how
significantly "American life and literature" had progressed by the late 1910s
foreshadowed Heap's fond memories of the prewar "revolution in the arts"
in 1929. Nevertheless, each of these commentaries is marked by silences and
ambiguities with respect to how race and interracialism figured into this
movement, which some of Braithwaite's critics and successors faulted for
the apparent focus on a "whites-only" cultural transformation of Jim Crow
America.

On the other hand, numerous archival and printed sources suggest that by
the early 1910s, a small but growing interest in reaching across racial lines
existed within and well beyond the publishing trade. In fact, dozens of Black
authors and intellectuals benefited from stronger demand for their work well
before the 1920s. The publisher Walter Neale, in a 1913 letter to one of his firm's
formerly enslaved, Chicago-based authors, raved about the recent rise of Black
authorship. "I am glad to say, there seems to me to have been greater activity
among Negro writers in America during the past five years than during the 200
preceding years," he wrote.[22] Ten years later, C. E. Bechhofer's introduction to
an esoteric book, *The Literary Renaissance in America* (1923), offered a comple-
mentary description of a conspicuous yet underreported feature of contemporary
print culture in the United States. "So far as I know," Bechhofer wrote, "no
attempt has hitherto been made to discover [the renaissance's] principal tendencies and to show how fundamentally these are connected with the development and interplay of the various cultural and racial forces inside the
country."[23] But by the time Bechhofer's little-remembered monograph was
published, critics such as Ezra Pound had already insisted for several years that
literary culture in the United States was getting "stung by the negroid lash of
Mr. Braithwaite."[24] Four years earlier in 1913, when Pound denigrated Braithwaite as "a nigger" who was not "a man of equal race," his vitriol initiated a
long, drawn-out war on a short-lived, egalitarian conception of modern American literature.[25]

THE
LITERARY RENAISSANCE
IN AMERICA

BY

C. E. BECHHOFER

LONDON
WILLIAM HEINEMANN LTD.

FIGURE 1.2. C. E. Bechhofer's *The Literary Renaissance in America* (London: Heinemann, 1923).

Here and elsewhere, Pound implicitly appealed to racist assumptions that Black intellectuals and artists such as Braithwaite were undoubtedly inferior to their white peers. Though it's difficult to measure how racial dynamics changed, a chronological survey of this period indicates why assertions of biological differences between Black and white Americans inhibited progressive interracialism during the well-documented and celebrated "Negro Renaissance" of the 1920s. In sum, if an "interplay" of "racial forces" had helped ensure

Braithwaite's professional victories after the turn of the century, Pound and his allies were resolute in deliberately and maliciously undermining equitable interracialism after World War I.

Defying Categories

In 1899 Braithwaite finished his first poetry manuscript. In a cover letter he sent to several white-owned publishing firms that year with samples from his collection, Braithwaite cautioned: "Do not be surprised therefore should I inform you that I am an American Negro, a Bostonian by birth, and received my M.A. from Nature's University of 'Seek, Observe and Utilize' and am now in my 20th year."[26] Braithwaite had always been proud of his racial heritage, but he also knew that Black accomplishments and expertise barely registered in the white public's consciousness. But given skills and qualification, facts like these rarely stopped Braithwaite from pursuing his dream of becoming a published author or gaining professional employment in the publishing trade.

While he searched for a publisher, Braithwaite also sought "employment on the newspapers and in the book stores" of New York City. He later estimated "that there was not a book store of importance in the city, to which I had not applied for a position as a book clerk." At the conclusion of his interviews, when white newspaper managers and booksellers asked him what his racial background was, he later recalled, "I would answer, as invariably I did, with the truth, that I 'am an American Negro.'"[27] Despite numerous assurances from prospective employers in the winter of 1900 and 1901 that his "knowledge of literature in general, current, or standard, or classical, was extensive and superior to that of any other applicant," Braithwaite was never offered a job. Then and decades later, he rightfully attributed this paradox to "the usual procedure" of being discriminated against on the basis of race.

It took Braithwaite five years to find a publishing house willing to work with him. Even then, the firm that recognized his talents in creative writing required him to secure a guarantee "of two hundred persons" before initiating the production process for his first book.[28] But once *Lyrics of Life and Love* finally appeared, in 1904, Braithwaite's literary and professional prospects rapidly improved. Over the next two years his book of poems was widely recognized as an unusually popular achievement in both resisting and deconstructing assumptions about Black authorship. As the literary scholar Kenny Williams explains, Braithwaite's "insistence upon being part of the American scene was not predicated upon a view that race could or should be denied;

rather, he felt race was simply a characteristic which did not have to be a motivating factor for one's life. Thus, he actually believed that the differences between races could be minimized."[29] Braithwaite's *Lyrics of Life and Love*, published by Boston's Herbert B. Turner & Company, featured a sketch of the author that clearly indicated he was African American. By contrast, the poems in this volume were far more racially ambiguous. This didn't stop the book's publisher from aggressively advertising that *Lyrics* was penned "by a Negro" and had still managed to sell "a great many copies."[30]

Braithwaite's audacious proposal to publish a Black-authored book of poetry that diverged from a dialect literary tradition popularized by Paul Laurence Dunbar was cutting-edge at the turn of the century. Braithwaite was thus aware that his first book held the potential to disrupt a tenacious standard that unwittingly buttressed white supremacist customs in the mainstream publishing trade. Indeed, many white contemporaries considered the appearance of Braithwaite's first book an unprecedented advancement of both American and African American letters. The *New York Times*, the *Washington Post*, and several other prominent newspapers echoed the *Minneapolis Journal*'s announcement that "[t]his young colored poet has been hailed, not only as the most gifted poet the negro race has yet produced, but also as being one of the most promising of the young generation of American singers. Many prominent literary people of Boston have spoken enthusiastically of Braithwaite's poetry."[31] In 1904, it was not unheard of for white critics and newspapers to endorse Black authors. But popular reviews positing that Braithwaite was one of "the most promising" creative artists of his generation—irrespective of racial heritage— were extremely rare in an era commonly termed "the nadir" of race relations in the United States.[32]

African American critics wasted little time in praising what Braithwaite had accomplished. The nation's foremost Black radical newspaper, Chicago's *Broad Ax*, cheered *Lyrics of Life and Love* just a few months after it was published: "Colored Americans may well feel proud of our youthful poet Mr. W. Stanley Braithwaite, of Boston, Mass., for he is proud of us, and if in doubt, learn for yourself by buying one of his books of poems or lyrics of life." This unnamed critic who endorsed Braithwaite's first book then warned: "We cannot establish a literature worthy of the name unless we encourage the genius of our race in all their noble, lofty, and worthy efforts."[33] Without question, the "we" in this statement was directed toward Black readers. But the aim was much broader: to disabuse readers across the anglophone world of the notion that America's most distinctive and versatile creative authors were white.

Promotions of Black authors such as Braithwaite in the summer of 1905, and "even Robert Browning [an English poet], who was an octoroon," in *The Broad Ax* and elsewhere, were probably viewed as counters to endorsements of Thomas Dixon. Dixon, an extremely popular white supremacist Baptist minister in North Carolina, had recently published *The Clansman: A Historical Romance of the Ku Klux Klan* (1905). Three months after the publication of *The Clansman*, the Florence, Alabama, Daughters of the American Confederacy publicized its formal motion to buy and deliver copies of the book to Alabama A&M, a historically Black college.[34] Dixon's family had been prominent members of the Klan since the late 1860s, and his reverence for the terrorist organization at the turn of the century was boundless. *The Clansman* was only the second novel in Dixon's pernicious "Trilogy of Reconstruction," published by Southerner Walter Hines Page, the vice president of New York's Doubleday, Page & Company. Offering a sense of how popular Dixon's fictive narratives of the Klan were, a 1907 advertisement for *The Clansman* boasted: "Within five years the public has paid two million dollars to hear and see the product of Dr. Dixon's work on this theme."[35] *The Clansman* was later adapted as a Hollywood film, debuted in Woodrow Wilson's White House, and broadcast in theaters across the United States under the title *The Birth of a Nation* (1915).

Shortly after *The Clansman* was first published in book form, racial tensions spiked when President Theodore Roosevelt dishonorably discharged close to 170 Black soldiers stationed in Texas in August 1906. These men were booted from the nation's armed forces in a drama known as "the Brownsville affair," sparked by an unproven allegation that Black soldiers were responsible for shooting a white police officer and killing a white bartender. Less than two months later, an estimated ten to fifteen thousand white males, including children, attacked scores of Black Americans in Georgia over a four-day period in an event memorialized as the "Atlanta Race Riot of 1906."[36] The sharp deterioration of race relations in this brief period of time jolted Northern elites, including many who were associated with the white and racially homogeneous publishing establishment.

Months earlier, at the beginning of 1906, hundreds of newspapers had mourned the death of Paul Laurence Dunbar, who had died at the age of thirty-three. Dunbar was, at that time, the most celebrated Black author in America. Among the subset of white liberals who connected the tragic passing of "the Chaucer of the negro race" and the mounting of racial conflicts and violence soon thereafter, no creative Black author benefited more than W. S. Braithwaite.[37] Seven days after Dunbar's death, the *Boston Transcript*, then the

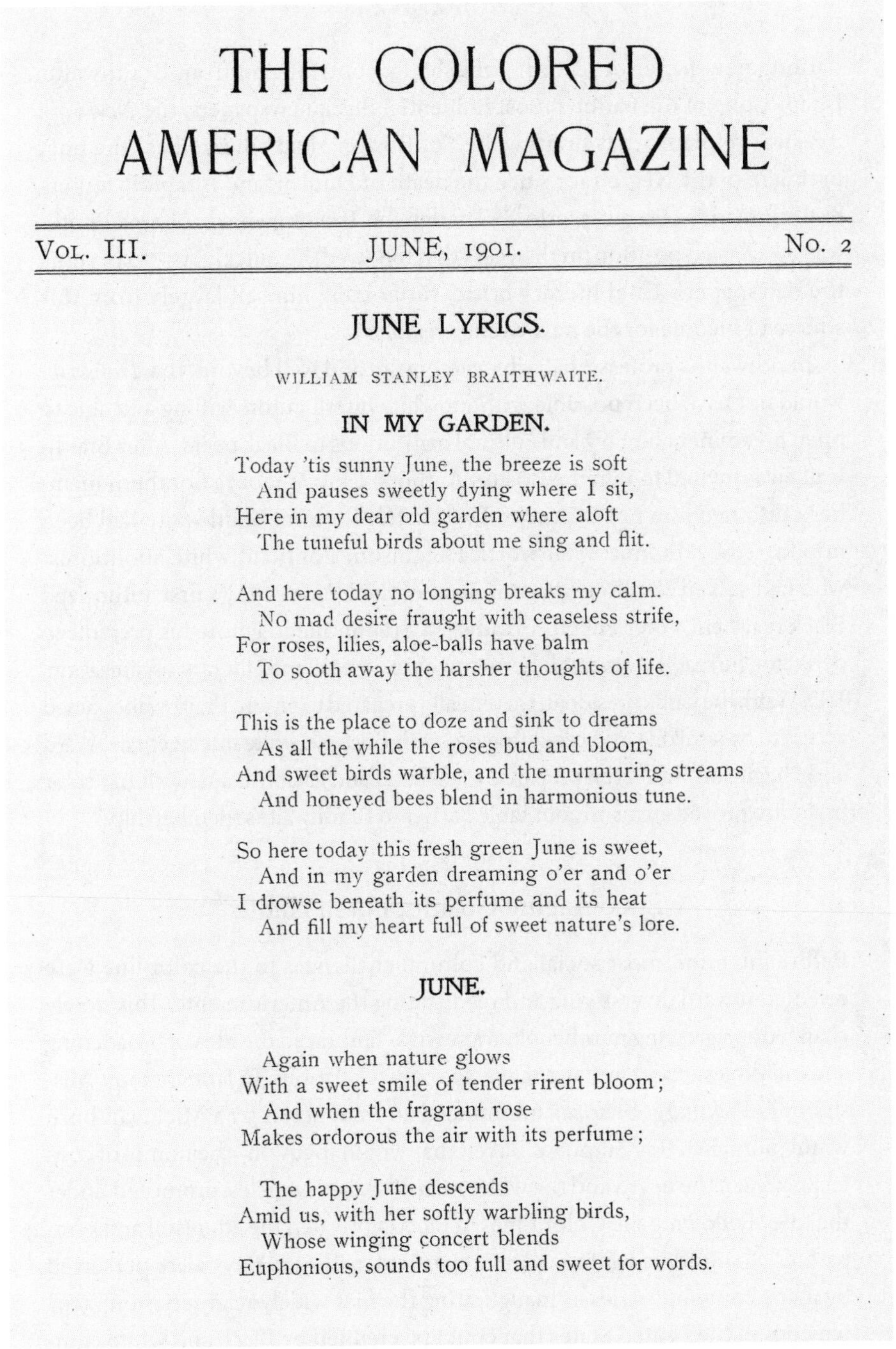

THE COLORED AMERICAN MAGAZINE

| VOL. III. | JUNE, 1901. | NO. 2 |

JUNE LYRICS.

WILLIAM STANLEY BRAITHWAITE.

IN MY GARDEN.

Today 'tis sunny June, the breeze is soft
  And pauses sweetly dying where I sit,
Here in my dear old garden where aloft
  The tuneful birds about me sing and flit.

And here today no longing breaks my calm.
  No mad desire fraught with ceaseless strife,
For roses, lilies, aloe-balls have balm
  To sooth away the harsher thoughts of life.

This is the place to doze and sink to dreams
  As all the while the roses bud and bloom,
And sweet birds warble, and the murmuring streams
  And honeyed bees blend in harmonious tune.

So here today this fresh green June is sweet,
  And in my garden dreaming o'er and o'er
I drowse beneath its perfume and its heat
  And fill my heart full of sweet nature's lore.

JUNE.

Again when nature glows
With a sweet smile of tender rirent bloom;
  And when the fragrant rose
Makes ordorous the air with its perfume;

The happy June descends
Amid us, with her softly warbling birds,
  Whose winging concert blends
Euphonious, sounds too full and sweet for words.

FIGURE 1.3. W. S. Braithwaite's poetry on the opening page of *The Colored American Magazine,* June 1901. A month earlier, the magazine announced that Braithwaite would run its newly established "Book Reviews" section, citing the poetry Braithwaite had contributed to the *Boston Transcript* since 1897.

nation's newspaper of record, published a contribution from Braithwaite. By 1910, one of the nation's most influential Black newspapers, the *New York Age*, was rejoicing that Braithwaite, "of Boston," had emerged as "the poet premiere of the Negro race since the death of Dunbar, and is rapidly forging to the fore in the literary world."[38] Though the *Transcript* never offered Braithwaite a salaried position, in the years that followed, he quickly rose to become the newspaper's chief literary critic, supporting himself largely from this source of income for the next twenty years.[39]

Braithwaite's professional achievements in and well beyond the *Transcript* would not have been possible without white interlocutors willing and able to open preeminent literary and cultural institutions to Black peers. After Braithwaite was invited to join the Boston Authors' Club in 1906, a Southern member cautioned him not to accept. Fortunately for him, Braithwaite had been nominated by Thomas Wentworth Higginson, a militant white abolitionist who had served as colonel in command of the Union Army's first authorized Black regiment. After Higginson advised Braithwaite to ignore his prejudiced detractor, he readily joined his hometown's most esteemed literary organization. Julia Ward, the club's president, was equally prepared to ensure Braithwaite gained access to fraternizing and brokering ties with Boston's white intelligentsia. Ward and Higginson were even prepared to disband and establish a new club if color prejudice proved an insurmountable barrier to Braithwaite's membership.[40]

Encouraging Cosmopolitan Habits

Before the 1910s, most social and cultural challenges to the color line were oriented toward diversifying and reeducating the American elite. This slowly changed as a growing number of progressives embraced the idea of broadening and building support for fairer coverage of race relations. In January 1907, Mississippi's *Vicksburg American* announced an essay series by a Michigan-born white journalist, Ray Stannard Baker, that would focus on "the points of contact between the negro and the white man."[41] Baker's articles, promoted under the title "Following the Color Line" in 1907, captivated the attention and sympathies of countless white readers in particular. These essays were perceived by many contemporaries as inaugurating the first widely read series on racial tensions in the United States that could be credited by Black and white commentators alike as "objective." Baker's reporting was not nearly as balanced or reliable as Black readers desired. Nevertheless, Baker listened to, and cared about, what his Black readers and critics thought. In a letter to W.E.B. Du Bois drafted on March 29, 1907, Baker assured him, "I should be very glad indeed to have any suggestions or criticisms you may see fit to make on my articles. I want them to be accurate and fair from every point of view."[42] Baker was thoroughly committed to racially balanced reportage, at least rhetorically.

Baker's popularity and reputation led Doubleday, Page & Company to sponsor a book of essays based on his *American Magazine* series, which was titled *Following the Color Line: An Account of Negro Citizenship in the American Democracy* (1908). It may seem ironic that Baker's book was published by the same firm that had already made a fortune selling Dixon's white supremacist novels. But this was how Walter Hines Page, who also represented the African American author Charles Chesnutt, worked. In a letter of rejection sent to Chesnutt a decade earlier, Page estimated: "A novel in these days must have some much more striking characteristic of plot or style to make its publication a good venture than was required a dozen years ago or less."[43] Still, Page always claimed that his firm was committed to cultivating a diverse base of authors and opinions. In truth, Baker's book was well positioned to be a moneymaker for Doubleday, which published *Following the Color Line* just a few months after another particularly deadly episode of white supremacist violence. This time, thousands of vicious attacks on African Americans were concentrated in Springfield, Illinois, in several days of terror that were commonly described as the first race riot in the North in over fifty years.[44]

In addition to prompting the founding of the white-led NAACP, Springfield's riots inspired a flood of Black and interracial-themed writing. Baker's authoritative coverage became a standard-bearer for many new and aspiring authors in this loosely defined literary genre. Indicating as much, in 1908, Brander Matthews of Columbia University received a draft of a manuscript by his former student James Weldon Johnson, *The Autobiography of an Ex-Colored Man* (1912), with a letter stating that this now-canonical novel was comparable to Baker's essays: "There has been an out[burst] of literature somewhat along the same line within the past year," Johnson wrote, including "Ray Stannard Baker's articles in 'American Magazine.'"[45] Matthews self-identified as a "conservative" and was close friends with Theodore Roosevelt. His scholarly expertise bore little relation to either Black literary culture or Black writing. But none of these factors kept him from mentoring and advising Johnson or promoting the *Autobiography* as an outstanding example of "American" realism once it was published.[46] Johnson later remembered of his "warm and lasting friendship" with Matthews that he had been "especially impressed" by his former teacher's "catholicity [openness]."[47]

WOMEN OF COLOR AND THE SUFFRAGE MOVEMENT.

By Mrs. Gertrude Cromwell. All that is being done by the women of our race in this great movement will be regularly supplied to our readers by one who is in most intimate touch with all the leaders, in fact she herself is one of "our" leaders in all that pertains to the real development of the suffrage movement among our race.

MEN OF VISION. By Pauline E. Hopkins.

The series of sketches prepared by Miss Hopkins some years since on "Famous Men of the Negro Race," will have a worthy sequel in this series entitled "Men of Vision." It will include the lives of those men of the race who have clearly demonstrated by their achievements that they are really "Men of Vision," and the entire series will be fully illustrated.

PLENYONO GBE WOLO
Treasurer of the
Harvard Cosmopolitan Club,
Cambridge, Mass.

FACTS PERTAINING TO THE EARLY GREATNESS OF THE AFRICAN RACE,

and the possibility of restoration by its descendants. This series of articles is compiled and arranged from the works of the best known ethnologists and historians. Among the subjects treated are Original Man, Division of Mankind into Races, The Brotherhood of Man or the Origin of Color, Early Civilization of the African, etc. No student of racial development can afford to miss this series.

NEGRO ARTISTS IN EUROPE.

This series of articles, by Clarence Cameron White, will comprise exhaustive data of Ira Aldridge and Coleridge Taylor of London, Henry Tanner of Paris, Pushkin the Russian poet, Edmonia Lewis (sculptress) of Italy, and many others.

Mr. White will give us "personal contact" writings of these famous people, having met them in his sojourn abroad as a student. He will endeavor to let us have each month a sketch of some one person of color who is doing commendable work abroad.

REFORMS IN LIBERIA.

Major Charles Young (Military Attache of the U. S. Army at Liberia) will give us a series of articles on the various reforms and methods now in vogue to make Liberia a Republic among Republics. This will prove one of the most timely as well as interesting series on what the race is really doing in "Darkest Africa."

HAYTI—POLITICAL AND HISTORICAL.

Mr. E. H. Leonard, a native of Hayti, having served in the army in that country, will do research work for our magazine. Mr. Leonard is an able scholar in several languages, including French, German and Italian, and will give us many interesting happenings, both political and historical.

A NORTHERN TEACHER AMONG SOUTHERN CHILDREN.

Miss Margaret A. Henderson, having had a varied experience as teacher among the race in the south, will give us her impression of a northern teacher among the southern children. A most valuable series for all those interested in any way in the vital question of modern education.

FIGURE 1.4. Pauline Hopkins's short-lived *New Era Magazine* (est. 1916) featured W. S. Braithwaite on the cover of its first issue (left) and a photo of Plenyono Gbe Wolo, Harvard's first African graduate, in the same issue (right). The caption under the photo of Wolo highlighted his recent election as treasurer of Harvard's Cosmopolitan Club, a group the *New Era* planned to collaborate with on future essays.

Comparable stimulating and productive interracialism took in a handful of newly established organizations on the eve of the 1910s. Harvard's Cosmopolitan Club, founded in 1907, and counterparts at Oxford and elsewhere, readily welcomed Black members. Mary White Ovington, one of several of the white cofounding members of the NAACP, belonged to New York City's Cosmopolitan Club. Years later, Ovington reminisced about how exceptional cultural activism in this vein still was when her chapter began meeting in 1908: "I have spoken of the Cosmopolitan Club, an organization made up of white and colored men and women for the discussion of present-day problems. While it was small, numbering about thirty members, for a moment it achieved fame." According to Ovington, the group's "doings were reported North and South and East and West," yet still "reverberate[d] in the South" more than anyplace else.[48]

Cross-racial friendship and intellectual customs at Harvard preceded the establishment of its Cosmopolitan Club, which welcomed members such as Plenyono Gbe Wolo, the first African to graduate from the university. Numerous other Black students graduated from Harvard well before Wolo. In fact, the preeminent philosopher William James gained a reputation for teaching and welcoming Black and other minority students that dated back to the early 1890s. Alain Locke, Leslie Pinckney Hill, and W.E.B. Du Bois are the most famous of James's African American students to later attain prominence, nationally and internationally.

Reflecting on James's influence in the mid-1920s, Du Bois wrote how his "teachers of Harvard," and James in particular, offered him "exceptional fellowship and contact" and "helped me so abundantly to find myself." Having arrived at Harvard with "no desire to cross the color line," Du Bois was utterly surprised to be "lifted to a larger world" by scholars like James who encouraged his capacity to "see this thing which I called my 'Problem' [race], less narrowly and more splendidly as a part of life." For decades, Du Bois preserved a personal invitation James sent him to a "philosophical supper" one Valentine's Day, signed "Yours truly, William James." Du Bois also affectionately described his frequent visits to the James family's home near campus: "I well remember that study: long, low and cheerful in its disorder; spacious so that the Master could walk to and fro in his nervous thinking and talking."[49] Until his death in 1910, James happily read and gave both candid and encouraging feedback on almost everything Du Bois published.

Three months after James's death, Du Bois directed the publication of the inaugural issue of the NAACP's *Crisis* magazine. Du Bois had been invited by Mary Ovington and the rest of the organization's white leadership to serve as the organization's sole Black board member. Du Bois tapped Braithwaite to help found *The Crisis*, and his name appeared alongside five other Black and white deputy editors from the periodical's very first issue at the end of 1910. Back in August, the *American Historical Review* published Du Bois's "Reconstruction and Its Benefits," making him the first African American published by that scholarly journal.[50] His historiographical essay challenged white supremacist interpretations of this period widely associated with the Dunning School, a cohort of white scholars who were either based or trained at Columbia University under the historian William Dunning. Dunning was effectively a scholarly complement to Dixon's novel *The Clansman*, arguing that the federal government's Reconstruction program and the granting of African Americans full citizenship after the Civil War were grave mistakes. James would have been proud of both literary accomplishments.

Though Du Bois was successful in the end, it was never a sure thing that *The Crisis* would secure the sponsorship it needed. Decades later, Du Bois recalled how frustrated and resistant one of the NAACP's white board members had been when he proposed to establish a periodical backed by the civil rights organization. "I remember Albert Pillsbury, former Attorney General of Massachusetts, wrote to me and said: If you have not already determined to publish a magazine, for heavens' sake drop the idea. The number of publications now is as many as the 'plagues of Egypt!'"[51] Pillsbury's perception of the publishing landscape at the time was correct—the number of periodicals was large and growing by the early 1910s. Before World War I, related growth in the print trade presented opportunities that Du Bois, Braithwaite, James Weldon Johnson, and dozens of other African American writers diligently pursued.

As Du Bois's recollection also implies, some whites greeted the space these authors claimed in the literary field with hostility. Hilda Satt Polacheck, who worked at Chicago's McClurg Bookstore in this era, explained in a letter to her fiancé that a number of her colleagues maintained an active boycott against the novel Du Bois published in 1911: "The book called *The Quest of the Silver Fleece* is a gem, but our boys [white salesmen] refuse to sell it, because it is written by a 'nigger,' about 'niggers.' What I mean by refusing to sell it, is they do not recommend it." Polacheck quit her job at the store, but not before "criticizing" the firm's leadership for its prejudiced "methods of doing business" with Black-authored books.[52] Yet Du Bois and his African American peers were by no means the only writers to face skepticism and opposition for their work on Black and interracial topics during this period.

Two years earlier, Gertrude Stein, also a favored student of William James, had no choice but to publish *Three Lives* (1909) at her own expense. Stein's first book was a work of fiction that had, at its center, "Melanctha," a novella-length romance centered on two Black, mixed-race characters from different social classes. Over two decades later, Stein described "Melanctha" as the "first definite step away from the nineteenth century and into the twentieth century in literature."[53] Corroborating this bold assessment, James Weldon Johnson informed Stein's friend Carl Van Vechten that the publication of "Melanctha" made its author "the first (I believe I'm right) white writer to write a story of love between a Negro man and woman and deal with them as normal members of the human family."[54] Stein attributed her breakthrough with "Melanctha" as a direct outgrowth of her exposure to pluralist psychology under James's tutelage during her undergraduate years at Radcliffe in the 1890s. James was by far Stein's favorite professor. And as with Du Bois, Stein and James remained close following her graduation from the women's college that was still known as the Harvard Annex.

In 1913, Georgina Goddard King, a professor of fine arts at Bryn Mawr College, offered a sense of how transformative reading "Melanctha" was for some white readers: "In reading *Melanctha Herbert* you were a Negro yourself. The whole world was Negro. The power was as undeniable as it was curious. You saw for a moment into somebody else's skin, sometimes by a sudden lightning flash of intuition."[55] The palpable sense of surprise, even wonder, in King's memories of reading Stein's short story is a reminder of how rare it was at the time for elite and educated white readers to consider a Black woman's perspective—especially in fiction. Innovative literary narratives like "Melanctha" found little interest in an era when Baker's *Following the Color Line* dominated the commercial market for Black and interracial literature.

Suggesting just how odd "Melanctha" was, the president of the Grafton Press, F. H. Hitchcock, advised Stein shortly after his firm published *Three Lives*, "I hope you will appreciate that you have written such an unusual book that it has been impossible for us to interest the buyers in the book stores in putting it in stock."[56] Despite several positive newspaper reviews for *Three Lives*, Grafton still struggled to get it represented in commercial outlets. Du Bois's endorsement of *Three Lives* in the second issue of *The Crisis* in 1910 was a modest sign of support, but it did little for sales.[57]

Although William James regularly implied that his brother, the novelist Henry James, had killed his own interest in fiction, less than three months before his death in 1910 he was unequivocal in his praise for Stein's first book: "I have

Men of the Month

J. E. SPINGARN.

Joel Elias Spingarn, president of the New York branch of the National Association for the Advancement of Colored People, stands in the front rank of the younger group of American scholars. He is widely known in this country and in Europe as an authority on literature,

versy with President Butler over a question of academic freedom and was "relieved from academic service" without explanation in March last.

Dr. Spingarn was the Republican nominee for member of Congress from the eighteenth New York district in 1908; this is a hopelessly Democratic constit-

J. E. SPINGARN.

GILCHRIST STEWART.

especially of the sixteenth and seventeenth centuries.

He was born in New York in 1875, and was graduated from Columbia in 1895. After four years of post-graduate study at Harvard and Columbia he received the degree of Doctor of Philosophy from the latter in 1899, and was immediately made assistant in literature, under Professor George E. Woodberry. He was promoted to tutor in comparative literature the following year; and when Professor Woodberry resigned from Columbia in 1904, Dr. Spingarn succeeded him as adjunct professor of comparative literature; he was promoted to a full professorship in 1908, and was elected chairman of the division of modern languages and literatures in 1910. Phi Beta Kappa poet, 1901; represented the university at the New York University Poe Centenary, 1909. He recently engaged in a contro-

nency, but Professor Spingarn received eight thousand more votes than any preceding Republican candidate. Besides numerous contributions to periodicals, chiefly articles of a scholarly nature and some verse, he has written the following books:

"History of Literary Criticism in the Renaissance," 1899; second edition, 1908; translated into Italian, 1905.

"American Scholarship: An Address Before the Congress of Comparative History at Paris," 1900.

"Critical Essays of the Seventeenth Century," in three volumes, published by the Oxford University Press, England, 1908-9.

"The New Criticism: A Lecture Delivered at Columbia University," 1911.

"The New Hesperides and Other Poems," 1911.

"Seventeenth Century Criticism," a

FIGURE 1.5. *The Crisis* featured Joel Spingarn and New York entrepreneur Gilchrist Stewart as its "Men of the Month" in its August 1911 issue.

a bad conscience about 'Three Lives.' You know (?) how hard it is for me to read novels. Well, I read 30 or 40 pages, and said 'this is a fine new kind of realism—Gertrude Stein is great!'"[58] James never mentioned which of the stories he read, but it would be a surprise if he had not turned to "Melanctha" first, like most readers. Stein, writing in the third person in *The Autobiography of Alice B. Toklas* (1933), implied that her capacity to reach across racial lines—in literary texts and in real life—was most nurtured by James: "The important person in Gertrude Stein's Radcliffe life was William James. [. . .] Keep your mind open, he used to say."[59] Stein landed at the Harvard Annex the year after the death of James's queer sister, the diarist Alice James. James had maintained a very close bond with his sister.[60] He was likely aware that Stein, a Jewish lesbian, would have been heartened by the pluralist tone of his intellectual mentorship.

In the early 1910s, the appearance of Stein's *Three Lives* affirmed and complemented Joel Spingarn's intellectual advocacy for racially inclusive cultural production, analysis, and recognition. Spingarn, a Jewish cofounder of the NAACP, became the first literary scholar in the United States to theorize and broadcast the term "New Criticism." In the winter of 1910, Spingarn argued in a public lecture on the "New Criticism" that cultural contexts were, and should be, vital to formal interpretations of literature: "To study these phases of a work of art is to treat it as an historic or social document, and the result is a contribution to the history of culture or civilization."[61] This work was highlighted when Spingarn was profiled in *The Crisis* in 1911. And it was also sold in advertisements placed in *The Crisis* for the remainder of the first half of the 1910s.[62] At the end of the decade, Spingarn entered a publishing partnership with Donald Brace and Alfred Harcourt, two of his former undergraduate students at Columbia University. Together, they ensured that this firm operated in accordance with Spingarn's philosophy of New Criticism. Spingarn's proposed methods were markedly dissimilar from the purportedly ahistorical "close reading" approach to "New Criticism" popularized by the white supremacists associated with Vanderbilt University decades later.[63] It would be a surprise if the white critics based in Nashville, whose use of the New Criticism eventually overshadowed Spingarn's, were unaware of the term's Jewish and cosmopolitan roots.

Prior to World War I, when the *Crisis* saluted white authors, activists, and intellectuals such as Stein, Spingarn, and numerous others, these efforts modeled a Black-led, multicultural agenda. Jessie Fauset, in her role as an occasional literary critic for the periodical from 1912, frequently promoted books about people of color penned by a host of white writers.[64] In a 1912 review of white author Percival Gibson's *Flower o' the Peach* (1911), a novel tracing the paradoxes and injustices of racial apartheid in South Africa, Fauset made her appreciation for this narrative clear: "The significant thing is that at last a dispassionate presentation of color-prejudice—its baselessness and its shamefulness—has found its way into modern literature. And, behold! the book sells."[65] Fauset knew that it was difficult to generate large sales of "modern" books like Gibson's. But the feat of challenging the color line for a global readership seemed to be far more important to her.

Often, sympathetic and entrepreneurial cultural professionals on both sides of the Atlantic both subtly and more bluntly referred to Braithwaite while challenging literary conventions. In the early 1910s, when more than one hundred thousand copies of Bengali poet Rabindranath Tagore's book of verse *The Gardener* (1913) were sold by the London-based Macmillan Company, the "poetic renaissance" was invoked to explain this phenomenal number. George Brett, the firm's American president, claimed in 1914 that a "change in the public's attitude toward literature" had emerged "with disconcerting suddenness."[66] Just a few months earlier, in October 1913, Macmillan's London office had used the title of Braithwaite's first volume of poetry, *Lyrics of Life and Love* (1904), in its advertisements for Tagore's *Gardener*.

Both Tagore and Macmillan knew that there was an advantage to invoking America's preeminent Black writer in 1913.[67] In a letter to W.E.B. Du Bois several years later, Tagore remarked on this cultural evidence of racial progress: "What is the great fact of this age? It is that the messenger has knocked at our gate and all the bars have given way. Our doors have burst open. The human races have come out of their enclosures. They have gathered together."[68] Tagore was perhaps too optimistic on the state of interracialism in "this age." On the other hand, if he was referring to cultural achievements since the turn of the century, books such as Braithwaite's *Lyrics of Life and Love* (1904) and Tagore's *Gardener* (1913) had done much to raise the standing of Black and brown writers in the anglophone world.

On the American East Coast, public and institutional reverence for Braithwaite's nascent legacy was ubiquitous in the 1910s. His efforts are largely forgotten today, but he played an outsized role in promoting and advancing Black and white writers in and beyond New England. The contract Boston's Sherman and French offered James Weldon Johnson for *The Autobiography of an Ex-Colored Man*, for example, stemmed directly from Braithwaite's use of his platform at the *Transcript* to elevate a broad range of American creative writing, including Johnson's early poetry. Based on Braithwaite's endorsement of the poems, Sherman and French offered Johnson a book contract for his novel.

In 1911, Johnson wrote Braithwaite to thank him for drawing attention to his recent work, alongside a racially eclectic cohort of rising American poets: "As a result of your review, Sherman, French and Company have written me regarding the possibility of bringing out a volume."[69] While the "volume" of poetry didn't pan out, Johnson's celebrated novel did.

Less than three months before Johnson's letter to Braithwaite, Edward Smyth Jones's book of poems *The Sylvan Cabin: A Centenary Ode on the Birth of Lincoln* (1911), which featured an introduction by Braithwaite, was also published by Sherman and French. Braithwaite praised Jones for giving his literary work "a unique value because [the poems] are in a deeply essential manner the rendering of a human document, as all poems must be, of an individual who speaks universally."[70] Jones's ability to do so was against the odds: the poet had been born to formerly enslaved parents shortly after the Civil War. Jones was intent on ascending from his humble origins to attend Harvard, but after traveling more than one thousand miles from Indianapolis to pursue his dream, he was arrested in Cambridge, Massachusetts, on a vagrancy charge. Remarkably, he was released from custody on the strength of his poetry.[71] By 1914, the publisher that Jones and Johnson shared was well equipped to publish a biography of Allen Allensworth, the U.S. army's first Black lieutenant colonel, by Black scholar Charles Alexander.[72]

In the world of publishing, Braithwaite was in a much better position than any of these African American writers. Sales of Braithwaite's poetry anthologies were far higher than the entire sea of "little magazines" that had cropped up in the United States by the mid-1910s. In a 1915 letter to his colleague Amy Lowell, the white imagist poet, Braithwaite estimated that sales of the *Anthology of Magazine Verse* that year would be "ten thousand copies at least this fall and winter."[73] By contrast, the avant-garde periodical *The Little Review* (est. 1914) reported a subscriber base of just one thousand readers in Chicago before moving its operation to New York in 1917.[74] In early 1916, author and literary critic Dorothea Lawrance Mann heaped praise on Braithwaite for "making American verse national" and for the recent multicity "influx of purely poetical magazines, and the forming of poetry clubs."[75]

Braithwaite later recalled that his promotional efforts on behalf of James Weldon Johnson and hundreds of others had supported this cultural momentum: "The publicity given to poetry in the press, the appearance of other poetry magazines in different parts of the country, and the space given in general periodicals like *The New Republic* and *The Freeman* [...] made the public so conscious of the art that the renaissance took full stride."[76] While poetry held pride of place in the renaissance that predated the 1920s, its rebirth in the United States fueled new experiments in both established and emerging literary genres.

In 1918, Braithwaite was awarded the NAACP's fourth Spingarn Medal, a prize named after Joel Spingarn for outstanding achievement by an African American. *Reedy's Mirror*, an influential literary journal based in St. Louis, readily credited Braithwaite as one of the leading figures revolutionizing American letters in this era: "He has done so much for poetry that he is ranked among its friends with those who have been most responsible for the poetic renaissance in the United States." According to this critic, Braithwaite had distinguished himself from other critics through his commitment to open-minded and inclusive leadership in the creative field: "[Braithwaite] keeps his readers in touch with every new poet. [. . .] He is hospitable to every new rhymer or free verser. No school claims him. [. . .] People who write poetry, north, south, east or west of Boston look alike to him as people. It is only as poets that he differentiates them."[77] For better and for worse, Braithwaite was more attuned to racial heritage than this commentary suggests. And fellow Black authors, critics, and publications were almost uniform in supporting and praising his contributions in the 1910s.

In 1916, the first issue of the Chicago-based *Champion Magazine*, edited by Fenton Johnson, boasted: "Braithwaite's laurels in the literary world are perhaps the greatest of the Negro's achievements. The young poet of Cambridge has proved his race to be the intellectual peer of the other race." Johnson and Braithwaite were at the top of a small but well-known cohort of Black cultural professionals making comparable gains. Just three years earlier, McClurg Bookstore had sold its entire stock of Johnson's first poetry collection, *A Little Dreaming* (1913), just two months after the volume was published. Cheering this breakthrough, the Black weekly newspaper the *Broad Ax* reported not only that the "head buyer" at McClurg's considered sales of *A Little Dreaming* "a phenomenal record for poetry" but that unparalleled demand for Johnson's book signaled that "[t]he Negro poet now takes his place among the 'best sellers,' and is a commercial as well as artistic success."[78] Black books that were this successful seemingly defied recent, covert boycotts on creative but less popular books such as Du Bois's *Quest of the Silver Fleece*.

As Black writers, periodicals, and books gained greater shares of the broader literary market by the mid-1910s, some African American commentators argued that this output upended white supremacist standards. As the *Kansas City Sun* insisted in 1914, since "Afro-American" women and men continued

THE NEGRO: "THOSE ARE MY ACHIEVEMENTS"
Cartoon by E. C. Shefton

FIGURE 1.6. *The Champion Magazine* (December 1916) included a cartoon by
E. C. Shefton, "The Negro: 'Those Are My Achievements.'"

to be "hung apart" from other Americans, supporting Black authors and establishing Black publications was "the epitome of common sense" for Black
readers: "We must read Negro papers, Negro periodicals, Negro magazines,
and Negro books to be in accord with the onward and upward march of the
race."[79] Black periodicals multiplied rapidly in the United States by the end of
1916. An eclectic sample of Black magazines published in that year alone

FIGURE 1.7. Black periodicals multiplied rapidly in the United States by the end of 1916. Two examples include (a) *Colored American Review* (March 1916) and (b) *The Champion Magazine* (October 1916).

FIGURE 1.7. (*continued*)

illuminates how closely their producers followed early modern Europe's Renaissance artists in borrowing liberally from Greco-Roman iconography.

These new and expansive Black print commodities also carried forward the unconventional perspectives of ancient writers such as Herodotus, who posited that ancient Greece had borrowed heavily from ancient African civilizations. "Herodotus gives us some remarkable information [on Africa] that he acquired by traveling four hundred years before Jesus Christ," Claude McKay explained. "And as late as the fifteenth century, in the high tide of the European renaissance, Leo the African adventured below the Sahara to give the world historical facts about the Negro nations."[80] Providing a corrective to imperialist notions about Africa and her descendants in the centuries that followed, in 1916, periodicals such as the Chicago-based *Pullman Porters' Review* emphasized announcements that they were "For All The People."[81] Countless new and established white writers and critics echoed Black calls for cultural unity in the 1910s, but their contributions to this inclusionary ideal were often at odds with racially egalitarian conceptions of the African diaspora promoted by McKay and numerous others.

Authenticating Negroes

When Harriet Monroe launched *Poetry* in late 1912, critics knew of her abiding love for Black and interracial culture.[82] In the same month that the first issue of *Poetry* was published, Monroe fulsomely praised Paul Laurence Dunbar in an essay on the state of "modern American poetry" in London's *Poetry Review*. In this piece, Monroe characterized Dunbar's literary acumen as reflecting the essence of "the Southern negro," which was not particularly unusual. But she went on to discuss Dunbar's legacy alongside—rather than in distinction from—a host of other popular, white-authored texts, including seventeenth-century Scottish poetry.[83] In short, Monroe was pulling oft-separated literary traditions together, rather than assuming or reinscribing cultural hierarchies.

Monroe lamented that Dunbar, who died in 1906, had "pass[ed] too soon, [leaving] as his supreme achievement not a plantation melody, beautiful as some of these are, but one of the finest death songs of the language."[84] Monroe also implied that new magazines such as *Poetry* held the potential to "unite and inform" rather than divide Americans from one another. "Public sympathy is not dead," Monroe wrote, "but remote and scattered and unaware." Albert Shaw's *American Review of Reviews*, with an estimated circulation of more than eighty thousand, reprinted Monroe's remarks on Dunbar, as well as her perspectives on the "poetic Renaissance," which, "if not yet here, may [...] be close on the way." Affirmations of Monroe's commentaries on "modern" poetry in the *American Review of Reviews*, and periodicals such as *Current Opinion*, ensured that a broad readership was aware of her new publication's pluralist ambitions—even if they never bothered to secure a copy of her avant-garde monthly.[85] Monroe's philosophy of racially inclusive poetry encouraged Fenton Johnson to send his unsolicited work to *Poetry* beginning in 1913, sparking a dialogue that lasted several years.[86]

In 1914, Monroe insisted in the "Comment and Reviews" section of *Poetry* that "[m]odern inventions, forcing international travel, and inter-racial thought, upon the world, have done away with Dante's little audience, [and] with his contempt for the crowd."[87] Her remarks were a counterclaim against Ezra Pound, the foreign correspondent for *Poetry*. Monroe had initially been enthusiastic about Pound's "recent distinguished [literary] success in London," the reason she tapped him for such an important role in her newly established publication.[88] Unfortunately for Monroe, decades before Pound famously claimed that "Adolf Hitler was a Jeanne d'Arc, a saint," who, "[l]ike many martyrs [. . .] held extreme views," his racism extended to contempt for multiculturalism.[89] In other words, Pound hated Monroe's "open door" motto for poetry, which for her included cultivating a heterogeneous audience. In 1914, Pound began to protest these values more openly, after having done so in private up to this point.[90] A letter he wrote to Alice Corbin Henderson, Monroe's coeditor at *Poetry* in 1913, offers a sense of the racism Pound had previously hidden. Writing from London, Pound made plain how perplexed he was by Braithwaite's racial identity in light of his preeminence in the publishing world: "Sorry [to learn that] Braithwaite is a nigger. [. . .] I have taken the trouble to be more contemptuous to him than I should have ever thought of being to any one but a man of equal race. [. . .] A Boston coon!! [T]hat explains a lot."[91] The following year, when Monroe defended interracialism, she was rebuking Pound's sordid obsession with Braithwaite's race.

Monroe's willingness to challenge white supremacist customs in the early 1910s paralleled other progressive, innovative treatments and interpretations of African and African American culture in this era. One of the first exhibitions of African sculpture in the United States also took place in 1914. Describing the *Negro Art Exhibition* he co-curated with photographer Alfred Stieglitz, the prominent New York gallerist and Mexican expatriate Marius de Zayas claimed that year that welcoming Black cultural perspectives was long overdue: "Negro art has re-awakened in us a sensibility obliterated by an education."[92] Zayas wasn't claiming that either African culture or the African diaspora was equal to white counterparts. Nevertheless, such declarations and creative activism challenged Western artistic and intellectual standards that had typically erased Black cultural achievements as a rule.

POETRY: *A Magazine of Verse*

TWO NEGRO SPIRITUALS

A DREAM

I had a dream last night, a wonderful dream.
I saw an angel riding in a chariot—
Oh, my honey, it was a lovely chariot,
Shining like the sun when noon is on the earth.
I saw his wings spreading from moon to earth;
I saw a crown of stars upon his forehead;
I saw his robes agleaming like his chariot.
I bowed my head and let the angel pass,
Because no man can look on Glory's work;
I bowed my head and trembled in my limbs,
Because I stood on ground of holiness.
I heard the angel in the chariot singing:
    "Hallelujah early in the morning!
    I know my Redeemer liveth—
    How is it with your soul?"

I stood on ground of holiness and bowed;
The River Jordan flowed past my feet
As the angel soothed my soul with song,
A song of wonderful sweetness.
I stooped and washed my soul in Jordan's stream
Ere my Redeemer came to take me home;
I stooped and washed my soul in waters pure
As the breathing of a new-born child

[128]

FIGURE 1.8. Fenton Johnson's "Two Negro Spirituals" appeared in the December 1921 issue of Harriet Monroe's *Poetry*.

Monroe's enthusiasm for "inter-racial thought" was similarly laudable but also less equitable than she was willing to admit. Her support for white authors such as the poet Vachel Lindsay, who popularized Black cultural themes with such works as the poetic narrative "The Congo: A Study of the Negro Race" (1913), irked peers such as Braithwaite, who were deeply suspicious of

Fenton Johnson

Lying on a mammy's breast at night.
I looked and saw the angel descending
And a crown of stars was in his hand:
"Be ye not amazed, good friend," he said,
"I bring a diadem of righteousness,
A covenant from the Lord of life,
That in the morning you will see
Eternal streets of gold and pearl aglow
And be with me in blessèd Paradise."

The vision faded.   I awoke and heard
A mocking-bird upon my window-sill.

THE WONDERFUL MORNING

When it is morning in the cornfield
I am to go and meet my Jesus
          Riding on His white horse.
When it is morning in the cornfield
I am to be there in my glory.
          Shout, my brethren!   Shout, my sisters!
I am to meet the King of Morning
          Way down in the cornfield.
                              Fenton Johnson

[129]

FIGURE 1.8. (*continued*)

exoticizing African American life. Monroe's frequent endorsements and publications of Lindsay's poems catapulted his career.

Initially, Black critics such as W.E.B. Du Bois welcomed Lindsay's interracial perspectives. In a letter that Du Bois published in the *Crisis* in 1915, Lindsay, who grew up in Springfield, Illinois, explained that "The Congo" was an outgrowth of his responses to the racial violence in his hometown in 1908.

FIGURE 1.9. The *Negro Art Exhibition* (November 1914) at Alfred Stieglitz's 291 Gallery in New York was one of the first exhibitions of African sculpture in the United States.

Lindsay recalled: "Way back in 1908 I had attempted several magazine articles, just after the Springfield anti-Negro riots. [. . .] Those riots shook my young soul. It was my first revelation of the savagery of the white man."[93] As this memory suggests, the catalyst for Lindsay's literary work shared much in common with James Weldon Johnson's attempt to situate *The Autobiography of an Ex-Colored Man* two months after Springfield's riots.

In 1914, Monroe hosted a banquet in Chicago to honor the Irish poet William Butler Yeats and enlisted Lindsay to recite his own work after dinner. Lindsay's performance of "The Congo" that evening captivated the entire room, including the Black waiters catering the event. A description of Lindsay's performance of "The Congo" written by an attendee for *The Dial* emphasized how taken wealthy white Chicagoans were by this young, handsome poet: "When Mr. Lindsay had finished, he was surrounded by women who wished to be his hostesses at dinner. The North Shore had discovered a lion who could roar! The young man who had come up to Chicago to stay three days remained three weeks."[94] In a letter to Yeats decades later, Lindsay remembered: "That instant remains, as it appeared then, the literary transformation scene of my life."[95] In a book of poetry and essays published just a few months after the Chicago event honoring Yeats in 1914, Lindsay observed that a "new" New England was on the horizon, "a New England of ninety million souls! An artistic Renaissance is coming."[96] The fact that a prosperous segment of Chicago's white community was captivated by "The Congo" bolstered claims like these, echoing other proclamations of a nascent literary renaissance.

For all of Lindsay's good fortune and enthusiasm, his hope that "The Congo" would valorize Black life and culture for white audiences fell short of the mark in critical ways. The poem's opening lyrics celebrate "[f]at black bucks in a wine-barrel room," under a subheading titled "Their Basic Savagery." For Lindsay, "The Congo" was "a scrap of grand black opera."[97] By imagining Congolese culture as a site for poetry at its most pure and formidable, Lindsay argued that his fetishistic conception of Africa and the African diaspora was untainted by the corrupting artifice of modern civilization. But for many readers, Lindsay's most popular poem was little more than a rowdy minstrel show.

In a defense of Lindsay and "The Congo" in 1915, Du Bois noted in *The Crisis*: "Colored readers may be repelled at first by Lindsay's great poem, but it is, in its spirit, a splendid tribute with all its imperfections of spiritual insight."[98] Braithwaite, however, did not share Du Bois's convictions. Despite vigorously supporting poems that Lindsay had published in 1913, Braithwaite wrote in his review of *The Congo and Other Poems* that this book did "not mark an advance" on the poet's earlier work—which had avoided foregrounding racial essentialism.[99] By 1916, Du Bois and Braithwaite both agreed that poems like "The Congo," with lines such as "kill the white men," were problematic, and Du Bois was even blunter in rejecting Lindsay's attempts "now and then to make a contribution to Negro literature."[100] White cultural professionals monitored this development. "Mr. Lindsay has written many poems about the negro," *Publishers' Weekly* reported, qualifying that "Mr. Braithwaite [. . .] thinks they misrepresent the race, and regard it 'purely as a spectacle.'"[101] Higher scrutiny from Braithwaite and Du Bois of Lindsay's "contributions" to Black and interracial literature was emblematic of a growing racial schism at the top of the publishing establishment.

By the second half of the 1910s, a growing number of white writers rebuffed toning down or eliminating exotic and downright offensive depictions of African Americans. At the same time, tensions between Black and white authors and critics grew over linguistic biases. The majority of white Americans, regardless of whether they read Black-directed publications, were well aware that their use of *nigger* made this term a racial epithet.[102] But rather than respecting and building upon the work of cultural activists to drop this epithet from the language, Carl Sandburg and other white writers countered that *nigger* should become common parlance.

In 1916, Sandburg published *Chicago Poems*, a volume that included a poem titled, simply: "Nigger." The poem conjures a wide-ranging sample of repugnant racial stereotypes, including "I am the nigger. Singer of songs, Dancer," with "Lazy love of the banjo thrum," and "Smiling the slumber dreams of old jungles," to name only a few.[103] Sandburg, like Lindsay, cast himself in what might best be described as literary blackface, in an ill-advised attempt to highlight the joys and struggles in what little of Black life he knew—or imagined. But well-read Black readers and critics had little patience for well-meaning white gestures like these. Poems like "Nigger" reflected neither literary modernism nor interracial cultural progress. As with his review of Lindsay's *The Congo and Other Poems*, Braithwaite was unimpressed with Sandburg's *Chicago Poems*.[104]

Sandburg was offended by Braithwaite's negative review of *Chicago Poems* in the *Transcript*. In a letter to Alice Corbin Henderson, Monroe's coeditor at *Poetry*, Sandburg claimed not to know what had incensed Braithwaite about his book: "Why should the writings of a Chicago Swede wop give any Boston nigger a headache"? Sandburg rhetorically asked: "Has B[raithwaite] a tapeworm? Or is he ashamed of his blood?"[105] But it is Sandburg's insistence that Braithwaite's review reminded him of "the mumblings of a Pullman porter making the bed of a berth occupant who didn't slip him the req[u]isite twenty-five cents" that makes plain his allegiances to white supremacist standards.[106]

Winners and Losers

The publishing market was once again in a state of flux following the end of World War I. By 1919, the cost of paper for book manufacturing in the United States was twice as much as it had been in 1917. There were fewer opportunities to publish and lower professional prospects for several of the Black authors who had found a modest yet significant toehold in the literary field during the previous decade. Boston's Cornhill Publishing Company had been an invaluable resource for Black writers seeking to publish books in a wide range of genres in the 1910s—especially during the years when Braithwaite helped run the firm.[107] When Brookes More assumed control of Cornhill in 1921, the firm simply stopped publishing Black authors. Speculating on the "bad financial straits" at Cornhill preceding More's decision to buy the firm, literary scholar George Hutchinson has observed: "Presumably More had no interest in publishing African American poets; in any case, he published no more of them."[108] But fledgling poets were not the only Black writers to see their precarious fortunes turn by the early 1920s.

African American letters and culture in the United States were becoming "blacker." In short, a growing number of writers, critics, and cultural professionals were asserting that there was an essential Black aesthetic. This trend was a biracial development, and many established Black authors who once held pride of place became increasingly unfashionable. Discriminatory practices, which had never been excised from the literary field, made these shifts more complicated. Ambiguities reigned as African American writers and editors such as Braithwaite, Fenton Johnson, and Charles Chesnutt lost ground in various areas of the publishing sector. In 1921, Chesnutt sent his novel *Paul Marchand: Free Man of Color* to his long-standing publisher, Houghton Mifflin. Highlighting his track record with the firm, Chesnutt explained, "I naturally think of your house first in this connection, since most of my other books are on your list. [. . .] [M]y books, as you know, still sell, and if I have written a good one, I imagine it would sell regardless of the others."[109] Houghton's staff was unmoved by Chesnutt's successes. Nor were they moved by a historical novel set in nineteenth-century New Orleans that foregrounded the story of an educated, affluent "quadroon." A representative of the firm explained: "Business conditions in the publishing trade are very badly mixed at present, as possibly you know."[110] *Paul Marchand: Free Man of Color* remained unpublished until 1999.

Changing tastes of white editors and publishers surely felled many Black authors after World War I. But for Fenton Johnson, discrimination in lending

Opportunity Wanted

FIGURE 1.10. Cartoons in *The Champion Magazine* such as (top) "Opportunity Wanted" (E. C. Shefton, February 1917) and (bottom) "Whose Move?" (unattributed, March 1917) drew attention to racial discrimination in hiring and prejudices in and beyond publishing.

arguably posed a greater threat to his literary career. Atypically for an African American, Johnson received a substantial inheritance following the death of his aunt. Following the war, the poet and editor sought to leverage this capital to salvage his second periodical, *The Favorite Magazine*. In the introduction to his self-published book *Tales of Darkest America*, Johnson described how a Chicago-based insurer refused to lend money to him or any other Blacks, irrespective of their assets: "One incident I can never forget as long as I live [...] is the case of Conkling, Price, Webb & Company, a bonding firm that refused me surety bonds to draw from my aunt's estate. [...] The only cause given [to] me was 'that colored people's estates were too risky.'"[111] Business conditions were indeed "very badly mixed" for African Americans—both during and following the heady 1910s.

For white authors writing about Black life in this era, there were simply not as many barriers to publishing. The tenacity of a mix of unintended, covert, and blatant racial discrimination exacerbated Black disadvantages across the publishing sector. While countless white writers produced Black texts that were well intentioned in the 1920s, others produced narratives undermined by an uneasy alchemy of pejorative stereotypes joined with progressive viewpoints. In sum, this cohort of white authors and cultural professionals were Vachel Lindsay and Carl Sandburg's successors.

―――――

Clement Wood, a white graduate of the University of Alabama, received his law degree from Yale in 1911. He went on to pursue a career as a writer, mainly of poetry, and in 1919, New York's E. P. Dutton published his collection *The Earth Turns South*. This volume contained three of Wood's popular Black dialect poems, most notably "Nigger Hebb'n."[112] In a highly positive review, a critic writing for the *Brooklyn Daily Eagle* singled out these poems as three of the four "most interesting and successful verses in the volume."[113] Even more mixed reviews of the book still praised these three poems as representing what the *New-York Tribune* called a "successful experiment in negro dialect poetry."[114] That summer, the *Montgomery Advertiser* assured its readers that Wood's poetry conveyed a "rare faculty of knowing and interpreting the true soul of the southern negro in its wilder and more primitive aspects."[115] His poems were, indeed, both wild and primitive, rendering Black speech with exaggerated misspellings and childlike glee. Wood made his name depicting Black protagonists who were comic, pitiable simpletons. In "Nigger Hebb'n," the tragic

Negro's aspirations were so limited that they could only hope to be "Wash[ed]" as "white as de dribb'n snow" and find "possum 'n' 'taters" in "Jerusalem land."[116]

Poems like these were so widely praised and commercially successful that Dutton readily sponsored Wood's *Nigger: A Novel* (1922), a 230-page book written from the perspective of its African American protagonists.[117] Wood's *Nigger* follows generations of a Black family from the last years of slavery to their disillusionment with sharecropping and their eventual relocation to "Bummin'ham [Birmingham]," the largest city in Alabama. As the title suggests, the book's dialogue continues in the same vein as "Nigger Hebb'n," with garbled spelling and primitivist portraits of Black life. The subject matter, however, gave substantially more breadth to the African American experience, with vivid depictions of the difficulties and injustices facing Black Southerners in a cruel, racist environment. Many progressive critics were won over by Wood's *Nigger*, praising his "touching" and "wonderful knowledge of the negro."[118] The *Montgomery Advertiser* congratulated Wood for his images of a "colored man" who was neither "sentimentalized over nor glorified nor made comic. He is shown as a human being."[119] Northern critical reactions to both Wood and *Nigger: A Novel* were more mixed.

In 1922, Hubert Harrison, Harlem's leading socialist, described Wood in the *New-York Tribune* as "seem[ing] to lack the necessary equipment" to portray the novel's African American protagonists in an "objective manner." The previous year, Cornhill's Brookes More urged Braithwaite to publicly denounce Wood, whom he described as a "wild-eyed radical." Claiming that he was far from alone in finding the author of "Nigger Hebb'n" repugnant, More declared: "I have had experience with Clement Wood and I have had a great many people express their opinions about him. He is absolutely unpopular and despised by a very large number of the better element in this country, and I seriously believe he deserves it."[120] As with Houghton's letter rejecting Chesnutt's *Paul Marchand: Free Man of Color*, there is no clear indication that More's comment had a racial dimension. At the same time, in outlining his animus for Wood, More's remarks signal a deep, unresolved tension between interracialists like Braithwaite and white men like Wood and Carl Sandburg.[121]

While it would be a mistake to characterize More as a racial progressive—especially after his firm stopped publishing Black authors—his letter did urge Braithwaite to use his cultural capital to rebuke Wood's poems: "[Y]ou have secured a reputation for praising everybody. [. . .] [T]hey do not realize that you do not criticize poetry that you do not like."[122] But Braithwaite did like Wood, despite criticizing *Nigger: A Novel* in 1925 for being based on "wholly illogical material."[123] Indeed, in spite of More's pleading, Wood's poems appeared in the 1922, 1923, 1925, and 1926 editions of Braithwaite's anthology. It helped that Wood acknowledged Braithwaite as "the leading anthologist of the country" in 1922.[124] It was also to his credit that Wood was kind to a rising generation of Black authors, writing glowing reviews of Black poets such as Claude McKay and James Weldon Johnson.[125]

Other white authors seeking to capitalize on the new cultural vogue for racial epithets were more ambivalent. Two years after *Nigger: A Novel* was published, Ronald Firbank, a young English author primarily known for sophisticated novels about British aristocrats, published *Prancing Nigger* (1924). The publication was sponsored by Brentano's, a boutique firm in New York. The novel follows the hijinks of a Black family residing on a fictitious Caribbean island that moves from their primitive village in an attempt to break into high society. Firbank's rendering of Black dialect was as denigrating as Wood's, if not more so.

A journalist for Honolulu's *Star Bulletin* accurately "suspect[ed]" that the racial dialect featured in Firbank's *Prancing Nigger* "was never heard either in the West Indies or in the Solid South."[126] Other detractors, such as the reviewer for the *Brooklyn Daily Eagle*, characterized Firbank's characters as "[s]illy, empty, and tiresome."[127] In a review titled "Dialect Hurdle Is High Hazard for New Firbank Yarn," Fanny Butcher, a literary critic for *The Chicago Tribune*, faulted Carl Van Vechten, the power broker responsible for recommending the publication of *Prancing Nigger*, and chided Firbank for perpetuating tired tropes of "most stories about Negroes" written by whites: "talk which the writer thinks they talk rather than talk that they do talk."[128] Criticisms like these, however, were rare. Most contemporary critics greeted the novel with praise. A decade earlier, Brander Matthews, James Weldon Johnson's mentor, published "The Rise and Fall of Negro-Minstrelsy" (1915), an essay commensurate with his broader aims of encouraging erudite and universal perspectives on Black literary and cultural themes.[129] By the mid-1920s, this work was thrown into question when publications such as the *New York Times Book Review* casually described the title of *Prancing Nigger* as a "triumph" that was a "hilarious invitation" to "a glorious blackface minstrel show."[130]

Carl Van Vechten was responsible not only for the publication of *Prancing Nigger* in the United States but also for the title. In a 1923 letter to Firbank, Van Vechten explained that "after reading this delightful opus, I suggested that Prancing Nigger would be a better title, and [the editors of the book] all agreed to this." While Van Vechten was aware that titles like these offended African

Americans, he suggested it would improve sales: "I may say, however, that beyond a doubt the new title would sell at least a thousand more copies."[131] Two years later, when Knopf published Van Vechten's infamous novel *Nigger Heaven* (1926), sales of this book were exponentially larger than those of *Prancing Nigger*. The enormous commercial success of the novel was like a knife in the back for Black authors and intellectuals who had established reputations long before the 1920s. But authors such as Charles Chesnutt, whose writing career in the 1920s was precarious—at best—feared speaking out against Van Vechten.

In a letter to W.E.B. Du Bois in 1926, Chesnutt wrote, "I could not criticize [*Nigger Heaven*] adversely [in public] even if I cared to, because of the fact that he had treated me so splendidly in his comments on my writing."[132] In a note to another Black friend the following year, Chesnutt similarly confessed, "I was shocked by the name of the book, and there were other respects in which [*Nigger Heaven*] is not above criticism."[133] True to his reputation, Du Bois wasted little time in condemning Van Vechten. In an essay initially published in *The Crisis* and reprinted by the African American *Pittsburgh Courier*, Du Bois, aware of Van Vechten's social and professional ties to some of the nation's leading Black cultural professionals, characterized *Nigger Heaven* as "an affront to the hospitality of black folk and to the intelligence of white. First, as to its title: My objection is based on no provincial dislike of the nickname. [. . .] It is worse than untruth because it is a mass of half-truths." Indeed, these problems were only compounded by the novel's title, which helps explain why Du Bois complained that "Carl Van Vechten's 'Nigger Heaven' is a blow in the face."[134] As strange as it may seem, this assessment would not have surprised Van Vechten.

Before his novel was published, Van Vechten's own father, Charles Duane Van Vechten, advised him to choose a less offensive title. In November 1925, Charles, the cofounder of an African American school in Mississippi, informed his son: "Your 'Nigger Heaven' is a title I don't like." Indeed, the cautionary letter Charles sent to his son insisted that his proposed use of this racial epithet ran counter to the elementary courtesy he had shown African Americans for several decades: "I have myself never spoken of a colored man as a 'nigger.' If you are trying to help the race, as I am assured you are, I think every word you write should be a respectful one towards the blacks."[135] Carl Van Vechten was in his mid-forties when *Nigger Heaven* was published. He knew that using this title would be perceived as a contentious if not retrograde choice by most African Americans.

Back in 1922, the year *Nigger: A Novel* was published, Eric Walrond, a twenty-three-year-old Black writer, published a searing essay explaining why white authors should not use the term *nigger*. Walrond complained, "The word [*nigger*] is a stigma of inferiority and its [white] users know it. Ever since its origin it was used to label the Negro as a member of an inferior race." Worse still, Walrond warned, was how this trend impacted racial perceptions: "Today the Negro, to a vast portion of the American public, is yet a 'Nigger.'"[136] Three years later, an unattributed essay published in the *Negro Year Book* (1925) expanded upon Walrond's concerns: "Now comes along the startling suggestion from Carl Sandburg, the Chicago poet and journalist, a man who is decidedly friendly and sympathetic. His suggestion is that we bodily adopt the term 'Nigger.'"[137] While conceding that the word was "commonly used among colored people themselves" as "a term of endearment," this essay cautioned that this should not be misconstrued as an endorsement for broader use: "[T]here is hardly a Negro in the United States so humble or so ignorant that he does not bitterly resent its use by any white person."[138] This message certainly had not registered with a host of white, male authors or corporate cultural professionals such as Alfred and Blanche Knopf, who published *Nigger Heaven* just a few months later.

According to an essay Van Vechten published in 1925, if African American authors were disturbed by how white writers depicted Black lives, these "idiosyncratic reactions" were "caused by an extreme sensitiveness."[139] Van Vechten frequently justified his mode of literary racialism by citing Black allies who defended and praised him, a group that included Wallace Thurman, Langston Hughes, Charles Chesnutt, and several other Black writers. It was convenient for Van Vechten to ignore the unequal power dynamics between him and writers such as Chesnutt, who clearly feared the professional consequences of publicly attacking *Nigger Heaven*.

Drawing the Color Line

More than two decades earlier, in 1901, Chesnutt informed his publishers that his "friend Mr. [William Dean] Howells," the foremost white literary critic of the late nineteenth century, "has remarked several times that there is no color line in literature. On that point I take issue with him. I am pretty fairly convinced that the color line runs everywhere as far as the United States is concerned."[140] Chesnutt was deeply familiar with a "color line" in the publishing sector that his white friends and professional interlocutors failed to see. But even for Chesnutt, it was difficult to ascertain how racial segregation in the literary field was changing over time.

After the turn of the century, the utopian vision of American literary culture heralded by Braithwaite and others signaled the fracturing of separatist impulses across publishing. Yet by the late 1910s, the color line was reemerging. One white author and critic lamented in 1922, "Art ought to be at least one field in which the color line might readily be dispensed with. It isn't. A publisher once told us that he found it impossible to sell an anthology of American poetry by William Stanley Braithwaite in the south because Mr. Braithwaite is a negro."[141] Braithwaite's knowledge and expertise threatened the fiction of white supremacy in American literature. In the 1920s, racist opposition to his stature stretched well beyond the South. Nevertheless, during the interwar period, Black and white cultural professionals continued writing and collaborating across racial lines. But a growing number of white interlocutors consciously and unconsciously assumed that Black authors and editors would be junior partners in biracial literary texts and cultural endeavors. The proliferation of a cottage industry for white-authored poems and books with *nigger* in their titles is emblematic of this profound shift.

Three years after Sandburg published *Chicago Poems* (1916), he wrote a series of newspaper articles on the 1919 race riots in Chicago. The NAACP's Joel Spingarn ensured that these essays were published by his friend Alfred Harcourt the same year as *The Chicago Race Riots, July 1919*. Walter Lippmann, a Harvard-trained author, contributed the introduction to Sandburg's book, which unambiguously argued that Black and white Americans needed to embrace segregation: "Since permanent degradation is unthinkable, and amalgamation undesirable for both blacks and whites, the ideal would seem to lie in what might be called race parallelism. Parallel lines may be equally long and equally straight; they do not join except in infinity, which is further away than anyone need worry about just now."[142] It would be difficult to overstate how convenient statements like these were for white men like Sandburg who had chafed at the cultural authority of Black men such as Braithwaite.

Three years later, Jean Toomer complained in a 1922 letter to his white Jewish friend Waldo Frank that another white Chicagoan, Sherwood Anderson, "[l]imits me to Negro."[143] When white peers, editors, and publishers forced Black writers to stay within a racially particular habitus, authors such as Toomer associated these schemes with the color line. Anderson's celebrations of a newly emboldened white South in *Vanity Fair* four years later, in 1926, illustrate that Toomer's fears were not overblown: "The South—the white

South—getting bolder. Southern white life will yet express itself—really—in song, prose, painting, music."[144] In the same essay, Anderson also complained: "The Negro contributing—doing too much of the contributing now. A second-rate Negro poet or artist [is] always getting twice the credit of an equally able white man. That's northern sentimentality." Of course, Black authors like Toomer knew that this "northern sentimentality" was running thin by the mid-1920s.[145]

Authors such as Anderson, Lippmann, and Sandburg and numerous other white writers and critics clearly and casually assumed that "Negroes" in general, and "Negro authors" in particular, were racially inferior. Writing for the *New York Times* in 1927, Herbert Gorman, a leading scholar of James Joyce, illustrates what this trend looked like in popular literary criticism: "Among the Americans Langston Hughes belongs to the colored race and it is therefore impossible to estimate him beside, say, Humbert Wolfe or Richard Aldington [white British poets]."[146] Summing up the annual production of American poetry for 1927 soon after Gorman's review was published by the *Times*, George R. Stewart Jr., an assistant professor at the University of California, Los Angeles, claimed that since Langston Hughes, James Weldon Johnson, and other Black writers were "more interested in interpreting their own race than themselves," they could "largely be placed under—[or considered] inferior to—the head [literary category] of objective poetry."[147]

Dominant literary categories and white authors were not explicitly marked by race. At the same time, Stewart insisted in 1928 that racial identity—and an "inferior" one at that—consistently diminished several now-canonical Black authors who flourished in this epoch. In a telling aside, Stewart singled out Countee Cullen as distinct from his allegedly subpar African American peers: "Countee Cullen must be separated from the other negro writers mentioned above, because his work is individualistic and lacks a specially racial touch."[148] Cullen didn't need to be "separated" from other Black authors. When Black authors like Toomer rejected how white writers and cultural professionals invoked these labels, they were not rejecting their racial identities. They were asserting a right to use their Black heritage strategically—and much more respectfully than white interlocutors.

Five years earlier, after Boni & Liveright requested that Toomer emphasize his "colored blood" in a description of himself they planned to advertise, he responded: "My racial composition and my position in the world are realities which I alone may determine."[149] Whenever he could, Toomer highlighted his aspiration to "take the color of whatever group I at the time am sojourning in."

FIGURE 1.11. Jean Toomer ice skating with friends, 1916.

He thus lamented the likelihood that "I shall doubtless be classed as a Negro" by white critics following Boni & Liveright's publication of *Cane* in 1923.[150] Jessie Fauset, the second Black author Boni & Liveright published, was indeed "classed" by the firm one year after *Cane* was published. Fauset's novel *There Is Confusion* (1924) foregrounded the lives and times of a proud, educated, and talented Black family.

In at least one advertisement for Fauset's novel, Boni & Liveright advertised the book to white readers as an "absorbing story" that affirmed "the belief of sociologists that the solution of our color problem lies in the development of a milieu that, self-contained, parallels the life of the white American."[151] In a combined review of Firbank's *Prancing Nigger* (1924) alongside *There Is Confusion* published by the Minnesota *Star Tribune*, Mississippi-born Herschel Brickell echoed Boni & Liveright's affirmations of racial segregation in this advertisement. Brickell concluded that Fauset had not produced "a remarkable novel," but he nevertheless appreciated the "thoroughly civilized" Black protagonists in her book. Fauset, a Cornell University alumna and a literary critic for over a decade, was familiar with biased critiques like these from white peers, which affirmed common assumptions that Blacks in the United States must "self-contain." When white critics such as Brickell estimated that Fauset's book illuminated how Blacks were "paralleling in culture that of the whites," they fueled, rather than tempered, racial divisions.[152]

When white writers, critics, and intellectuals like Monroe advocated for "inter-racial thought" back in the mid-1910s, they were advancing, albeit gradually, a common cultural agenda. A decade later, a growing number of their successors recklessly substituted cooperative rhetoric with hierarchical conceptions of interracialism. In 1925, one white journalist's article published by newspapers in West Virginia and Tennessee offers a sense of how anti-egalitarian popular commentary on multiculturalism often was in descriptions of the Harlem Renaissance: "The African, with his love of color, warmth, rhythm and the whole sensuous life, might, if emotionally liberated, do things interesting to a 'Nordic' stock, so bustling and busy, so pre-occupied with 'doing things' in the external world."[153] Summarizing the literate public's growing awareness of the "Negro renaissance," this critic also pointed out that the French author Alexandre Dumas *père* "was the grandson of a Negro—but [...] these American Negroes are expressing for the most part essentially Negro feeling and standing squarely on their racial inheritance."[154] Ironically, in the 1920s, Dumas remained an important model for numerous aspiring and established African American writers. Back in the 1830s, Dumas closely monitored the trajectory of the African diaspora, "not only in France, but everywhere I can count my brothers in race and friends of color."[155] Much the same was true of the mixed-race Russian author Alexander Pushkin, whose Black African heritage Dumas researched and commemorated in the 1860s. Pushkin also decried "the fate of my brothers the Negroes," irrespective of where they were held in "unendurable slavery."[156] A century later, when white commentators laid bare their preoccupations with racial differences during the Harlem Renaissance, their widely circulated musings obscured long-standing calls for pan-African unity in this spirit.

In 1926, William H. Ferris, a Black Yale graduate and scholar, acknowledged that it was "very gratifying to colored people to see a renaissance of interest in the aspiration and activities of the Negro." On the other hand, Ferris warned that "there is also a tendency to a cultural segregation of the Negro."[157] Ferris's remarks echoed other prominent Black critics in this era who decried "the constant presentation of the Negro in novels, short stories, plays and movies as a savage," which appeared in Van Vechten's *Nigger Heaven* through his "over-emphasis of the grotesque." Like numerous other detractors, Ferris argued that the 1920s had inaugurated a new "segregation wave [...] which rose to its crest in the present year [1926]." Ferris's lengthy essay was featured on the front page of the *Pittsburgh Courier*, the nation's Black newspaper of record. The paper's editor explained in a note above Ferris's reflections that his opinion on the "latest craze for typifying the Negro" had been solicited "[b]ecause of the un-doubted wave of 'Niggerism' sweeping over the country, and because of the obvious support many so-called Negro leaders are giving this propaganda." In his autobiography, Claude McKay offered a similar critique when he character-ized the 1920s as "the highly propagandized Negro renaissance period."[158] Like Toomer, McKay indicted both sides of the color line for belaboring and ac-centuating racial and ethnic differences in this era.

In 1927, when McKay informed Alain Locke that he didn't want to be mar-keted as a "Negro author," the perplexed editor of the now-canonical anthol-ogy *The New Negro* (1925) wrote back: "The movement suffers—but that is your prerogative. I hope you will find the abstract universal recognition you desire. My opinion is that your previous work and acceptance of racial repre-sentativeness and spokesmanship will follow you through life and posterity."[159] Five years later, Locke boasted in another letter to McKay that he should "visit over" and observe "'The Newest Negro,' who after all is quite a strange animal. Among other things, he seems to be in a strange state of sexual transformation. Whether this conforms to the Renaissance formula as laid down by yours truly, I can't say."[160] While it would be unfair to take his disparaging comments literally, Locke's letter helps clarify why McKay was so ambivalent about "the exotic flower of the Negro renaissance" in his autobiography.[161]

Back in 1925, Braithwaite, who was a close friend and colleague of Locke's, confessed in a letter that the "last four years [had] been a heavy and steady drain" on him. Braithwaite was referring to his health, but the tenor of his note to Locke suggests that these problems were somehow related to the reemer-gence of the "color line in literature" after the 1910s: "[A]s youth begins to subside I realize with increasing conviction that the [racial] barriers grow more stubborn. There is no doubt, my dear Locke, had I been white, the whole course would have been paved for me, and all I would have had to do would be to travel steadily."[162] Braithwaite was worn down after years of personal and professional setbacks, but they did not keep him from making one of the most expansive contributions to Locke's *New Negro* (1925) anthology or from pursu-ing literary work across racial lines elsewhere. A month before Braithwaite wrote Locke, *Survey Graphic* issued a special issue titled "Harlem: Mecca of the New Negro." Several months later, on the eve of 1926, Albert & Charles Boni—which was no longer affiliated with Boni & Liveright—published Locke's edited adaptation of *Survey Graphic*'s Harlem issue as *The New Negro: An Interpretation* (1925). The volume established Locke's reputation as the midwife of the Harlem Renaissance.

The following year, in 1926, Braithwaite issued a special edition of his annual anthology, which was dedicated to America's sesquicentennial. Truly epic in its scope, this meticulously edited collection of poetry and essays was nearly nine hundred pages, a full third longer than Braithwaite's *Anthology of Magazine Verse for 1925*. In the *Anthology of Magazine Verse for 1926*, there were fifteen essays, including a contribution Braithwaite commissioned from Locke called "The Negro Poets of the United States."

The additional fourteen essays covered the poetry of eight geographic regions (New England, the South, the Midwest, etc.), as well as verse by "Amerindians," Catholics, and Jews. Other essays in Braithwaite's 1926 anthology outlined the influence of Asian (mostly Chinese and Japanese) poetry on American verse and the "'New' Poetry" (modernism). In his essay, Locke identified a historical pattern in Black poetry, from a racially specific form often written in dialect up through the best of contemporary work he considered both universally accessible and valuable: "Negro poetry in the year of America's entry into the Great War, through the work of Roscoe Jameson, Claude McKay and James Weldon Johnson was linked up with the main stream of English poetry, and [...] began to attain universality."[163] While it is true that Locke undermined his "formula" for the Harlem Renaissance by accentuating its "Negro" character, Black writers were far more willing to discover and promote commonalities with their white counterparts by the mid-1920s. Or as William H. Ferris noted in 1926 after lambasting the literary establishment for the "cultural segregation" of African Americans across the publishing sector: "Colored writers are discouraged from writing on philosophy, sociology, science, literature, art and music per se and are advised to write purely on Negro themes."[164] Structural biases and inequalities were at the root of the habits and behaviors Ferris detailed. But when white writers, editors, and publishers denigrated the acumen of Black cultural professionals, they personally benefited from biased customs that protected their dominant positions.

A Vicious Assimilation

Between the second half of the 1910s and the late 1920s, the torrent of racial prejudice in the publishing world was often far more surreptitious than is commonly recognized. One of the best examples of this dynamic is the secret boycott launched against W. S. Braithwaite during World War I. Ezra Pound faulted Braithwaite for destroying literary culture in the United States. In a letter to *Poetry*'s Alice Corbin Henderson, Pound complained that the United States was Braithwaite's "country not mine" and fumed that "America has disappeared. What does it matter whether one's books are sent there, or read there or reviewed there."[165] Henderson sympathized with Pound's white supremacist critiques during the war years, when Braithwaite was still regularly credited for establishing and promoting a literary renaissance in America. Alongside many other witting—and countless unwitting—defenders of racial hierarchies, the bond Pound and Henderson shared was crucial in affirming and reestablishing a "color line" in publishing that Braithwaite's ascendance had called into question.

At the same time, these two were far from alone in their contempt for Braithwaite. "The bad grammar and proofreading can be forgiven, but who can cleave his way through the jungle of [Braithwaite's] incoherent thought?" a young, wealthy white lawyer complained months earlier. Despite the connotations of remarks like these, Braithwaite was urged not to object, "if our lips writhe back at the cup which you have held out to us and if our tongues are twisted to a sincerity that sounds like malice."[166] Several of Braithwaite's white colleagues, peers, and competitors increasingly perceived his dominance and authority in the American literary field as a threat by the second half of the 1910s. But it was Henderson who initially proposed the boycott of Braithwaite's anthology. Her intention was to shrink the number of prominent contributors to Braithwaite's annual volume. In a 1916 letter by Henderson to Harriet Monroe, her colleague at *Poetry*, she noted: "Braithwaite certainly writes 'darky' English. When I was in High School I entered an oratorical contest, in which I won 2nd place and $10. A darky who was working at Mrs. Moody's got 1st place and $15. He was talking about the future of the 'cullud' [colored] race, and he talked just as Braithwaite talks about poetry—hardly a trace of logic or sequence and almost less than the ghost of an idea. My family never got over it."[167] If Monroe "hammered away at the racial and sexual exclusivity" promoted by America's intellectual establishment in the mid-1910s, as one scholar has argued, it is unclear whether she ever tried to counter Henderson's views.[168] What is less ambiguous, however, is that Henderson's unapologetic mocking of Black achievements went hand in hand with her ardent promotions of racial essentialism.

The year after Henderson accused Braithwaite of writing like a "darky," in an essay Henderson wrote for *Poetry*, she claimed that "["the negro's"] emotional reactions, his religious feeling and his imagination are racially different from those of the white man." Henderson then argued that if Black "art" hoped "to amount to anything," the African American would "have to seek to give expression to what is essentially his."[169] Clement Wood, the author of *Nigger: A Novel*, echoed this sentiment in an essay on African American poetry, when he called for the Black poet to abandon the poetic styles of the "broader way of humanity" and return to the "toe-tickling song that is his."[170] Literary scholar Koritha Mitchell has recently characterized the pernicious legacy of white commentaries like these, as examples of "know-your-place aggression."[171] During World War I, when Henderson insisted that "[a]s soon as the negro is educated he begins to think the white man's thoughts, or to try to think them[,] it is impossible for him to do otherwise," her aggression was effectively a direct attack on Braithwaite's literary stature.

Only two months earlier, *Poetry* had published a lengthy, satirical poem titled "On Reading The Braithwaite Anthology for 1916," by Willard Wattles, a lampoon of the anthology's references to ancient Greco-Roman culture—the period underpinning countless features of the "renaissance" in early modern Europe. Wattles packed in as many overwrought allusions to Greek and Roman mythology as he could, scattering in a few tamely outré jokes about nudity and women's underclothes, as well as references to "moonbeams," frolicking "nymphs," and "fauns."[172] The overall effect of the poem is reminiscent of a learned if not clever schoolboy poking fun at the English Romantics' lesser imitators and old-fashioned, pedantic teachers. Nevertheless, it misrepresented the actual content readers found in Braithwaite's anthologies.

While they did indeed include the sort of poems Wattles satirized, Braithwaite also regularly accepted, promoted, and published a wide variety of poetic styles. No one could possibly fault Vachel Lindsay or Amy Lowell, to name just two contemporary authors who had appeared in a Braithwaite anthology, for tired classicism. In the end, subtle takedowns like these complemented Henderson's assertion shortly thereafter in *Poetry* that Black writers were racially unfit to work in European modes. In 1917, Carl Sandburg stated his support for Henderson's scheme to boycott Braithwaite's anthology. Braithwaite had not included Sandburg's work in the 1915 and 1916 anthologies, and Sandburg's supporters noticed these absences.[173] Braithwaite also had published a negative review of *Chicago Poems* (1916) and had criticized Sandburg's work in the introduction to the 1916 anthology.[174] In a letter to Henderson in 1917, Sandburg denounced Braithwaite as a "pathetic personage" who had been "permitted to grow into a fungus mistaken for what it grows on."[175] In spite of this, Braithwaite included Sandburg's poems in the 1917, 1919, and 1920 editions of the anthology.

In a comment relevant to this perplexing paradox, the poet John Gould Fletcher breezily noted in his 1937 autobiography: "Braithwaite I knew to be harmless and lacking in critical standards. His poverty and, still more, his negro blood had worked so long against him that he was prepared to be any-one's sworn defender from the moment he was invited to dinner."[176] Just two years after Fletcher's disparaging remarks about Braithwaite's "negro blood," Fletcher became the first Southerner to win the Pulitzer Prize, a prize also won by Carl Sandburg in 1919 for his poetry collection *Cornhuskers* (1918), the volume that included "Singing Nigger."

Tellingly, many of Braithwaite's covert detractors, such as the essayist H. L. Mencken, who privately referred to him as the "Braithwaite coon," couldn't agree on why the nation's foremost anthologist was inferior to them.[177] While Henderson argued that it was obvious that Braithwaite wrote "darky" English, other white writers such as Allen Tate asserted in the mid-1920s that Braithwaite was "only Negro by an accident of blood and has as little of the Negro temperament as Longfellow."[178] Like John Gould Fletcher, a fellow Southerner, Tate stated that his justification for joining Braithwaite's detractors was that he found the anthologist "too inclusive."[179] For countless white supremacists, such judgments were coded terms for conveying objections to interracialism. Tate was more than happy to acknowledge Braithwaite as a Black man once it became convenient to both reject and undermine his professional standing. In 1926, Braithwaite noted in a letter to NAACP veteran Joel Spingarn that he was greatly pained by coordinated and institutional efforts to smear his reputation. "These individual attacks do not in the least disturb me; the organized denouncements such as those of the Author's League and the Poetry Society must be nullified; they carry an authority which the unthinking and dependent obey," he stated, lamenting how easily Black expertise could be thwarted in this era.[180]

Worse still, in extreme cases, white authors were intent on cutting off virtually all contact with Black peers as Braithwaite's cultural influence waned. One of the clearest examples of this trend centered on the "Fugitive" poets, a group of twelve white writers who later became known as the "Southern Agrarians." Tate was both the youngest and most prominent member of the Fugitives. The group's manifesto, published in 1930, was a collection of essays titled *I'll Take My Stand*.[181] Even illiterate Americans in the northern United States recognized "I'll take my stand" as a line in the song "Dixie," the de facto national anthem of the Confederacy. Tate explained, "I would call the Fugitives an intense and historical group as opposed to the eclectic and cosmopolitan groups that flourished in the East."[182]

In a letter sent to the editor at the University of North Carolina Press during the early years of the Great Depression, H. C. Nixon, a contributor to *I'll Take My Stand*, wrote, "I cannot go with them in their unwillingness, as I understand them, to give the Negro a square deal; that's carrying damn yankee-ism too far for me."[183] Written while he studied at Oxford University, Robert Penn Warren's contribution to *I'll Take My Stand* reflects the segregationist mentality Nixon came to doubt: "There are strong theoretical arguments in favor of higher education for the negro, but those arguments are badly damaged if at the same time a separate negro community or group is not built up which is capable of absorbing [. . .] those members who have received this higher education."[184] This was the newly emboldened South that Sherwood Anderson had saluted four years earlier in *Vanity Fair*, while bemoaning that too many "second-rate" Black poets were "doing too much of the contributing now."[185]

Ironically, it was W. S. Braithwaite who helped launch the careers of the best-known Agrarians. In 1923 alone, Braithwaite's *Anthology* featured at least twenty-three poems written by the poets who later became the "Fugitives."[186] In the introduction to the 1925 anthology, Braithwaite singled out *The Fugitive* magazine as "the best edited" of all the poetry magazines in the country and named Tate and his fellow editors there as "poet[s] of rare significance and achievement."[187] This didn't stop Tate from building on Alice Corbin Henderson and Ezra Pound's deeply biased interpretations of American and African American cultural standards. Tate's highly publicized refusal to meet Langston Hughes and James Weldon Johnson in the early 1930s in Nashville was the most infamous example of this legacy of prejudice.

In this instance, Tate "took his stand" by refusing to attend a party in Nashville to honor Langston Hughes and James Weldon Johnson in 1932. "My theory of the race relations is this: there should be no social intercourse between the races unless we are willing for that to lead to marriage," Tate noted.[188] In addition to circulating this statement among Vanderbilt's English faculty, Tate also sent it to New York in an effort to have it published. He informed Tom Mabry, the young white man who proposed holding this party, that he'd be willing to meet Hughes and Johnson anywhere, in fact, outside of the South. Calling Tate's bluff, Mabry responded: "Certainly a more vicious assimilation is going on because of the attitudes of people like yourself."[189] A year later, Tate was once again pitching similar dogma in response to a request from Lincoln Kirstein, the editor of *Hound and Horn*, a literary quarterly cofounded by Harvard undergraduates. Kirstein was seeking an essay from Tate outlining the Agrarians' perspectives on race. In a wide-ranging denouncement of interracialism, Tate insisted: "The negro race is an inferior race."[190]

The flawed progressivism of white writers such as Clement Wood and Carl Van Vechten, who had at least attempted to elevate Black culture, was further diminished by a broader pattern of poorly scrutinized—yet increasingly accepted—notions of racial difference over the 1920s. Dissimilar from that during the previous decade, this trajectory supported rather than challenged the logic of racial difference (and in some cases, segregation) in the publishing sector. Blacks and whites didn't stop working and writing across racial lines, but neither did they build on the egalitarian spirit of the 1910s, which became far less common as the Harlem Renaissance gained traction. Moreover, outright racists like Henderson and Anderson could present themselves publicly as supportive of Black writing and culture, as long as this sympathy did not challenge the underlying validity of white power and authority in the publishing world. Harriet Monroe did not truly challenge the status quo among her peers when she advertised Braithwaite's ringing endorsement of *Poetry* or when she published Fenton Johnson's work the following month.

Recovering a deeper sense of the racial essentialism and demands for white cultural leadership affirms literary scholar James Smethurst's observations on American literary culture prior to the 1920s: "Black writers of the Nadir, then, were far more important to the shaping and reception of an 'American' bohemia and artistic avant garde than has been generally acknowledged."[191] Failure to acknowledge the significance of these Black authors goes hand in hand with a general erasure of the racially inclusive literary renaissance of the 1910s. Or as C. E. Bechhofer claimed in *The Literary Renaissance in America* (1923), when a writer such as Sinclair Lewis poked fun at provincial obsessions like "Klassy Kollege Klothes" in Minnesota, he offered a "perfectly honest" account of "present-day America at its most intolerable."[192] To be sure, Bechhofer failed to properly acknowledge the sheer volume of related Black-authored contributions in this period. On the other hand, an influential set of his white contemporaries were far less generous. Literary critics such as Henderson insisted on the erasure of Black contributions to this epoch, as the following letter to Harriet Monroe back in 1916 illustrates: "Tell Carl Sandburg that he is too big a man to put himself on a level with Brait[h]waite. Sandburg will be remembered when Braithwaite is forgotten. You could not cut out the nigger."[193] Henderson was referring to Sandburg's poem "Nigger," which, like Braithwaite, has also been by and large forgotten.

Henderson's racism had far-reaching implications. In 1939, H. B. Hunting, the president of Berea College, searched in vain for research materials on Braithwaite's life. In a letter to W.E.B. Du Bois, Hunting noted, "I have searched the Boston Public Library for material about him, but have not found much.

I think your July number is, not only the best issue you have ever printed, but the best issue of any poetry magazine that I have ever seen.
William Stanley Braithwaite

Vol. XIX No. II

POETRY *for* NOVEMBER, 1921

		PAGE
The Lions	*Edwin Curran*	59
The Jilt I-VI—The Blunted Age	*Agnes Lee*	69
From the Day-book of a Forgotten Prince	*Jean Untermeyer*	74
A Fillet of Thorn	*Anita Grannis*	75
The Wages of Sin	*Jessica Nelson North*	76
Fog	*Kathryn White Ryan*	76
Geyser	*John R. C. Peyton*	77
Gargoyle	*Kate Buss*	77
Don Juan in Portugal	*Florence Wilkinson*	78
The Passers-by	*Dorothy Butts*	80
The Parade—To the Hills around Northampton—A Vanity—Audience—Listening—May Basket—The Transient—Difference—Please		
Poems	*Henry Bellamann*	85
Gargoyles of Notre Dame—Edges—Lullaby—Peaks—God—The Artist		
From Queen Anne to George the Fifth	*H. M.*	90
Reviews:		
Drinkwater as Poet and Playwright	*Laura Sherry*	94
Of Dreams and Stitches	*Pearl Andelson*	100
Correspondence:		
Poet and Composer as Allies	*Louise Ayres Garnett*	102
Reactionary Composers	*Kay Boyle*	104
Announcement of Awards		107
Our Contemporaries:		
A New "Youth"		115
Notes and Books Received		115, 116

Manuscripts must be accompanied by a stamped and self-addressed envelope. Inclusive yearly subscription rates. In the United States, Mexico, Cuba and American possessions, $3.00 net; in Canada, $3.15 net; in all other countries in the Postal Union, $3.25 net. Entered as second-class matter Nov. 15, 1921, at the post-office, at Chicago, Ill., uuder Act of March 3, 1879.

Published monthly at 543 Cass St., Chicago, Ill.

Copyright 1921, by Harriet Monroe. All rights reserved.

FIGURE 1.12. The November 1921 issue of *Poetry* included W. S. Braithwaite's praise on the contents page.

I hoped to find there, the files of The Crisis, thinking that it might contain something [on Braithwaite] but they do not seem to have said files. Is that one more manifestation of race prejudice?"[194]

A decade earlier, Ezra Pound, who hated Braithwaite, had been commissioned to write one of the first comprehensive and authoritative essays on the literary renaissance of the 1910s. Pound traced a whites-only history of "the active phase of the small magazine in America" for readers of *The English Journal*.[195] Crucial and influential Black contributions to this cultural movement—most conspicuously, Braithwaite's—were ignored altogether. If Henderson had assured Sandburg fifteen years earlier that he would be "remembered when Braithwaite is forgotten," it bears remembering that Pound helped ensure that it happened.

Only in hindsight did Black authors and critics gain a collective sense that the vogue for "Negro literature" in the 1920s—or in the case of far too many white writers and readers, "the nigger"—had inhibited moves toward egalitarian interracialism. Most of those who were aware of these shortcomings before the 1960s did not end up forswearing literary interracialism. Instead, they became even more adamant in rejecting professional inequities that were reinscribed by Black primitivism and racial essentialism. After all, for at least some white interlocutors, the Harlem Renaissance was hardly a segregationist movement.[196] For better and for worse, cultural integration remained a widely shared goal for progressive artists of all backgrounds.

2

Integration and Its Discontents

WHITE AUTHORS like Allen Tate and Ezra Pound who opposed working and fraternizing with their Black peers did not kill progressive literary interracialism. At the same time, skeptics and enemies of racial equity did not disappear. Nor did deeply prejudiced publishing standards or broader cultural ephemera that accentuated Black primitivism. Encouraging fairer cross-racial partnerships, as well as Black cultural representations, demanded rigorous analysis and a willingness to learn from previous mistakes and shortcomings.[1] Or as James Weldon Johnson maintained in his 1934 book of essays, *Negro Americans, What Now?*: "For a number of years we have given vent to loud lamentations over the treatment we have received in literature and art. Well, what ought we to do about it? Beg white writers and artists to treat us with more consideration? Of course not."[2] Johnson was sixty-three years old when this book was published. He wasn't going to waste his time pleading with white supremacists.

On the other hand, Johnson explained in *Negro Americans, What Now?* that white Americans who refused to collaborate—or even be in the same room—with Black authors were stoking racial hostilities and separatist tendencies more broadly. Johnson thus cautioned his Black readers not to take the bait: "There come times when the most persistent integrationist becomes an isolationist, when he curses the White world and consigns it to hell. [. . .] With our choice narrowed down to these two courses, wisdom and far-sightedness and possibility of achievement demand that we follow the line that leads to equal rights for us [e.g., integration], based on the common terms and conditions under which they are accorded and guaranteed to the other groups that go into the making up of our national family."[3] Johnson's book was published by Viking, a firm cofounded by two highly educated white Jewish men. Johnson sincerely believed in the need for African Americans to cultivate "our interrelationship with the country as a whole."[4] But he was also keenly aware that white liberals would read *Negro Americans, What Now?* if it was published by a white-owned publishing house that, like himself, believed in the power and promise of nurturing interracialism.[5]

This chapter investigates the ascendance of idealistic multiracial literary culture during the 1930s and 1940s.[6] While the term *integration* often elicits skepticism or hostility in the twenty-first century, the historic, literary roots of this cultural and civic aspiration remain poorly understood. To be sure, there was also little agreement on the scope and significance of integration in the 1930s and 1940s, which is one reason it inspired heated debates among African Americans from the early years of the Depression. On the other hand, critics and observers generally celebrated the cultural achievements of Black and white authors alike who broke commercial records while challenging racial essentialism and hierarchies. Indeed, such contributions on and off the page led countless contemporaries to perceive these writers as promoting formidable challenges to the color line in and beyond mainstream print culture.

A comment by Richard Wright in 1940 offers a sense of how he used his position and influence to criticize tenacious racial divisions in American popular culture. "Negroes are segregated in flickers [movies] the same as in real life," Wright stated in an interview published by *The New York Sun*. "You're not supposed to show a Negro eating with white people, and all that. I wouldn't go out there [to Hollywood] if I had to write around those Jim Crow taboos."[7] Four years later, a newspaper profile of the white novelist Lillian Smith, after the publication of her contentious yet enormously popular interracial romance, *Strange Fruit* (1944), illustrates how ambiguous related cultural promotions of "integration" often were: "For both races, Lillian Smith wants to see the end of the segregation pattern. She believes it will end. 'If I didn't believe it,' she says, 'I wouldn't want to live.'"[8] Despite the tenacity of racial segregation in American life, Smith and Wright were far from alone in framing social and cultural interracialism in these terms.

Connections between aspiring and established authors and cultural professionals who contributed to writing and working across racial lines were more common in this period than one might expect. *Ebony*, founded in 1945, and other Black publications of the time are generally seen as operating under the exclusive purview of African Americans. But even *Ebony's* first issue disrupts this common understanding: Of the seven boys from New York's Henry Street Settlement in its striking cover photograph, only one is not white. In a letter to the editor published in the magazine's second issue, Langston Hughes exclaimed that *Ebony* "is terrific! I like it very much, and hope it goes places!"[9] Historian Adam Green argues that after World War II, *Ebony* "grew into one of the most variegated enterprises in African-American cultural life at the time, as well as one of the more integrated (racially and otherwise) within the United States generally."[10] As a description published in *Ebony* explained, the white photographer tapped to capture the image featured on its inaugural cover, Marion Palfi, was a young woman "who had come to the United States from Europe in 1940 to escape the mania of Adolph Hitler."[11] When *Ebony* commissioned this photograph from an artist fortunate enough to flee Amsterdam shortly before the Nazis invaded, racially unifying symbols like these were enormously popular. The first issue of *Ebony* sold out—25,000 copies—within hours.

FIGURE 2.1. The first issue of *Ebony* (November 1945) featured a photo by Marion Palfi.

In the 1930s and 1940s, building a dynamic, racially and ethnically integrated literary culture was a widely shared goal among Black authors. In short, there wasn't a particular way to be a Black or white writer during this period. New cultural perspectives rendering commonalities and complex interactions among Black and white Americans, elsewhere separated by either de facto or de jure racial distinctions, expanded mental worlds warped and bound by Jim Crow. Dozens of writers, editors, and intellectuals maintained biracial cultural networks that pushed these boundaries both from the margins and within the literary establishment. While many of these interracial ties dated back to the 1910s and 1920s, during and after the Great Depression Langston Hughes and numerous other men and women were at the forefront of reimagining who counted as American—and how they might come together. But at various stages, Black-led efforts to defy social divisions pervading the public sphere were inhibited by white interlocutors, who often failed to see (or adequately counter) how racial prejudices were perpetuated in and beyond corporate publishing.

In hindsight, this lack of awareness curtailed the dismantling of racial barriers in the literary field. Moreover, several of the most popular interracial narratives produced in this era were later dismissed as "assimilationist" when a relatively empowered generation of African Americans gained cultural authority. Black authors such as Juanita Harrison, Willard Motley, and Frank Yerby, who captivated readers on both sides of the color line prior to the 1950s, barely registered as literary trailblazers during the 1960s Black Arts Movement. Their stories, professional relationships, and initiatives led them to unexpected popularity in difficult circumstances.

Americans Dreaming

Six months before Juanita Harrison turned forty in December 1927, she embarked on close to ten years of travel around the world. Harrison was born in Columbus, Mississippi, in 1887 to Rosa Crigler, a woman who was listed in the 1870 federal census as a "mulatto."[12] In 1936, New York City's Macmillan Company published Harrison's document of her experiences in letters and diaries as a three-hundred-page book titled *My Great, Wide, Beautiful World*.[13] Unlike other books in this genre, Harrison's exceptionally cosmopolitan travelogue of more than twenty countries in Africa, Asia, and Europe could in no way be considered a narrative of an elite, highly educated African American woman abroad.[14] Like most Black women in the United States employed outside of their own homes at mid-century, Harrison worked as a domestic. A full decade before Ann Petry's first novel, *The Street* (1946), introduced American readers to the hardships of a Black woman in Harlem, who worked as a maid in suburban Connecticut, *My Great, Wide, Beautiful World* foregrounded Harrison's lighthearted yet affecting experiences laboring around the globe.[15]

A Macmillan ad from the period warned potential readers to "beware" of Harrison's travelogue "if human interest bores you" or "if you are a firm stickler for race and class-consciousness." Macmillan's jocular marketing of Harrison's *My Great, Wide, Beautiful World* as "universal" dared potential readers to consider her life and times a model of how to gracefully defy cultural boundaries: "For Juanita treads on the toes of propriety, right and left. She loves the human race, she loves strange places, she's a gourmet of the first order, and her boundless curiosity and lawless grammar are grandly exhibited in this hilarious and penetrating tale." The publishing house instructed readers to make connections between Harrison's literary acumen and late medieval European humanists such as Giovanni Boccaccio, as well as to early nineteenth-century radical, romantic, white essayists such as William Hazlitt.[16]

Macmillan's modernist design for Harrison's international travelogue was also unusual for a Black-authored text expected to boost this firm's sales. Unlike the case for numerous other titles published by the overwhelmingly white, commercial publishing trade in this era, neither Harrison's race nor her nationality could be easily discerned from the cover of *My Great, Wide,*

Beautiful World. Literary scholar Cathryn Halverson, Harrison's foremost biographer, has observed that even the "original outer cover" of this book "evokes a contemporary sphere of cultural relativism" that, like its author, "resists classification."[17] As Halverson points out, "Harrison references but does not emphasize her identity as African American, choosing instead to portray herself as a newly minted world citizen."[18] Nevertheless, Macmillan balanced this worldview by accentuating stereotypes widely associated with America's Black working class elsewhere in Harrison's book.

The dedication page is the first place in *My Great, Wide, Beautiful World* where Harrison's racial heritage is revealed by design, as suggested by flagrant spelling and grammatical errors:

To

Mrs. Myra K. Dickinson

Your great kindness to me have made my traveling much happier if You hadnt been interested in me I never would have tryed to explain my trips also your True and Kindness encourage me and made me more anxious to tell you the way I spent my time.

By presenting this uncorrected, error-riddled manuscript written by a woman with little formal education, Macmillan hoped to attract readers seeking an authentic expression of the Black experience. In this era, most white readers did not associate highly educated, cosmopolitan African Americans with the cultural essence of Blackness. Their stories, fictional and otherwise, were not best sellers.

The preface to Harrison's book explains that Juanita's education in Mississippi had been limited to "a few months of schooling" before the age of ten.[19] According to numerous white critics who reviewed her manuscript in the 1930s, Macmillan's decision not to copyedit or standardize the style of *My Great, Wide, Beautiful World* beyond its cover made Harrison's travelogue much more authentic and entertaining.[20] Harrison seems to have embraced her atypical literary celebrity, at least initially. In one letter to a friend after the book was published, Harrison boasted: "Since the Book came out I have read letters from [dozens] of fine unseen friends of America[']s best."[21] Although Harrison's name is not well known beyond the academy, her travelogue was one of the most popular of numerous Black and interracial books, plays, and pamphlets countering assumptions that African American lives were thoroughly bound by Jim Crow.

In various ways, the help Harrison received from white "friends" and critics in and beyond the publishing world hearkened back to nineteenth-century abolitionism. For several years in the 1920s Harrison worked for George Dickinson, a Los Angeles real estate magnate, and his wife, Myra, who invested in property on Harrison's behalf. Their investments in her name generated slightly over $200 annually until shortly after the 1929 stock market crash. In 1935, Ellery Sedgwick, the editor of the *Atlanta Monthly*, published two excerpts from Harrison's forthcoming book, based on a recommendation from Mildred Morris, the daughter of Harrison's first employer in Paris.[22] Morris was instrumental in ensuring the publication of *My Great, Wide, Beautiful World* and wrote the preface to the book—much the way published narratives by enslaved people were published with introductions from white abolitionists between the 1830s and 1850s.

Harrison's travelogue was enormously profitable for Macmillan. Less than a year after publication, the book had already been reprinted nine times, and the Black press in Los Angeles proudly reported that the city's former resident had, against all odds, managed to publish "the first work by a colored author to get on the 'best seller' list of the New York Herald Tribune."[23] Indeed, this was the same newspaper where Macmillan had placed its quasi-provocative advertisement for *My Great, Wide, Beautiful World* four weeks earlier. Writing for the Associated Negro Press in 1936, Frank Marshall Davis described Harrison's travelogue as "one of the few travel books by a writer of color" in existence.[24] Large sales and countless endorsements of this title in the mainstream press made Harrison an outlier in breaking out of the commercial book trade's literary ghetto following the 1920s. Several years later, in Sedgwick's autobiography published in 1945, he offered an exaggerated synopsis of Harrison's overall track record in resisting Jim Crow, asserting: "For her exists no barrier of class or color, and when men brown or white find her too attractive, she is superlatively competent to look after herself."[25] However naive this statement may be, Sedgwick's claim that Harrison effortlessly evaded segregationist customs (including sexual threats) offers a sense of how her independence was regarded by the white publishing establishment at mid-century.

Several years before Richard Wright, Ann Petry, Willard Motley, and Frank Yerby gained fame with crucial support from socialist interlocutors, networks, and publications, Harrison helped establish a larger commercial market for Black books. Moreover, Harrison's unwavering commitments to her personal autonomy foreshadowed this small yet influential cohort of Black authors, who frequently rebuffed being pigeonholed as "leftist" during, and especially after, World War II. A provocative quote from Harrison featured in the opening pages of *My Great, Wide, Beautiful World* clarifies how emphatic she was about remaining untethered during the 1930s: "I will sail far away to strange places. Around me no one has the life I want. No one is there for me to copy, not even the rich [white] ladies I work for. I have to cut my life out for myself."[26] While Harrison's book didn't inaugurate perspectives like these, the combination of her travelogue and countless popular endorsements brought this expansive philosophy of Black personhood to a broad audience at mid-century. A brief note on Harrison's popularity published by the *Afro-American* in 1938 conceded that despite her book's grammatical flaws, "[i]t's the story of a servant girl who was born in Mississippi but demonstrated the fact that she didn't have to stay there."[27] In the years prior to the second Great Migration, in the middle of a global depression, Harrison's extensive domestic and international travels were indeed no small act of defiance for a Black woman with limited means.

At the time, Harrison's steadfast independence, protection of her privacy, and capacious cosmopolitanism might have inspired a rejoinder from at least one of her forebears, Jean Toomer. Toomer's poem "Blue Meridian," published in the annual literary survey *New Caravan* (1936), echoes the utopian, liberating character of the stories collected in Harrison's book. Just a few months after *My Great, Wide, Beautiful World* appeared, Toomer's poem defiantly stated: "Free the sexes, / I am neither male nor female nor in-between; I am of sex, with male differentiations."[28] Toomer's feminist sentiments, published in this edited volume along with some of Richard Wright's earliest Black, proletarian fiction, led the *New York Times* to champion the "Wide Diversity" of the *New Caravan* of that year.[29]

In the end, prior to the 1940s, neither Toomer nor Wright was anywhere near as popular with book buyers as Harrison's *My Great, Wide, Beautiful World*. Toomer, Jesse Fauset, Charles Chesnutt, Walter White, W. S. Braithwaite, Nella Larsen, and many other well-established authors were already intimately familiar with the paradox of being a mixed-race or light-skinned Black celebrity in Jim Crow's America. Not infrequently, white commentaries on African American writers in the 1930s and 1940s casually denied their shared heritage, culturally or otherwise. In 1944, H. L. Mencken recalled how incensed numerous Black readers of *The Atlantic* were when its editor, Ellery Sedgwick, referred to Harrison as a "negress" in the periodical a few years earlier. A letter from Isadore Cecilia Williams to Sedgwick chiding the editor's insensitivity thus stated: "*Negress* [. . .] is obnoxious to Negroes chiefly because of the sordid, loose, and often degrading connotations it has been forced to carry. [. . .] Certainly Miss Harrison, whose honesty you commend [. . .] deserves at least common courtesy at your hands."[30] The type of disrespect

A RARE BOOK . . .

My Great Wide Beautiful World

by JUANITA HARRISON

The hilarious but penetrating travel diary of an American negress who, untutored and inexperienced, set out at the age of thirty-six to tour the world. In the eight years covered by her narrative she lived and worked in *twenty-two* countries. Her shrewd, kindly summing-up of the people met, her naivete combined with a unique understanding, her untrammeled enthusiasm, make the book a sheer delight.

The clamorous demand for "More!" which followed publication in ATLANTIC MONTHLY last Autumn of condensed portions, is now met with the complete diary.

"There is a sincerity—a gusto—a real sense of values and human interests that takes it out of the ordinary. Primarily a unique human document. I have a hunch this book will go."
—VIRGINIA KIRKUS

PUBLISHED MAY 12th   PRICE $2.50

The Macmillan Company • New York

FIGURE 2.2. A 1936 Macmillan advertisement for Juanita Harrison's *My Great, Wide, Beautiful World* in *Publishers' Weekly* describes the author as "an American negress."

Williams outlined in her letter to Sedgwick offers a sense of why this intergenerational cohort often rejected being categorized—and effectively pigeonholed—as either "Negro" authors or authors of "Negro" literature. Negative associations with these labels were exacerbated when Macmillan, Juanita's own publisher, described her as an "American negress" in advertisements for *My Great, Wide, Beautiful World* in venues such as *Publishers' Weekly*.

W.E.B. Du Bois was one of the most respected Black writers of the twentieth century to regularly complicate these labels and categories by drawing attention to his white ancestors. In 1940, this included carefully detailing the life story of the white father of his paternal grandfather, Alexander Du Bois, in his autobiography, *Dusk of Dawn* (1940).[31] A host of popular and canonical African American writers followed Du Bois's lead in interviews, correspondence, and their own autobiographies. "I have no doubt," Ralph Ellison once asserted in a letter, "that the light skin, blue eyes and reddish hair which have turned up in [his own] family spring from" a mixed-race grandmother, who "was never talked too much about, and when she was it was always with a guarded air." Ellison also confessed, "[A]s a novelist who has learned much from Faulkner, I am interested in the linkages, in the hidden sources of the confluent blood," in his family members hailing from South Carolina.[32] After becoming famous in the mid-1940s, the novelist Frank Yerby, who was born in Augusta, Georgia, in 1916, often summarized the multiethnic heritage of his working-class, Black Southern parents as effectively constituting a "mini–United Nations."[33] But in 1983, Yerby cautioned Madrid's Associated Press bureau chief: "[D]o not call me black. That word bugs me. Besides, I have more Seminole than Negro blood in me anyway. But when have I ever been referred to as 'that American Indian author'?"[34] Yerby wasn't denying his Black heritage. Rather, like many of his African American peers and forebears, for decades, Yerby chafed at the American public's general inability to comprehend how racial distinctions— and by extension, belief in white supremacy—were constructed.

Langston Hughes published a remarkably similar statement to Yerby's regarding his Southern family's lineage. "You see, unfortunately, I am not black," Hughes declared in his first autobiography, *The Big Sea* (1940). He then commented: "But here in the United States, the word 'Negro' is used to mean anyone who has any Negro blood at all in his veins. [. . .] On my father's side, the white blood in his family came from a Jewish slave trader in Kentucky." The other great grandparent Hughes mentioned in this book "was said to be a relative of the great [white] statesman, Henry Clay, his contemporary."[35] Five years later, in his own autobiography, *Black Boy* (1945), Richard Wright described his illiterate, maternal grandmother, Margaret Bolden Wilson, as "old, white, [and] wrinkled" in the very first paragraph of the book.[36] Wright also noted that his "tardiness in learning to sense white people as 'white' people came from the fact that many of my relatives were 'white'-looking people. My grandmother, who was [as] white as any 'white' person, had never looked 'white' to me."[37] Wright's grandmother was emancipated from slavery around the age of twelve but did not know the actual date or place of her birth, as was the case for many formerly enslaved persons. And much like Juanita Harrison's mixed-raced, immediate relations, Wright's family lived precariously in Mississippi's plantation belt for generations, but on the other side of the state, in Jackson.

———

Harrison likely knew who her mother's white father was (and the whereabouts of her other white relatives), but the particulars of this Black author's lineage were either obscured or hidden from white readers. Prior to the 1940s, even fiction related to, or centered on, interracial liaisons remained taboo. In 1933, when Langston Hughes pitched a short story to *Scribner's* entitled "Mother and Child," centered on "a little farming village of the mid-west when a white woman bears a Negro child," the magazine's associate editor rejected the story due to its plot.[38] "There is nothing I'd like better than to see a story of yours in Scribner's, and even this particular story," Hughes's contact at the periodical noted, "but because of the theme it just isn't possible. We make a stab at being broad-minded [...] but this would frighten our good middle-class audience to death."[39] Four years later, when Hughes's play *Mulatto* (1935) was set to open in Philadelphia after a successful legal petition against a mayoral ban, its white producer, Joseph Becker, backed out. As these examples indicate, explicitly interracial cultural challenges to Jim Crow by Hughes and other Black authors in the 1930s were often contentious.

A decade later, a collection of essays edited by the Black scholar Rebecca Chalmers Barton recognized the social and professional barriers this generation had overcome in a volume titled *Witnesses for Freedom: Negro Americans in Autobiography* (1948). Harrison's *My Great, Wide, Beautiful World* (1936) was the first of seven autobiographies represented in the third section of Barton's survey, which was devoted to African American authors she termed "the experimenters." For Barton, Harrison's bravery hearkened back to "the same trait in Matthew Henson [*A Negro Explorer at the North Pole* (Frederick A. Stokes, 1912)] and we could even surmise that in both cases membership in a minority group had taught them the dangers of [racial] dogmatism."[40] Recalling how Harrison's book related to Henderson's celebrated travelogue published in the early 1910s was Black literary history at its finest. Rather than a narrow conception of African American literature, statements like these in *Witnesses for Freedom* invited readers to trace an expansive twentieth-century history of Black writing, celebrating texts that eluded racial and national boundaries.

At the same time, Barton's generous assessment of *My Great, Wide, Beautiful World* and its author indicated how Harrison challenged long-standing racial conventions that were overwhelmingly associated with Black elites: "In Juanita Harrison we have evidence that not all cosmopolitans come from the privileged classes. [...] There is a wisdom of common humanity in her that embraces all customs and all creeds."[41] Barton's discussion of Harrison's travelogue, and other authors represented in this collection, made a compelling argument that Black writing had become much more capacious after the classical 1920s "Negro Renaissance" period than was otherwise commonly assumed.

Indeed, analyses foregrounding this argument were subtle yet unmistakably political refutations of preoccupations with racial essentialism over the second half of the 1920s. According to Barton's overview of "experimenters" like Harrison, in "the 1930's and the 1940's Negro-American autobiography expands. The number and variety of books increase [. . .] and the subject matter becomes more complex. [. . .] Except for the word 'dark' in one title, there is not the slightest hint of Negro authorship."[42] A foreword by Alain Locke echoed these sentiments: "This volume reveals no 'Negro mind,' no 'minority temperament,' or 'personality.' There is wide variation from high optimism to deep cynicism, from minority self-reliance to socialistic integration." Like Barton, Locke emphasized the incredible range of Black thought in this collection. Racial stereotypes and "popular-oversimplification," Locke suggested, had inhibited both "interracial understanding" and "dynamic democratic thought and action."[43] Harrison's refusal of the racial categories that constrained her in Mississippi and elsewhere in the United States aligns closely with Locke's perspectives. Harrison wasn't passing in the interwar period—she was refusing to be simplified.[44]

Cathryn Halverson has suggested that *My Great, Wide, Beautiful World* "sometimes sounds just like Gertrude Stein."[45] This observation may be more apt than it seems. For at least some of Harrison's readers, her travelogue was indeed reminiscent of the lighthearted yet commanding verve of Stein's mixed-raced protagonist Melanctha in *Three Lives* (1909). Carl Van Vechten, one of the earliest influential critics to endorse *Three Lives*, eagerly promoted Harrison's travel vignettes in his correspondence with both Stein and Langston Hughes. In a letter to Hughes in early 1936, Van Vechten asked: "Do you know about Juanita Harrison? She appeared in the [October] and [November] numbers of the Atlantic and I LOVE her."[46] Five days later, Van Vechten was still raving about Harrison's literary debut, this time in a letter to Stein in Paris: "If there are any Atlantic Monthlies handy around your parts, please read Juanita Harrison's My Great Wide, Beautiful World in [the] Oct. & Nov. issues."[47]

Van Vechten's enthusiastic response to *The Atlantic*'s excerpts of Harrison's book at the beginning of 1936 sheds light on some of the continuities and changes in literary interracialism during the Depression. In the late 1920s, Van Vechten was an outsized promoter of African American literary culture. In

James Weldon Johnson's autobiography, *Along This Way* (1933), he explained: "In the early days of the Negro literary and artistic movement, no one in the country did more to forward it" than Van Vechten.[48] By the mid-1930s, Van Vechten was no longer regarded as a singular voice in promoting Black authors. Nevertheless, with unwavering—albeit covert—institutional support from Alfred and Blanche Knopf's publishing house, he remained an important interlocutor for several established and newly prominent Black authors.

During the Depression, Van Vechten and the Knopfs sought to honor their maturing social and professional connections to preeminent Black authors such as James Weldon Johnson and Langston Hughes with symbolic gestures of their friendship. Hughes later recalled: "For several years [Van Vechten] gave an annual birthday party for James Weldon Johnson, young Alfred A. Knopf, Jr., and himself." They were all born on the same day. Hughes's vivid recollection of their final joint celebration at the end of the 1930s implied that their ties to one another had only become more egalitarian—or at the very least, their birthday cakes were: "At the last of these parties the year before Mr. Johnson died [in 1938], on the Van Vechten table there were three cakes, one red, one white, and one blue—the colors of our flag. They honored a Gentile, a Negro, and a Jew—friends and fellow-Americans."[49] In a fictional summary of social ties that crossed racial lines in this era, W.E.B. Du Bois once stated: "Naturally, as time went by, inter-racial friendships arose over trifles—adjacent backyards, the democracy of children, the unity of misfortune." Despite various difficulties, Du Bois estimated that "in a few" cases, "gradually, real friendship across the color line persisted."[50] It would be difficult to ascertain whether interracial ties within Van Vechten's circle had in fact become more equitable, but this crew clearly valued pluralist culture long after the Harlem Renaissance took root.

In and beyond the Federal Writers' Project

The Great Depression years were not easy for Black writers, whether aspiring or established. Hughes later joked, "I was never able to enroll in the Federal Writers Project [in the 1930s] because I had two small volumes of poems published and a novel, so the government presumed I was well off—not realizing that a writer cannot eat poems, even when handsomely bound by Alfred A. Knopf."[51] African American authors and creative professionals had more experience with deprivation than the majority of their white counterparts. This was arguably a comparative advantage for Black writers: When they published and mentored younger generations of African American intellectuals, their motives were by and large altruistic.

In 1934, W. S. Braithwaite maintained that his teaching position at the historically Black college Atlanta University was driven by a long-standing interest in encouraging Black authors and culture, but without question he also needed the steady income it provided. Writing to Nella Larsen that year, Braithwaite outlined his goals for cultivating a lifelong interest in supporting Black-authored literary culture:

> This work will stun the country into a recognition and acceptance of the spiritual and cultural equality of the Race. [. . .] For twenty-five years I gave my best for the poets and poetry of America; it was a labor of love that cost me dearly; at the same time I proved something that no other man of the [Black] race dared even so much as to attempt; I won something precious for the future hope and aspiration of the artistic and creative youth of the Negro; now I want to add a tower to that foundation, a tower that will stand glowing in the reflection of that heavenly and divine sun of the Imagination, a tower on the hill of our sufferings and repressions, our denials and persecutions [. . .] which will throw its beams far out over the troubled waters of the Racial sea.[52]

Braithwaite never finished this collection, but his passion for completing it was certainly helped by his affiliation with Atlanta University, where Du Bois rejoined the faculty, during and after the Great Depression.

More than two decades earlier, Braithwaite's public support for James Weldon Johnson's poetry had led directly to the first published edition of *The Autobiography of an Ex-Colored Man* in 1912. Johnson repaid Braithwaite with his friendship and reciprocated Braithwaite's unquantifiable work on behalf of "the poets and poetry of America" by similarly remaining committed to mentoring the next generation of Black authors. Johnson influenced many college-aged Americans of all backgrounds as a professor at New York University and Fisk University in the 1930s. One of his youngest Black mentees in this era, Frank Yerby, went on to become the most commercially successful African American author of his generation.

Yerby was still a teenager when he started corresponding with Johnson in 1933.[53] In his first letter to Yerby, Johnson warned the aspiring writer to avoid essentializing African Americans in his creative work: "Let me say that poems atavistic [primitivist] by Negro poets leave me cold. Such poems are generally not written out of any experience or genuine emotion. The majority of the

FIGURE 2.3. W.E.B. Du Bois celebrating his seventieth birthday with friends and family at Atlanta University, 1938. Back row, left to right: Charles Johnson, Yolande Du Bois, James Weldon Johnson, Ira De A. Reid, Rufus Clement, William Stanley Braithwaite. Front row, left to right: W.E.B. Du Bois, Nina Du Bois, Joel Spingarn. W.E.B. Du Bois Papers (MS 312), Special Collections and University Archives, University of Massachusetts Amherst Libraries.

poems harking back to Africa that our young poets write strike me as second hand, even as third hand, poetry."[54] Apologizing for the mediocrity of his Afrocentric poems, the seventeen-year-old Southerner responded, "It was without either my knowledge or consent that the delightful little manager and self-appointed press-agent, who is my sister[,] carried these specimens of my work to you."[55] As this poignant and contrite response indicates, it was Yerby's sister who deserves credit for bringing this young writer's work to Johnson's attention.

Johnson kept close tabs on Yerby's writing for several years. He advised Yerby to seek out cultural opportunities on both sides of the color line in his efforts to get published. In 1933, Johnson encouraged Yerby to submit his poems and other literary work to Black periodicals such as *The Crisis* and *Opportunity*, as well as to "some of the big magazines," presumably led by whites.[56]

Yerby followed Johnson's advice but was nevertheless rejected across the board. Although somewhat embarrassed that he had accumulated "a very imposing collection of rejection slips" by the spring of 1934, Yerby promised Johnson that he would keep trying to place his writing while pursuing his undergraduate studies at Paine College.[57]

After World War II, Johnson's advice that Yerby attempt more expansive creative narratives paid off handsomely for both the author and his white interlocutors. Yerby's first novel, *Foxes of Harrow* (1946), sold more than a million copies in hardcover and paperback. *Foxes* was also the first book penned by an African American to be adapted as a big-budget Hollywood film. Soon after *Foxes* was published in early 1946, one white reviewer for *The Philadelphia Inquirer* astutely noted: "At first and last glance, it would seem that Frank Yerby had deserted the ranks of Negro writers to pen a mere historical novel intended for popular sale, rather than one of the provoking books of social significance which the authors of his race have been turning out." Assuring readers that this was not the case, the reviewer explained that after reading the first pages of *Foxes*, "it becomes obvious that Mr. Yerby is fashioning a subtle yet powerful exposé of the degradation of slavery, and an equally strong indictment of the caste system of the South."[58] Close to a decade later, in August 1955, the Dial Press, Yerby's long-standing publisher, could boast that "[t]o date his books have sold 13,114,459 copies."[59] (At the time, Dial was announcing the publication of Yerby's tenth novel.) Sharing much in common with both W. S. Braithwaite and Juanita Harrison, Yerby's commercial successes in the literary field were undoubtedly rare. On the other hand, before the twenty-first century, most accounts of his literary career exaggerated how sharply his connections and achievements diverged from his most successful peers and forebears.

Back in the late 1940s, critics like Carl Van Vechten countered these assumptions by connecting Yerby's work to a widely acclaimed nexus of Afrodiasporic authors, anchored by Alexandre Dumas *père* and Alexander Pushkin.[60] Recalling early coverage of Yerby's Blackness, his agent later stated, "[T]hey christened him the Modern Dumas, and book-review readers rushed to their encyclopedias to figure it out, making two discoveries in the process."[61] The latter of these "discoveries" was that Dumas was not white. Van Vechten was probably aware that Yerby's mentorship from James Weldon Johnson had been especially influential. After Johnson died in a car crash in 1938, his widow, Grace Nail Johnson, continued the relationship. A few weeks after the publication of Yerby's first book in 1946, Grace sent the novelist a warm letter of congratulations, expressing the wish that "Mr. [James Weldon] Johnson could see you,

FIGURE 2.4. Grace Nail Johnson and James Weldon Johnson, photographed in 1932 by Carl Van Vechten. Beinecke Library Collection © Van Vechten Trust.

Mrs. Ann Petry, and others winning [literary] awards."[62] Johnson's untimely death was a tremendous loss not only for Grace but also for the rising generation of Black writers he had instructed to make space within—rather than at the margins of—the American literary field.

Shortly after Johnson died, Yerby moved to Chicago after earning a master's degree from Fisk University in 1938. His northern migration was well timed. While enrolled as a doctoral student at the University of Chicago, Yerby moonlighted as an employee of the Illinois Federal Writers' Project (FWP) and thus gained exposure to several preeminent Black authors from his recently deceased mentor's generation. Chicago's seasoned FWP cohort included luminaries such as the poet and magazine editor Fenton Johnson, in addition to a younger set of emerging Black authors, artists, and intellectuals, such as Katherine Dunham, Margaret Walker, and Richard Wright.[63] When Harper & Brothers advertised Wright's *Native Son* in 1940, the firm reminded booksellers that his collection of novellas, *Uncle Tom's Children* (1938), had recently "won a nation-wide contest for the best fiction produced by a WPA [Works Progress Administration] writer."[64] A decade later, one of the FWP's mid-career authors, Arna Bontemps, claimed, "Chicago was definitely the center of the second phase of Negro literary awakening."[65] This declaration has only become more important for interpreting the synergy generated by the Illinois FWP and the eclectic mix of African Americans it employed.[66] And yet, Bontemps would have been one of the first Black authors to acknowledge that this latest "Negro literary awakening" had not occurred independent of new collaborations with enterprising, antiracist white peers and counterparts. The literary scholar Anne Meis Knupfer has noted that these writers based in Illinois, which was a much more racially integrated, federally funded writers' community in comparison with most states, readily experimented with blurring both genres and the color line: "The W.P.A. not only provided an income during lean times but also offered camaraderie for both black and white writers."[67] In fact, as other literary scholars have pointed out, Bontemps was just one of several Black writers the white proletarian author Jack Conroy befriended through his work with the Illinois FWP.[68]

After the project ended, Conroy and Bontemps continued their collaborative work on at least three books that they managed to publish with major publishing houses in New York City, including a novel, *They Seek a City* (Doubleday, 1945), and two books for juvenile readers: *The Fast Sooner Hound* (Houghton, 1942) and *Slappy Hooper: The Wonderful Sign Painter* (Houghton, 1946). James Weldon Johnson likely would have been extremely proud of these interracial literary projects, sponsored by enormous, highly respected corporate publishers.

Sociological Best Sellers

Despite his long-standing interest in publishing stories with Black and Afrocentric themes, at the end of the Depression, Yerby claimed to know the white, commercial world of publishing much better than his successes up to that point would indicate. Bragging to his friends and colleagues in the Illinois FWP, Yerby once declared before World War II: "You intellectuals can go ahead and write your highbrow stuff. I'm going to make a million [from book sales]."[69] After years of rejections, it is unclear whether Yerby was simply joking or evading reality. At the time, he was still enrolled as a doctoral student at the University of Chicago, and the prospect of making a million dollars in the late 1930s was certainly not on the horizon for an African American academic.

Worse still, Yerby's own memories of attempting to publish in this era illuminate how disinterested the commercial world of publishing was in what he
wanted to publish: "I wrote a novel in which the chief character is a Negro Ph.D.
The publishers suggested that I have him quit school in his early high school
days and become a prize fighter!" According to Yerby, white publishing houses
realized that there were plenty of "fine, well-educated, clean, intelligent, moral
Negroes. But the book buying public—which is 99 percent white doesn't
know and doesn't care to."[70] If anything, the frequent rejections he received were
more than enough evidence that publishers weren't interested in what Yerby
had to say about Black intellectuals.

On one hand, there was much truth in Yerby's complaints about the literary
field. On the other, commercial publishing was beginning to open up to new
Black and interracial narratives in the 1940s, but this state of flux also fueled
new disagreements over how to measure this literature's role and impact.
In 1944, one of the nation's leading book critics, Harry Hansen, published a
statement on the matter, entitled "Novel May Awaken Readers to Study of
Negro Problem." This article appeared in Hansen's syndicated *Chicago Tribune*
book review column. Rather than an endorsement of Black authorship, Hansen's essay made a case for the social power of literature more generally. "Books
are not only weapons; they are tools," Hansen maintained. The two books at
the center of Hansen's case study were Lillian Smith's *Strange Fruit* (1944) and
Gunnar Myrdal's sociological study of race relations in the United States,
American Dilemma (1944). Like countless other northern white liberals, Hansen supported racial and cultural "tolerance"—but his time and patience were
limited, which seems to have led him to offer similarly inclined readers some
opinions on the matter during World War II.[71]

Hansen observed that Myrdal's book, which was almost fifteen hundred
pages long, was "unlikely to have a wide, popular circulation because it is serious, bulky, and expensive." In sharp contrast, Smith's book was a 168-page
novel. Hansen observed that Smith's interracial romance, "by its very honesty,"
held the potential to awaken "Americans to the danger of sleeping out the
Negro problem." Despite how reasonable estimates like these were, they were
arguably more problematic when white critics and editors cast newly minted
Black authors such as Richard Wright as a foil. "[Smith's] novel did not make
the furore that greeted Richard Wright's 'Native Son,'" Hansen explained, "but
it deserves just as wide [of a] reading. In this connection it is interesting to
note that a reviewer [...] predicted that Miss Smith would be welcome everywhere as a writer of great promise."[72] It was captivating novels like Smith's,

which were intentionally designed to challenge Jim Crow and other white supremacist norms, that fans and detractors labeled "sociological best sellers."[73] In a revealing biography of Lorraine Hansberry, Imani Perry has recently pointed out that the playwright listed Smith's "interracial romance" as one of her two favorite books in "a kitschy quiz she filled out during high school."[74] Smith's narrative of a youthful love affair between a wealthy, white college dropout and an attractive, working-class Black woman of a similar age was set in the Jim Crow South. But despite Hansen's optimism, Smith's *Strange Fruit* was not, in fact, welcomed "everywhere."

The novel was banned in Detroit and Boston shortly after it was printed. Yale professor Henry S. Canby, who had penned a crucial endorsement of Wright's *Native Son* circulated by the Book of the Month Club four years earlier, was asked to testify in the latter city on behalf of Smith's novel. The request came from a fellow public intellectual, Bernard DeVoto, a novelist, historian, and lecturer at Harvard. In the spring of 1944, DeVoto's letter to Canby explained, "I have been asked by our concert of lawyers and agitators to ask you if you would be willing to come to Boston and tell the Superior Court that you regard Strange Fruit as a serious and decent novel. [...] The idea is to offer the testimony of several literary critics, several ministers, and several psychiatrists or educators."[75] White professionals in these fields typically shirked the label of racial "activists." But in this era, it was virtually impossible for progressive white Americans to avoid race-related scrutiny if they were brave enough to challenge Jim Crow–styled strictures.

In 1946, Smith rebuffed the mainstream media's accusations that she had some progressive agenda: "I'm not the reformer everybody insists I am. I think being called a crusader has hurt me the most."[76] Frank Yerby, Gertrude Stein, and dozens of other Americans of all races made similar remarks at midcentury, both publicly and privately. Regardless of how Smith and her white peers identified, growing public support for narratives like *Strange Fruit* challenged a cultural standard that frequently minimized—or feared drawing any attention to—racial mixing. Here it is also worth remembering how unlikely it would have been for a Black author such as Langston Hughes to rally as much legal and institutional support as *Strange Fruit* for either *Mulatto* (1935) or any of his other interracial projects during the 1930s.

To be sure, it was by no means easy for Smith to ensure the publication of her interracial drama during World War II. Indeed, she was forced to contend with countless vocal opponents of *Strange Fruit* after the book was published in early 1944. Over the first half of 1944, bans on *Strange Fruit* multiplied rapidly and eventually included one implemented at the federal level by the end of the year. Briefly, Smith's novel was prohibited from distribution via the U.S. Postal Service, until Eleanor Roosevelt asked F.D.R. to intervene and have the ban withdrawn. The Council on Books in Wartime, an organization that worked closely with the federal government during World War II to publish books for soldiers, also issued a resolution condemning various bans on Smith's novel. In the end, these controversies only fueled consumer demand for *Strange Fruit*. By the middle of June 1944, more than 285,000 copies of this novel were in the hands of the reading public.

In the midst of this controversy, Yerby launched his commercial literary career with his own sociological best seller: "Health Card" (1944), a short story. Prior to its publication by *Harper's*, Yerby was virtually invisible to New York's publishing world. "Health Card" was a fictive rendering of Johnny, a Black G.I., and his wife, who are forced to navigate their way through multiple encounters with degrading racial discrimination in the wartime present. The story, set on and around a Southern military base where Lily, Johnny's wife, is visiting, focuses on the conflicts that ensue after white soldiers arbitrarily assume that Lily is a prostitute. Prostitutes were required to carry a "Health Card," which Lily doesn't have, jeopardizing the couple's time together. The dialect in Yerby's story is reminiscent of the poor spelling and grammar that was so pronounced in Juanita Harrison's travelogue published eight years earlier. In an effort to defend his wife by appealing to a white superior, Johnny stutters: "It's about Lily, suh. She my wife. She done worked an' slaved fur nigh onto six months t' git the money t' come an' see me. An' now you give th' order that none of th' cullud boys kin go t' town. Beggin' yo' pahdon, suh, I wasn't in none of that trouble."[77] As the timing and theme of "Health Card" suggest, Yerby was both preoccupied with and infuriated by racism and segregation during World War II.

After several years of trying, and a great deal of rejection, Yerby had finally managed to craft a powerful, compelling literary rendering of Black encounters with quotidian racial prejudices. Of course, Yerby's artful dialect story was squarely aimed at offering white readers a clearer sense of just how unjust Jim Crow was. And this constituency was particularly taken by the narrative this young Black author was selling. "Health Card" received the O. Henry Memorial Award for 1944, a prestigious prize administered by Harry Hansen. Hansen also edited an annual collection of O. Henry Memorial Award stories with assistance from Muriel Fuller, who soon thereafter helped Yerby secure his first literary agent based on one of his submissions to *Redbook* magazine.

Not everyone was pleased with Yerby's breakthrough story. Indeed, for some Black readers, "Health Card" shared too much in common with the negative stigma and racial stereotypes associated with Wright's "protest" novel, *Native Son* (1940). One Black G.I., John S. Cousins, wrote Yerby after the story was published, complaining that several of his Black peers in the armed services objected to this fictionalized narrative of their mistreatment. "Color, not character [in "Health Card"], is the deciding factor," Cousins maintained. "They believe that your depiction of these two does nothing to set them off as moral Negro Americans, even though you do make the concession of marriage [the relationship between the G.I. and his wife]." Cousins thus faulted Yerby "[for] produc[ing] a piece of propaganda that will find its mark on the mind of every thinking reader of <u>Harper's</u>."[78] It would be surprising if these objections did not remind Yerby of James Weldon Johnson's advice several years earlier that he should avoid writing essentialist African American poetry.

But Johnson was dead. And with "Health Card," Yerby refused to back down from his creative interpretation of racial discrimination. In an unmistakably respectful response, Yerby noted that he had, in fact, written this short story "with the high purpose of pure educational propaganda to help make things better racially." Yerby also informed Cousins that his successes with "Health Card" were just the beginning of his career as a literary propagandist. "I hope there will be many, many more stories. I'm working on a historical novel of promise now," he stated.[79] This novel was *Foxes of Harrow* (1946), the book that would make Yerby far more famous than either Lillian Smith or any of his commercially successful Black peers who were on the verge of following in Juanita Harrison's footsteps.

———

In addition to garnering fellowships, awards, and widespread critical acclaim, the novels Yerby, Wright, Ann Petry, and Willard Motley published before the onset of the Cold War were enormously popular. A veritable cohort of best-selling Black authors was emerging for the first time in decades. Because Harrison generally refused to reengage with the literary world following the success of *My Great, Wide, Beautiful World* in the late 1930s, it was often assumed that Wright was the first author of this cohort to escape the literary ghetto and break into the commercial market. "A writer ought to make as much damned money as he can," detective novelist Chester Himes declared in 1946. "It doesn't add to your prestige or comfort as a craftsman to be eternally broke.

I've been broke, I know. Oh boy, I know."[80] Himes's description of Wright's successes in the late 1930s and 1940s reflected this understanding: "The Black Renaissance [of the 1920s] was an inward movement; it encouraged people who were familiar with it, who knew about it and were in contact with it, but the legend of Richard Wright reached people all over."[81] While the statement is an apt description of how the books published by this cohort (including Himes's novels) circulated in this period, Wright was never a singular voice at any stage of his career.

On the other hand, Wright's commercial success with *Native Son* (1940) was so foreign to some white critics that they couldn't name any of his Black literary forebears. In 1941, a white contributor to *Of Men and Books*, a nationally broadcast radio program, estimated, "I'm fully convinced that Richard Wright belongs to the long line of Negro singers which began with the spirituals."[82] Two decades later, Edward Morgan would echo this sentiment in his glowing recommendation of Lorraine Hansberry's Broadway play, *Raisin in the Sun* (1959).[83] Aside from his references to "Negro spirituals," Wright and Langston Hughes were the only other Black authors Morgan identified as Hansberry's forebears.

The parallel Morgan drew between Hansberry and Wright in 1959 was apt. But during the 1940s, even readers who had initially liked Wright's *Native Son* later denounced the novel. And yet, before his critical reputation began plummeting in the years leading up to the Cold War in 1947, Wright was widely hailed by white critics for "universalizing" the Black novel. Moreover, and more so than he is commonly credited for, Wright delighted in repeatedly challenging the color line in American literary culture in the course of his career. By the mid-1940s, Wright's commitment to this work was cheered by Gertrude Stein, one of his most prominent white friends and advocates in this era. On the eve of her death, Stein was confident that Wright had become her successor in advancing American literary culture.

In a fascinating reversal of the letter Van Vechten had sent to Paris regarding Juanita Harrison's travelogue ten years earlier, in 1946, Stein returned the favor, with a letter full of praise for Wright. Stein had recently spent a lot of time with the novelist in Paris helping his family settle in France. "[Wright] interests me immensely, he is strange, I have a lot of theories about him," Stein noted. She then added that Wright "has made quite clear to me the whole question of the Negro problem, the black white the white black, are they white or are they black." Though Stein jokingly claimed that Wright had "clarified" racial matters for her, the elliptical "blacks" and "whites" that followed—including "is Dick

[Richard] white or is he black"—make plain how moved she was by Wright's capacity to challenge racial essentialism. Stein informed Van Vechten: "I said to him, your next book can't be Black Boy, that is camouflage, you got to find out more than that, I think he knows what I mean."[84] Wright did in fact know what she meant, but it was incredibly difficult for his cohort of Black authors to ignore the allure of large-scale commercial publishing after the long Depression.

Despite having printed 170,000 copies of Wright's first novel, Harper & Brothers had to reprint Native Son just days after it was released to the public. Wright's novel was the best-selling title the firm had seen in twenty years. Native Son sold more than two hundred thousand copies in just three weeks.[85] Black Boy (1945) was even more commercially successful than Native Son had been. Wright's fame generated sales of close to six hundred thousand copies of Black Boy in its first six months on the market (195,000 as a Harper trade book; 351,000 copies as a Book of the Month Club selection). Overall, Black Boy was the fourth best-selling title of 1945. Stein's advice paled in comparison to numbers like these.

———

After sales of the novel Knock on Any Door (1947) approached one hundred thousand copies, the author, Willard Motley, noted in his diary in 1947, "My book is tied for first place as the Best Seller in Chicago with 'The Vixens' [Yerby's second novel, published that year]."[86] The fact that these Black authors were the top two best sellers in Chicago that May supported a growing sense of racial inclusivity in the literary field. In September, an Ebony profile of Motley led with a quote from the novelist that stated: "If you know people, you can write about any race."[87] A few months later, Ted Purdy, the white editor of Knock, informed Motley that he had "[j]ust got through hearing your book and name mentioned over the University radio station [. . .] wh[ich] was using your book and Yerby's as examples of the Negro's gradual acceptance as 'just people.'"[88] As strange as it may seem, this concept was still unthinkable for most white Americans in the second half of the 1940s.

Motley's commercial success with Knock on Any Door in 1947 was far from certain. Initially, neither he nor his editor assumed that readers would find this novel—which, like Yerby's first novel, was adapted as a Hollywood movie—entertaining. And it was somewhat of a mixed blessing that an academic sociologist and Work Projects Administration veteran, Horace Cayton, planned

FIGURE 2.5. *Ebony* published a profile of Willard Motley
following the publication of his novel *Knock on Any Door*
(New York: Appleton-Century-Crofts, 1947).

to review *Knock* for *The New Republic*. To be sure, Black literary culture in this
period frequently confounded categorical limits. Cayton was the coauthor of
Black Metropolis (1945), which is now a canonical study of Chicago's Black
community. Richard Wright was asked to write a lengthy introduction to this
academic study, which generously credited both William James and Stein's
Three Lives (1909) as precursors. "Gertrude Stein's *Three Lives*, which contained 'Melanctha,' the first long serious treatment of Negro life in the United
States, was derived from Stein's preoccupation with Jamesian psychology,"
Wright noted.[89] A year and a half later, Motley informed Ted Purdy that Cayton could publicly endorse *Knock* because *The New Republic* "allow[ed] him
2,000 words" to review "serious books."[90]

While Motley was hopeful that educated readers would appreciate his "serious" novel, he never imagined selling 47,000 copies of *Knock* within three
weeks of its debut. Motley was thrilled by his diverse readership. In another
diary entry less than two months after *Knock* was printed, Motley noted to

himself, "Amazing the different types of people from different strata of society who are reading my book. Even the people from the Skid Rows."[91] By that point, tens of thousands of readers across the United States were reading and discussing *Knock on Any Door.*

Nick Romano, the queer, attractive twenty-one-year-old protagonist at the center of *Knock*, roamed and hustled on the mean streets of Chicago with impunity. The following description of Nick's movements offers a sense of why so many readers purchased Motley's book in 1947: "He hung on West Madison Street, at the Pastime and at the Nickel Plate. He went jackrolling, or mooched, or played the queers for his money. He was never going back home again. [. . .] He started to ask Juan if he wanted to work tonight." An unanticipated run-in with Owen, the older man who pays Nick for sex, saves him from pursuing other illegal activity with Juan that evening. Before parting ways, Nick, who identifies closely with his Catholic, Italian American heritage, "angrily" rebukes Juan for his skepticism of Owen: "Do you think something's wrong with every-body? He's a good friend of mine!"[92] According to Motley's narrative, none of this stops Nick's plans to take anything he could from Owen that night.

Though literary historian Alan Wald has made explicit comparisons be-tween James Baldwin's *Giovanni's Room* (1956) and *Knock on Any Door*, few other literary scholars have. Wald observes that "*Knock on Any Door*'s status as a gay novel has yet to be assessed."[93] And unlike Baldwin, most historians of the twentieth-century United States have never heard Motley's name. Given that Baldwin was at the very beginning of his literary career when *Knock* was published, it is likely that he read Motley's novel as soon as he could. Baldwin's *Giovanni's Room* foregrounds unequal yet romantic exchanges of a poor, young, queer Italian, hustling a relatively mature, wealthy American Protestant.

Nick's many crimes in Motley's novel come to an end after he murders a policeman, which eventually leads to his execution in the electric chair at the age of twenty-one. This is a variation on the plot of Wright's *Native Son.* But rather than vilifying Nick, Motley's lengthy, naturalist saga inspired immense sympathy for this young, handsome Italian American. Countless readers reported crying at the end of the novel, when Nick, a clear victim of his slum environment, is finally executed.[94] As others would say about Yerby's fictional narratives, Motley's protagonist was everything Wright's "Bigger Thomas" was not.

Moreover, over the late 1940s, Motley received an overwhelming response from fans of *Knock*, congratulating and thanking him for publishing a sym-pathetic portrayal of same-sex relationships. Gay and queer identities were highly stigmatized after World War II, which made *Knock* that much more exceptional. In 1947, H. W. van Couenhoven, the chaplain at the jail complex on Rikers Island, wrote Dana Ferrin, the executive vice president at the publisher Appleton-Century, praising Motley's novel. "All that is stated [in *Knock*] needed to be proclaimed from the housetops," he said. Couenhoven appreciated *Knock* for its "compassion" and "sensitiveness," which he argued were more powerful than the literary realism of Theodore Dreiser and James Farrell. Indeed, this prison chaplain was "especially glad [Motley] was frank about homosexuality." According to Couenhoven, "homosexuality" was "all about us today on all levels. Fear makes most of those who come into contact with it become brutal and hysterical." Couenhoven "wished" he "could get a paper-covered edition; and give it out like a tract for [Rikers prisoners] to read. I shall preach from it one of these Sundays; a sort of review in sermon form."[95] Couenhoven's words suggest that familiarity with Motley's first novel might temper firsthand, inhumane reactions to sex and relationships between men in prison.

During 1948 and 1949, Motley maintained an active correspondence with William Samilov, who was released from New York State's Dannemora prison toward the end of their first year of exchanging letters. Samilov initially wrote Motley because *Knock*'s protagonist, Nick, reminded Samilov of Rick, his lover. Rick remained incarcerated at Dannemora after Samilov was released. "You see I love Rick like a brother. Maybe some people like Freud or someone would call it homosexual, but in prison, just like in a war, you get real close to a guy," Samilov explained.[96] In a third, despairing letter to Motley on New Year's Eve in 1948, Samilov lamented yet again the stigma associated with his intimate relationship with Rick: "Strange isn't it that the very love that society condemns is what made Rick want to live on the up and up. That love is also what has changed me so that I want to make something of myself and lead a good life with Rick. Can a love like that be bad? Is it degenerate?"[97] As these reflections indicate, Samilov chafed at widespread perceptions that his romantic relationship and future plans with Rick were inappropriate.

Motley's letters to Samilov were remarkably affirmative. In a touching response to Samilov's New Year's Eve letter, Motley confessed, "Your letter moved me deeply. No, no a love like that isn't bad. It isn't degenerate. [...] It is perhaps the best thing that could have happened to either of you [Samilov and Rick]."[98] Samilov was heartened by Motley's kind words and understanding; he assured the novelist in early 1949 that his positivity and willingness to correspond had "helped a lot."[99] On the eve of 1949, Motley even volunteered to write Rick on Samilov's behalf. Earlier, upon learning of Samilov's relationship with Rick, prison officials had prohibited correspondence between the two lovers. Curiously enough, sharing much in common with the prison chaplain at Rikers Island, the only person who did not object to Rick and Samilov's relationship was Dannemora's Catholic priest.[100]

Gratitude for Motley's sensational narrative extended well beyond jails and prisons in New York State. Several other fan letters related to *Knock on Any Door* credited the novelist for humanizing gay and queer lives. Sheldon Eckfeld, a forty-six-year-old from Ohio, noted, "I was glad that you had courage enough to stress the part homosexuality plays in the life of city youngsters. [...] Too many have the wrong idea of the homosexual and his relation to youth and overlook the fact that many of them exert a <u>good</u> influence over youngsters." Eckfeld also remarked, "I saw so much of this during the war and know that hundreds of thousands of service men got a far better 'deal' as they call it from the homosexuals they met than they did from women—yes, even their own sweethearts and wives."[101] Another fan, Glenn Clawson, a twenty-seven-year-old radio announcer, described himself as a "very unusual fellow and I say this without bragging if you will follow. [...] I have led a most unusually dull life that has been most unusual. Even my desires are unusual."[102] Clawson's coy allusions to his own nonheteronormative sexuality illuminate how exciting it was for readers like him to encounter agentive queer characters in a contemporary novel.

Some of Eleanor Roosevelt's biographers have discussed the First Lady's amatory relationships with women as well as men.[103] With or without these intimate ties, coming from an extraordinarily influential white ally, the First Lady's advocacy on behalf of women, African Americans, and queer persons was arguably "intersectional."[104] Roosevelt endorsed Motley's first book soon after it was published, and queer fans of *Knock* such as Clawson took notice when she did. In his 1948 letter to Motley, Clawson claimed to "know nothing about style but Eleanor Roosevelt says [*Knock* is] good and I'm a good Democrat," subsequently describing himself as "the new Deal variety."[105] For Roosevelt, *Knock* was "one of the best written and most disturbing books I have read in a long time. [...] [T]he book puts together and marshals before you all the evils of our democratic society." Roosevelt also assured the millions of Americans who read her syndicated newspaper column of the universality of Motley's protagonists: "[Y]ou can recognize them as you walk down almost any street."[106] Roosevelt's capacious progressivism was exceptional among American politicians in general but less so among radical progressives. In March 1948, Henry Wallace's Presidential Committee requested permission to print five hundred thousand political advertisements with Motley's name and the title of his book on them, in an effort to get out the vote.[107] The request suggests that Wallace, mocked by Motley's publisher as a "leftist candidate," wanted to run a campaign that followed other contemporaries in capitalizing on *Knock* as a unifying symbol.[108]

With overwhelmingly positive responses to his book, Motley went on to establish himself quickly as a public expert on troubled youth and slums. Even in the late 1940s, this was still an unusual but important achievement for a Black author. After Motley participated in a panel on juvenile delinquency hosted by CBS's radio show *The People's Platform*, one female fan wrote in 1947: "I think this is the first time CBS ever had a really representative panel discussing a public topic." She observed that CBS, like other radio companies, "usually exclude[d] women and colored people. I must say that they always excluded Negroes except on questions involving the race problem. Maybe a new day is dawning."[109] Days later, Motley's own private reflections offer a sense of how empowering he found this radio debut: "I was pretty nervous at first. It seemed to go off well. I got pretty tough about the slums, about America [as] a land of opportunity."[110] Like several of his successors—most notably, queer Black authors such as James Baldwin and Lorraine Hansberry—Motley eventually became overwhelmed by his position as a prominent, peripatetic public intellectual.

Between promoting *Knock* and countless civic obligations, Motley had little time to write his next novel or to respond to the many readers who sent him letters. By early 1948, Motley was even apologizing to fans for how busy he was. "There were launch parties launching the book," Motley explained, and "trips to New York to appear on radio programs, radio programs in Chicago, books to autograph, speeches to make, so many speeches, and people, god so many people, and more speeches, and women's clubs, and rounds of cocktail parties."[111] Despite how taxing this schedule often was, Motley still enjoyed his moment of fame immensely.

Motley's publisher, however, feared that Motley's notoriety was a liability. Ted Purdy, his editor at Appleton-Century, regularly chided the novelist for not spending more time on his second book: "I am a little alarmed to hear that you are still so much involved in radio work and other extra-curricular activities. Really, you ought to remember that you are a novelist first of all and a public figure secondarily!"[112] Purdy, of course, was more interested in Appleton-Century's profits than he was in seeing his star author become a leading Black public intellectual. But Purdy was also vitally aware that Motley had few alternatives to pursuing work—and pleasure—beyond the predominantly white publishing realm. Or as Purdy noted pessimistically in a letter to Motley toward the end of 1948: "The slicks are back in a romance-and-roses escapist mood."[113] Describing his own suspicions of this paradigm, white leftist Jack Conroy warned Motley that writers like themselves were not likely to benefit from America's postwar economic miracle. "Somebody has just commented that the intellectual air was much freer in the depression thirties than in the prosperous present, and that this intellectual freedom helped to bring out a richer literary development than we are enjoying today," Conroy noted in 1948.[114] Several years after he began collaborating with Arna Bontemps, Conroy knew, but likely struggled to articulate, that the publishing woes of his Black friends and colleagues were compounded by racial biases in the white publishing world.

Motley's correspondence with *Holiday* and *Look* magazines shortly after *Knock on Any Door* illustrates how skittish white publications still were about Black subjects and anti-Black discrimination. Motley corresponded with dozens of magazine editors in the months after his book became a best seller. Paradoxically, after numerous eager letters soliciting writing from him, Motley was rejected almost across the board. On its surface (at least for white readers), *Holiday* was a fairly apolitical publication in the years after World War II. But for a brief moment, its editors pondered shaking things up a bit. *Holiday* wrote to Motley in late 1947 or early 1948 asking whether he was interested in writing an article on various prejudices affluent Black vacationers encountered. Motley eagerly replied to *Holiday*'s editors, affirming that he was "surely most interested in doing it. Whatever you suggest as a beginning [...] is agreeable to me." Motley, who was already a seasoned traveler, volunteered to "investigate" a broad range of prospective getaways. His pitches included investigating how Black skiers were accommodated on Mount Rainier and even looking into "the situation" on Catalina Island, to see whether Blacks were discriminated against in places ranging from "tourist cabins" to "glass-bottom fishing boats." Motley also suggested shedding light on the relative lack of discrimination in locations such as Banff, which "might be a good place in Canada, [and] Mexico City in Mexico."[115] The range of Motley's proposals to *Holiday*'s editor, who claimed that "we are thinking precisely [along] the same lines," lends insight into the types of writing projects Black authors might hope to pursue if given the opportunity.[116] But in the end, two decades would pass before *Holiday* managed to publish an essay on how African Americans were affected by racial discrimination in the domestic hospitality sector.[117]

As the Cold War ramped up in the late 1940s, so did a marked embrace of racial biases and exclusion in the predominantly white publishing industry. These people were somewhat more open-minded than many white authors and literary professionals were a few decades earlier. But the outcomes for Black writers in such exchanges were often quite similar. *Look* magazine's decision to erase Motley's image from an extensive photo essay he arranged and codirected in 1947 is arguably one of the most conspicuous examples of this dynamic.

After this issue of the magazine was published, Henry Ehrlich, an editor at *Look*, secretly wrote to Motley explaining last-minute edits to the *Knock on Any Door* photo essay. Ehrlich's dramatic language made plain how embarrassed—and defensive—he was about the erasure of Motley's Black image from the story. "You'll die when you see what's happened to [the representation of] your book. I've already died a couple of times myself. But now Willard: This is all off the record, strictly between you and me," Ehrlich stated. "I request that you destroy this letter after you have read it." Ehrlich then outlined the particulars of how *Look*'s essay had changed: "[Y]ou are not to be [in the] 'Behind the Scenes' [section]—for the reasons I gave you [Motley's race]. The publisher has said nothing about your being a Negro—why should we? And instead, I seem to be the subject of the piece. But again, now Willard, this is between us strictly."[118] Of course, it was Motley's choice to write a novel centered on a white Italian American during and after World War II. Yet it was deep-seated prejudice that kept him from pursuing other literary projects that foregrounded the African American experience.

———

It was the literary editor and children's book author Muriel Fuller who was responsible for connecting Frank Yerby to his long-standing literary agent Helen Strauss, just before he planned on giving up on writing, and rejection slips, for good.[119] In a 1949 letter to Fuller, white author Cameron Shipp characterized Strauss as "[a] gem with a heart of gold and a will of iron."[120] Strauss had helped Shipp make a great deal of money as a ghostwriter. But she was indeed as tough as she was successful. In a letter to Strauss, Yerby credited her for "the supreme tribute of being the *meanest, roughest, hardest hitting* critic I ever encountered." At the same time, Yerby assured Strauss that she had also been a "good friend, an honest agent and a grand person," whom he loved "dearly."[121] For decades, Strauss was considered one of the leading agents in

New York's publishing business. In 1946, toward the beginning of her illustrious career, Strauss was hired by the William Morris agency, an important firm at mid-century. Based on Fuller's recommendation, Strauss accepted Yerby as one of her first clients.

Two decades later, Fuller explained in a 1963 essay published in *The Christian Herald* that "on the strength of 'Health Card' and the outline of a new novel [*Foxes of Harrow*], the late George Joel, then head of Dial Press, offered [Yerby] a contract." Fuller also recalled that it was Yerby's novel featuring a Black doctoral student that had inspired her recommendation: "The story was about a young colored man who was honest and decent, everything that [*Native Son's*] Bigger Thomas [. . .] was not. It was not a very good novel but there was something about it that made me feel I could not send it back with the usual rejection slip."[122] Strauss had a similar reaction to this story. "While [it was] not publishable," she praised Yerby's first manuscript for offering "a vivid picture of the anguish and despair of his race."[123]

It is somewhat unexpected, then, that Yerby ended up selling more books than any other Black author of his generation. And Yerby's commercial successes were less straightforward than many scholars and commentators later claimed they were.[124] When *Ebony* published a lavish photo spread on Hollywood's adaptation of *Foxes of Harrow* in 1947, the magazine reported that the movie exhibited "little resemblance to the original story and all controversial chapters" from the novel were "completely omitted from the screen script."[125] *Ebony* faulted "censorship rules of the Motion Picture Production Code" for "pull[ing] the teeth [out] of the script" and emphasized how the "miscegenation angle" of Yerby's book was virtually invisible in the movie.[126] In the years that followed, writers and critics regularly accused Yerby of disavowing his racial identity. Ben Burns, the white editor of *Negro Digest* and later *Ebony*, suggested as much in his autobiographical reflections on the 1940s: "Yerby himself refused to answer our letters and phone calls preferring to leave mundane business matters to his publisher and agent. Dial Press seemed anxious to keep Yerby's race a secret as part of the promotional build-up for the then unknown author." Burns also asserted that Yerby "preferred not to have anything to do with a Negro publication."[127] In reality, the particulars of Yerby's personal and professional choices, and the reception of his work, were far more complex than Burns was willing to acknowledge.

Yerby's white neighbors on Long Island responded violently after realizing that he was the Black author receiving so much national attention after the publication of *Foxes* in 1946. In a letter to Strauss two decades later, Yerby

FIGURE 2.6. The Hollywood adaptation of Frank Yerby's *Foxes of Harrow* received coverage in the December 1947 issue of *Ebony*.

"remind[ed]" her, in the unlikely event that she had forgotten, "that that was my house they threw those milk bottles against in Valley Stream, Long Island; that I was able to move into Jackson Heights only because two Jewish families held out against signing the petition to bar me."[128] The solidarity of these families is reminiscent of the Jewish solidarity Yerby's mentor, James Weldon Johnson, occasionally enjoyed and benefited from. Shortly after arriving in Jackson Heights, Yerby moved his wife and children to Europe to escape the virulence of American racial discrimination in this period—which is too often commonly misunderstood as a practice exclusive to the South.

In Fuller's case, her enthusiasm for cultural interracialism pitted her against her Southern mother, who maintained an unwavering allegiance to Jim Crow in this period. Olive Muir Fuller, a novelist, journalist, and noted lecturer, was a veteran of New York's literary establishment nearer to the turn of the twentieth century.[129] By 1903, she served as the secretary of the Professional Woman's League of New York and was elected as an executive member of New York City's Women's Press Club the following year. But for her daughter, Olive was primarily a harsh reminder of how deep and widespread racism was back in Charleston, South Carolina—even for a woman who had previously worked in New York City's relatively liberal publishing world. (Olive, a widow, moved to the South with her young daughter in 1909.) Personal correspondence between the two women suggests how much professional practices in the literary field had changed by the mid-1940s. Their letters also clarify just how extreme racism and racial tensions were in South Carolina, as Black and white cultural professionals in the North challenged various manifestations of segregation in earnest.

According to Muriel, Olive was a typical white Southerner. Her aversion to African Americans extended to avoiding virtual contact with them in print, even though she begrudgingly employed a Black maid. In a representative letter to Muriel in 1939, Olive complained about a *Life* magazine profile of Eleanor Roosevelt fraternizing with a Black woman: "I expect you saw the lovely picture in Life—that ape-like woman sitting with Eleanor [Roosevelt] standing beside her. Really of the two, the ape-like woman is to be preferred. At least she is true to her type while E. is a hybrid [interracial]." In the same letter, Olive also took aim at the rest of the "rotten [Roosevelt] administration," which she feared was on the verge of admitting "nigs [Black men] in among the Citadel cadets."[130] As these comments indicate, Olive was particularly bothered by the prospect of desegregation and any signs of social integration.

Olive's racial paranoia included worrying that Roosevelt's Supreme Court might force the state of Missouri to desegregate its law schools. Confident that such mandates for integration would lead to violence at the University of South Carolina, Olive gloated that the school's white students would have no choice but to lynch such an "intruder."[131] Muriel found her mother's racist diatribes very upsetting. She cut out the portion of Olive's letter imagining this murder, as well as her mother's vitriolic comments about Eleanor Roosevelt, and enclosed these snippets with her reply. Muriel wrote that she wished Olive would be forced to view this lynching in person, "to watch a human being, not an animal, though one who is black, not white, like yourself, tortured— illegally put to death by his fellow human beings—for the crime of wanting an education." Muriel's response also suggests how common her mother's prejudices were among whites in Charleston: "It is difficult for me to believe that the Williams's, your friends the Luhns, Simons, and others—for you say others feel this way—also desire this. I hope all of you will have front seats at such a spectacle."[132] Muriel's presumption that watching this lynching would be a punishment, though well intended, is somewhat naive given how popular these murderous spectacles had been for several generations of white Southerners.[133]

Olive never budged from assuming that Black Americans were inferior to their white counterparts. "We both know the negro race as manifested in the south where we have lived so long. We are first last and always against the mixing of the races," she insisted. According to Olive, who also considered herself a deeply religious woman, efforts at integration were "doomed to failure; it is against that which has been laid down by Almighty God."[134] Olive's opposition to progressive interracialism in the 1930s and 1940s was manifold and easily included rejecting cultural achievements such as Paul Robeson's performance in a 1943 Shakespeare production:

> I expect we [she and Muriel] shall always be miles apart on several matters. Othello is one of them, if and when the leading part is played by a negro and a white woman must endure his embraces. The thought of those great black hands touching one's body gives me the shudders. How any white woman with the slightest regard for her person would submit to a negro embracing her is beyond me—I mean a white woman as I know the Desdemona is. (I don't recall her name at present.) Of course I didn't read what [Paul] Robeson had to say in the [Herald Tribune] Forum. I skipped several others too.[135]

Olive's second husband was in full agreement with positions like this, as she made clear just a few months later: "Neither Burt nor I would go to a thing like Carmen Jones. [. . .] And this isn't prejudice. Prejudice can only exist where the thing prejudiced against is not known."[136] Muriel's correspondence with friends and colleagues in this era indicates that she hoped more African American representation and cross-racial interactions in popular media might challenge bigoted perspectives like those of her mother.

As her letters indicate, Olive deliberately avoided performances, films, and printed matter by and about African Americans. In 1943, Olive reminded Muriel that whenever and wherever she might encounter Blacks "as a race, I must always shrink from them. And I will not willingly live where they are taken on terms of equality [and] familiarity with the white race."[137] It was thus a great surprise three years later for Olive to find that Yerby's *Foxes* was dedicated to her daughter. Muriel's decision not to inform Olive—who was otherwise aware of virtually all of her daughter's professional activities—that she considered Yerby a friend and colleague is telling. Indeed, Olive only discovered that *Foxes* was dedicated to her daughter after an unexpected visitor arrived with a copy of the book. "I was amazed," Olive recalled in 1946. "I penned it in and concealed my amazement I thought very well and said, 'Yes, I expect Muriel has made very many books "possible."' It was the FOXES OF HARROW by Frank Yerbee [*sic*]." Upon realizing that Muriel had hidden her social and professional relationship with an African American man, Olive pled, "I really would like to know if you ever told me that Frank Yerbe [*sic*] had dedicated the book to you. I am very sure you did not but of course my memory slips of recent years. But please tell me."[138] Unlike in the 1920s, the most popular Black-authored books in this era—for example, Juanita Harrison's *My Great, Wide, Beautiful World* (1936)—circulated in large numbers across the United States and beyond. White supremacists like Olive couldn't ignore *Foxes*.

Yerby's first novel was extremely popular, even in the South. "I wrote you what I thought of it. I had no idea you even knew the author," Olive explained to her daughter. "If I 'hurt your feelings,' I am too sorry," she claimed. "So please forgive me if I was too frank. Will you tell me if you think the ENDING of THE FOXES made sense?"[139] The book in general and its ending in particular were incompatible with Olive's discriminatory impulses. There were many ways in which Yerby's novel was different from popular predecessors such as Margaret Mitchell's *Gone with the Wind* (1936). Yerby's story included several politically conscious Black characters who were unafraid of planning violent retaliations aimed at white slaveholders. Also containing a handful of unusually positive vignettes detailing sex and romance across racial lines, Yerby's *Foxes* symbolized many of the social and cultural changes Olive decried. Worse still, Olive was likely infuriated that her own daughter's name might always be associated with a man who quickly became the best-selling African American author of the twentieth century. As the literary scholar Stephanie Brown has argued, *Foxes* was a "profoundly interracial" novel penned "by a biracial writer."[140] Popular books like this were a severe blow to white Americans who were mortified by any form of interracialism whatsoever.

———

Interracial literary productions in this period, with all their potential and inequities, reflected how difficult it often was—personally and professionally—to live and work across racial lines. Recalling the adaptation of Yerby's first book in 1947, Langston Hughes stated: "When the motion picture made from *The Foxes of Harrow* had its highly publicized premiere in Augusta, [Georgia,] Yerby's relatives were relegated to the Negro section of the theatre. Such are the strictures of race in America even against an author whose books are translated around the world and whose earnings from writing total well over a million dollars."[141] For Yerby and the handful of other Black authors fortunate enough to break into the commercial market, their fan bases were larger and broader than ever. Between hardcover and softcover sales, Black authors such as Willard Motley and white authors such as Lillian Smith sold hundreds of thousands of books in the 1940s. By the 1950s, sales of paperback reprints would ensure that their once-controversial novels were read by millions of readers around the globe.

These literary successes weren't simply luck. Mentorship and advice from an older generation of authors and cultural entrepreneurs on both sides of the color line—for example, James Weldon Johnson, W. S. Braithwaite, and Gertrude Stein—encouraged the "universalism" that a younger cohort of Black writers was regularly praised for. "The day Frank delivered the final manuscript of *Foxes*," Helen Strauss remembered, "he came directly from the aircraft factory, still in his working clothes. I recall at the time looking at him and saying, 'You're going to make a lot of money from this book.'" Yerby responded: "I knew it would."[142] Preoccupations with racial purity, "selling out," and being "too American" during and after the 1960s frequently inhibited deeper insight into the nature of professional exchanges like these in the publishing world.

The next chapter examines the successes and shortcomings of interracialism in the commercial children's book sector. By the early 1940s, New York's corporate publishers were producing several of the most prominent Black and interracial children's books in the United States. Black children's book author Ellen Tarry later recalled of these years, "With Franklin Delano Roosevelt in the White House, Negroes began to feel that they would get a fair share of the prosperity. [...] The need for a Federal Writers' Project was diminishing."[143] A white artist, Myrtle Sheldon, helped Tarry mock up a version of her first children's book, *Janie Belle* (1940), which Grace Nail Johnson encouraged her to pitch to some of the biggest firms in Manhattan. Though uneven, racially progressive changes were occurring not only in publishing for adults but also in the corporate juvenile trade, which boomed during and after World War II.

3

Challenging Little Black Sambo

"THE PURPOSE OF BOOKS FOR CHILDREN IS, of course, to throw open new doors and wide portals, to give the child a vision of the world as it could be were men more understanding," Muriel Fuller reported in publisher E. P. Dutton's trade newsletter in 1939. Fuller was a published author, established editor, and the first literary agent for the Black novelist Frank Yerby. Like many white women in the corporate publishing world at mid-century, she had wide-ranging professional tastes, which included representing authors of children's books. On the eve of World War II, Fuller was pitching a children's book on Mexican history: "By reading of other countries, of other boys and girls of another color, race and language [. . .] he learns they are children like himself, whom it would be fun to know."[1] Fuller's claims echoed a growing awareness among editors associated with major publishing houses in New York by the late 1930s that children's books provided an easy and accessible platform for teaching "neighborliness" and "brotherhood" as early as possible.

Fuller liked marketing and promoting diverse juvenile literature. She did not consider herself an activist for civil or human rights. Neither, really, did any of the aspiring Black writers she befriended, mentored, and occasionally represented. Like other educated white progressives, however, she feared that inter-racial and interethnic tensions might lead to the undoing of humankind. An essay she published for booksellers in September 1939—just days before Nazi Germany's invasion of Poland—illuminates concerns that would inform the publication of pluralist children's books until the early 1970s. "We must learn understanding along with our scientific bridging of space as we run the girdle around the earth," she wrote, "so that at last we may learn to live with one another in harmony, or at least in tolerance."[2] When the global war erupted just a few days later, teaching younger generations the power and utility of peace through children's books became a more urgent cultural imperative than ever in the United States.[3]

In the years after the United States entered World War II in 1941, the nation's top publishing houses became leading producers of racially progressive juvenile texts. Summarizing popular American assumptions about the global conflict, historian Mary Dudziak has commented: "The thinking that World War II was a war against racial and religious intolerance, and that the United States stood to gain from promoting equality at home was so widespread that Frank Sinatra even sang about it." Dudziak also notes: "To be 'American' was to practice equality, at least toward one's wartime allies."[4] The rhetoric, and occasional actions, of white children's book editors during the war fit this pattern: Several of Fuller's white friends, colleagues, and peers joined their Black counterparts in committing to working across racial lines in the juvenile book trade.[5] Their attempts to model more egalitarian professional relationships and literary content marked an important turn away from conspicuous inequities in corporate children's book publishing prior to the war.[6]

Recent scholarship on mid-century children's literature has stressed the remarkable influence, scope, and continuity of progressive ideals in the production and promotion of juvenile texts and education.[7] But fully appreciating how these successes ebbed and flowed—and how tenuous they were, even when support for reforms was less precarious—requires a closer examination of white publishing insiders like Fuller. Even during World War II, children's book editors, and the organizations they formed, could fight for Black and interracial book projects one moment, only to distance themselves from such efforts in the next. After Fuller began working as a children's book editor during the Great Depression, she regularly documented, in passing, the details of how her white peers challenged and affirmed white supremacist customs in the children's book business.[8]

A host of reforms, though slow and uneven, radically changed the depiction of Black protagonists in American children's books from the turn of the twentieth century to the 1970s. At the same time, for most of this period, white publishers and readers struggled to make distinctions between Black and brown populations in and beyond the United States. Global reprints and adaptations of Helen Bannerman's *The Story of Little Black Sambo* (1899) and white authors Berta and Elmer Hader's *Jamaica Johnny* (1935) are just two examples of books that most white literary professionals claimed could or did represent African American children. *Jamaica Johnny* is a picturesque vision of the former British West Indian colony, published decades before this

Caribbean nation gained independence. Bannerman's narrative traces a grotesque caricature of a South Indian child outwitting four tigers. Dozens of
variations on *Little Black Sambo* were by far the most popular "Negro"
children's books in the anglophone world; scores of white editors who identified as liberal or progressive once claimed that both titles noted above helped
rectify racial inequities—even in the mid-1940s.[9] In 1945, one of these women,
Alice Dalgliesh, maintained in *Publishers' Weekly*: "Little Black Sambo is not a
comic character to children, he is a very intelligent little hero."[10] Declarations
like these mystified African American authors, critics, and cultural activists.

On the other hand, white-authored children's books such as *Jamaica Johnny*,
which critics credited as far less racist than *Little Black Sambo*, once heralded
the lofty promises of progressive literary interracialism: thoughtful writing and
illustrations that crossed racial lines and future-oriented but imperfect narratives that Black Americans still sometimes found worthy of their endorsement,
mass-produced for a large, diverse readership. Other modes of interracialism
in the juvenile sector in this era included white financial sponsorship of books
by Black writers and illustrators or simply bringing different racial groups into
the same fictional or nonfictional text—on fairer terms. As the president of
Publishers' Weekly insisted in 1947, the United States was unique in "hav[ing]
the big mass market for books, so rapidly and recently developed," where there
was a demand "for books which will illuminate and constructively face our
domestic problems," including "interracial frictions and friendship."[11] Two
decades later, in the late 1960s, there was exponential growth in the quantity
and quality of Black and multiracial children's books. Somewhat paradoxically,
this was also the era when it became common to dwell on deficits and to overlook or dismiss progressive forebears.

It would be impossible to cover the history of twentieth-century interracial
collaborations in children's publishing in one book chapter. Instead, this survey investigates continuities and changes in working across racial lines on
children's books (and related print) between the turn of the century and the
early 1970s. Doing so offers an unusual but important perspective on the work
and cultural attitudes of white editors (e.g., Fuller and her peers and predecessors), who once commanded an outsized influence over the production of
Black and interracial books for young readers. With and without support from
African Americans, the white publishing world made texts in both genres a big
business, one that was more complex, more contradictory, and sometimes less
racist than is commonly assumed. A variety of published and unpublished
sources from Fuller's manuscript collection, the archives of other literary

professionals, and popular and trade publications (e.g., *Publishers' Weekly*) help shed new light on the cross-racial habits and perspectives of the white women who directed this work—and those who refused to.

The apex of interracial collaborations and productions was the 1940s, when a growing number of attractive texts transcended primitivist renderings of Black children. Long before (indeed, from the very beginning of the twentieth century), African Americans wrote, illustrated, and sponsored the most inclusive, least demeaning juvenile texts in the United States. In the next section I briefly outline the four decades leading up to the 1940s, considering precursors (both reformers and racial chauvinists) to the white children's book writers and editors who were tasked with working across the color line during World War II. I then focus on the literary professionals and organizations that reinvigorated vital yet insufficient racial reforms in the juvenile sector as the Depression waned and outline the uptick in resistance to these changes; opposition within the trade started to grow several months before World War II was even over. A general failure to build on progressive interracialism in New York's small but powerful juvenile book business anticipated some conservative impulses that are more typically associated with the onset of the Cold War in 1947. More than two years earlier, growing conflations of socialism and antiracist cultural activism ensured that many of Fuller's colleagues (predominantly white women) were not supportive of—or even sympathetic to—addressing biases in books for younger readers.

Finally, I summarize the reemergence of high demand for Black and interracial children's books by the mid-1950s and the backlash against white supremacist texts in the years that followed. I also consider several white literary professionals and publishers who, several decades earlier, were directly responsible for some of the most racially offensive books in wide circulation.

The Early Twentieth Century

Before the late 1920s, children's books that defied a once-ubiquitous white supremacist literary tradition were by and large published independent of New York's largest commercial firms. While most of these books were financed and produced by African Americans, some of these initiatives benefited tremendously from interracial collaborations. As such, they were the predecessors of those with similar aims and cross-racial ambitions published decades later. At the very least, continuities between these periods—particularly in the realm of cultural interracialism for younger readers—remain understudied.

FIGURE 3.1. Otis Shackelford's *Seeking the Best: Dedicated to the Negro Youth,* illustrated by Grant Tayes (Kansas City, MO: Burton Publishing Co., 1911).

To be sure, scholarship on the history of Black children's literature published in the twentieth century has increased exponentially in the past few decades.[12] These narratives often begin with W.E.B. Du Bois and Jessie Fauset's *Brownies' Book* (1920–1921), a magazine designed specifically for African American children. This short-lived publication, backed by Black capital and leadership, was incredibly important for rehabilitating children's literature for African Americans. Much the same is true of related literary work Fauset and Du Bois directed in the 1910s. More than a century later, their predecessors have not received nearly as much credit (or criticism).

Shortly after the turn of the century, John A. Hertel, the president of J. L. Nichols, a white publishing house, financed the publication of *Floyd's Flowers, or Duty and Beauty for Colored Children* (1905).[13] This text—usually marketed as a "book for colored children"—was written by Silas Xavier Floyd and illustrated by John Henry Adams, two African American educators. Decades later, similar book projects produced by Black writers and illustrators were sponsored by New York's major publishing houses—in the 1960s, related work

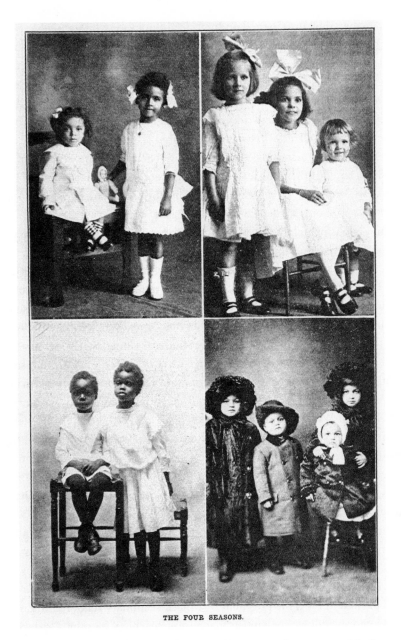

THE FOUR SEASONS.

FIGURE 3.2. "The Four Seasons" appeared in *The Crisis*, October 1913, one of the first issues that W.E.B. Du Bois devoted to photos of Black children, before he cofounded *The Brownies' Book* less than a decade later.

was furthered by the Council on Interracial Books for Children, founded in 1965.[14] Hertel, a very successful commercial publisher with offices in Chicago and Atlanta, was an outlier in brokering comparable deals. As the primary locations of his firm's bases indicate, J. L. Nichols operated outside of the center of the publishing world based in New York and greater New England. Its sales and distribution networks diverged accordingly. So too did its hiring practices: In 1903, Hertel's vice president hired Jesse Max Barber, a Black college student, as a managing editor in the J. L. Nichols "Negro department," a position based at the firm's headquarters in Georgia.[15] In an overview of Barber's early career, which centered on directing the firm's Black newspaper, *Voice of the Negro*, Louis Harlan has argued: "Barber soon became the dominant editor, and though he was cautious at first it soon became clear that he was idealistic, a hater of injustice, and a champion of civil rights."[16] Harlan also explained, "When Barber's magazine joined with the Niagara Movement and the Constitutional League, an interracial civil rights organization," the young editor "correctly identified [Booker T.] Washington as the leader of opposition to the proposal."[17] Most of the firm's other Black employees were hired "at will."

To sell the company's books, in the Southern United States Hertel's firm relied overwhelmingly on Black sales agents, several of whom were ministers. With the help of these canvassers, the firm sold a broad range of printed matter to African Americans, from Bibles to Booker T. Washington's *The Story of My Life and Work*, first published by the firm in 1900.[18] In a business letter addressed to Washington's chief adviser in 1907, Hertel reminded him that the firm's literary business was a reflection of his progressive values: "I want to contribute my little mite towards the solution of the negro problem in which I have been intensely interested."[19] Civic commitments aside, Hertel's investments in popular Black writers such as Washington and Floyd were enormously profitable for J. L. Nichols. As Katharine Capshaw Smith has pointed out, Floyd "edited the 'Wayside Department' of the important periodical *Voice of the Negro*," further noting that some of his writing for the publication was "reprinted in *Floyd's Flowers*."[20] Weeks before *Floyd's Flowers* was printed in 1905, the president of a Black secondary school in Arkansas informed an audience of Baptists that he was "teaching" his pupils "to take an evening with Homer, Carlyle, Milton, Shakespeare" and encouraging them to "read the books of" exemplary Black authors such as Paul Laurence Dunbar and Silas X. Floyd.[21]

A month later, a journalist for the *New York Age* described *Floyd's Flowers* as a "juvenile publication issued expressly for 'colored children'" that heralded

FIGURE 3.3. Two of John Henry Adams's illustrations for Silas Floyd's *Floyd's Flowers, or Duty and Beauty for Colored Children* (Atlanta: Hertel, Jenkins & Co., 1905).

"[a]n innovation in the line of book making."[22] Perhaps it is less surprising, then, that five weeks after the book hit the market, Hertel's firm placed advertisements claiming sales of ten thousand copies of *Floyd's Flowers*.[23] Moreover, high demand for Black books like *Floyd's Flowers* established an important precedent at J. L. Nichols.[24] More than a decade after sponsoring Floyd's juvenile text, the subscription-book firm published Alice Moore Dunbar-Nelson's *Dunbar Speaker and Entertainer* (1920), a literary anthology designed for young Black readers. It is unclear how lucrative this Black juvenile text was for J. L. Nichols. But the firm's financial leverage, and its army of independent sales representatives, certainly ensured that *The Dunbar Speaker* was sold "in every town or locality" possible.[25] Dunbar-Nelson was an author, educator, public intellectual, and political activist whom literate white Americans recognized as "one of the most noted women of her race in America."[26] Affirming as much, poetry she originally published in Bombay's *Indian Social Reformer* was reprinted in newspapers across the United States shortly after World War I ended.

On the eve of the printing of *The Dunbar Speaker* in 1920, Dunbar-Nelson was publicly commended by Delaware's white publishing establishment for her "excellent war work."[27] Her combination of patriotism and cultural activism anticipated the generation of racially progressive children's book authors who were backed by white publishers during and after World War II. Dunbar-Nelson's literary anthology featured an empowered African diaspora—for example, Russia's preeminent poet, Alexander Pushkin, whose Black ancestors served at the highest echelons of the imperial court for close to a century—young African American readers could commemorate as forebears.[28] Walt Whitman, William Wordsworth, John Greenleaf Whittier, and a handful of other white authors were also included in *The Dunbar Speaker*. Dunbar-Nelson's dedication in this Black and interracial anthology of transatlantic literature stated: "To the children of the race which is herein celebrated, this book is dedicated, that they may read and learn about their own people." The range of contributions indicates that doing so wouldn't be a racially exclusive exercise.

Harvard alumnus Leslie Pinckney Hill provided the foreword to *The Dunbar Speaker*. In this essay, Hill passionately argued that American "reading courses have been almost necessarily one-sided and undemocratic. Devised and executed exclusively by experts of the white race, they have naturally reflected only the ideals of that race." In the realm of publishing, J. L. Nichols was an important challenge to white supremacist images of Black protagonists in children's books. Hill warned that ubiquitous cultural affirmations of "the white man's superiority" had promulgated "patronizing" attitudes toward "that vast, brooding world of colored folk—yellow, black and brown—which comprises by far the largest portion of the human family."[29]

Thirteen years later, another Black Harvard alumnus, Carter G. Woodson, similarly lambasted the nation's "so-called school" system in *The Mis-education of the Negro* (1933). One of the system's worst crimes, Woodson argued, was that the majority of America's children were taught that "black face[s]" were a "curse." Woodson cited numerous factors inhibiting a more equitable society in his time, thus prompting many more questions and reflections: "It is strange, then, that the friends of truth and the promoters of freedom have not risen up against the present propaganda in the schools and crushed it. [...] Why not exploit, enslave, or exterminate a class that everybody is taught to regard as inferior?"[30] Woodson also warned that teaching racially biased children's

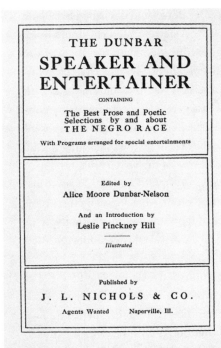

THE DUNBAR
**SPEAKER AND
ENTERTAINER**

CONTAINING

The Best Prose and Poetic
Selections by and about
THE NEGRO RACE

With Programs arranged for special entertainments

Edited by
Alice Moore Dunbar-Nelson

And an Introduction by
Leslie Pinckney Hill

Illustrated

Published by
J.   L.   NICHOLS   &   CO.

Agents Wanted   Naperville, Ill.

BASHFULNESS

FIGURE 3.4. Title page (left) and a photograph (right) from Alice Moore Dunbar-Nelson's anthology *The Dunbar Speaker and Entertainer: Containing the Best Prose and Poetic Selections By and About the Negro Race* (Naperville, IL: J. L. Nichols & Co., 1920).

books remained a standard rather than an exception in the early 1930s: "For example, the author [Woodson] has just received a letter from a lady in Pittsburgh complaining that the librarian in one of its schools insists upon reading to the children 'a great deal of literature containing such words as "nigger," "Blackie," "Little Black Sambo," etc.'"[31] The same year Woodson published *The Mis-education*, Muriel Fuller mused in *Publishers' Weekly* that Hollywood was missing out on "a gold mine" by not bringing "Little Black Sambo" to the big screen: "Think of him in a Silly Symphony dressed in his red coat, blue trousers, and purple shoes with crimson soles, eating 169 pancakes!"[32] As Fuller's remarks suggest, New York's white publishing community casually fueled demand for the most racially offensive juvenile texts that Black cultural activists were objecting to—in the same era.

Offering unqualified praise for white author Ellis Credle's *Across the Cotton Patch* (1935), the editor and critic Virginia Kirkus maintained, "Children will love the adventures of the [Black] plantation children."[33] In the mid-1930s,

Kirkus published glowing reviews of Credle's books and described her Black protagonists as "darkies" more than once.[34] A decade later, children's book editor Alice Dalgliesh, Kirkus's colleague, conceded in an overview of the books and professionals in her sector for *Publishers' Weekly*: "We have undoubtedly been guilty of too much emphasis on Negro comic characters, on rather overdrawn plantation life, and on exaggerated dialect. If we have published a really charming book about a Negro child, bookstores have reported it 'hard to sell,' while comic Negro books have sold by the thousands."[35] She wasn't exaggerating. As an example of just one of the writers this tendency authorized, Credle's *Across the Cotton Patch* (1935), *Little Jeemes Henry* (1936), and *The Flop-Eared Hound* (1938) each fit a pattern—Black protagonists typically rendered as degrading stereotypes of ignorant children—that was an industry standard before the 1940s. And Dalgliesh was still defending the intelligence and humor of "Little Black Sambo" in 1945.

It was Oxford University Press that published Credle's *The Flop-Eared Hound*, a book featuring unvarnished professional photography of Black children in North Carolina taken by the author's husband, Charles de Kay Townsend.[36] Dissimilar from Credle's other books with Black protagonists, this story did not feature unconvincing, offensive dialect. Still, the book's flaws did not go unnoticed by Black commentators such as Beatrice Murphy, the chairwoman of the children's literature committee of the Washington, D.C., Capital Press Club. Despite her appreciation for the images of African Americans included in *The Flop-Eared Hound*, Murphy warned that Credle's "text is not quite as pleasing as the photographs, however. [My] objections are to rather subtle insinuations rather than outright insults." Murphy was particularly disappointed by Credle's depictions of Black parents in *The Flop-Eared Hound*. "The hark back to the 'mammy' and 'pappy' days; the inference that washing clothes is every colored woman's profession detract from the beauty of the book as a whole," she noted.[37] In Credle's narratives, African Americans were always explicitly or ambiguously subservient to white counterparts, which hardly fazed Virginia Kirkus and her intimate circle of female colleagues in the corporate juvenile trade. When addressing the Child Study Association in 1936, Louise Bechtel, the first women to direct a "Children's Department" for a major American publisher, expressed deep reservations about socially progressive juvenile literature. This extended to a joke she told, which began with the story of a white "boy of 13" who defined a "grown up" as "a person who is always busy about not very much, and she usually has two children, a colored maid, and headaches."[38]

Literary scholar Trysh Travis has observed that despite a body of influential scholarship on women and the history of the book, most of this work has centered on what these women read—or in the case of female authors, published. Travis thus argues that "feminist book history" has yet to extend to "the workings of the communications circuit that transforms manuscripts into books and brings them to market."[39] Related absences are even more conspicuous in professional histories of authors, editors, and illustrators who at various moments produced, welcomed, and resisted publishing children's books with racially and ethnically progressive themes. Kirkus's support for Credle's books in the 1930s is emblematic of a corporate culture that was conspicuously slow in reassessing renderings of Black people before World War II.

Kirkus was still in her early thirties in 1926, the year she established one of the first children's book departments in the United States at Harper & Brothers. She cemented her professional reputation with the establishment of *Kirkus Reviews* in 1933. This pioneering work in the literary field made Kirkus an important symbol both within and outside of the publishing trade. For decades, Kirkus remained an outsized advocate for the white women who followed in her footsteps by making more space for themselves in a rapidly consolidating publishing business. The title of one of Kirkus's most influential essays during the Depression, "The Women Back of Books" (1936)—which Muriel Fuller kept a photocopy of—is an apt illustration of her lifetime commitment to promoting gender equity. She advised women to get into the business at any level that they could and to scramble their way to the top: "After all, doesn't that make it more of a challenge to us, doesn't it make it more interesting to see where girls and women do fit in, what they are doing now in the world of books, and what opportunities lie within their grasp?" Even if women with college degrees were forced to start out as secretaries, Kirkus insisted that it was worth it. She explained that the one sector of the publishing business where women were already dominant was "in the realm of books for boys and girls." Lest there be any confusion, Kirkus informed aspirational readers that work in this subfield was tough. She observed that corporate publishers had "all faced the fact that publishing must be a business, first and foremost, if it is to survive the mad orgy of competition in this field."[40] Unfortunately, before the 1940s, Kirkus and too many of her peers remained unaware that their preoccupations with "business" went hand in hand with profiting from books that perpetuated exaggerated images of African Americans and Afrodiasporic cultures.

The 1930s and 1940s

Shortcomings and racial inequities in the corporate trade motivated several Black women to direct the production of their own children's books in this era. As was the case during the first quarter of the twentieth century, most of these books were either self-financed or sponsored by Black publishers and publishing houses. Jane Dabney Shackelford wrote *The Child's Story of the Negro* (1938), a book illustrated by the acclaimed artist Lois Mailou Jones. The book was published by Associated Publishers, the publishing firm founded and led by Carter G. Woodson since 1920.

Like her Black peers, Ellen Tarry was initiating similar projects on the eve of the 1940s. But unlike most aspiring Black authors, Tarry successfully pitched her books to major publishing houses in New York City owned and operated by white Americans. Tarry trained in writing books for young readers for two years at the progressive Bank Street School of Education (est. 1916); it was Lucy Sprague Mitchell, one of the school's white cofounders, who ensured that Tarry was awarded its inaugural "Negro Scholarship."[41] Summarizing her early books set in Harlem in an interview with Katherine Capshaw Smith published in 1999, Tarry recalled: "Nobody had been doing books by recognized publishers like that before, and that meant a great deal to my people." Tarry was responding to Smith's recognition of the author's children's books: "I'll brag for you. I think they're groundbreaking in their depiction of urban life and interracial relationships." Tarry then explained that African American children in cities were virtually unrepresented by major commercial publishers prior to her books published in the early to mid-1940s: "Before that, all we had was [white author Stella Sharpe's] Tobe, a little boy who was picking cotton somewhere."[42] Tarry's comment wasn't intended as an attack on *Tobe* (1939), a white-authored African American juvenile text set in the plantation South. Rather, she was describing a transformative moment during World War II when at least some of New York's white publishing establishment were in the earliest stages of welcoming more dynamic Black books. After the publication of *Janie Belle* (1940), her first children's book, Tarry frequently worked across the color line with editors associated with flagship publishing houses.

Tarry was thoroughly committed to brokering trust and more equitable partnerships with white literary professionals.[43] Literary scholar M. Tyler Sasser has noted of Tarry's willingness to work across the color line in and after the 1940s: "Her partnership with Viking, which also published Keats [white

FIGURE 3.5. Ellen Tarry in 1950 (left) and Grace Nail Johnson in 1940 (right), both photographed by Carl Van Vechten. Beinecke Library Collection © Van Vechten Trust.

author Ezra Jack Keats, author of *The Snowy Day*], and her professional friendship with Lucy Sprague Mitchell and Margaret Wise Brown illustrate her acceptance of cooperation across races."[44] Tarry's collaboration with white author and illustrator Marie Hall Ets was published as *My Dog Rinty* (1946) by Viking. The book centered on a handsomely dressed Black youth and his cute puppy. In less than a decade, Viking sold close to forty thousand copies of *My Dog Rinty*. Tarry was well known among Black readers as the "most successful" Black children's book author by the mid-1950s. But markedly dissimilar to the case of either self-financed Black books or those sponsored by white publishers before the 1940s, selling tens of thousands of copies of juvenile texts such as *My Dog Rinty* proved lucrative for Tarry.[45]

In her autobiography, Tarry explained that it was James Weldon Johnson's wife, Grace Nail Johnson, who encouraged her to connect with May Massee, the founder of Viking's juvenile department. "Following Mrs. Johnson's advice, I went to Viking," Tarry recalled, in addition to explaining that "Massee also understood my desire to have a Negro illustrate the little story of Hezekiah and

"Just wait," Hezekiah used to say to himself.
"As soon as I get to be eleven or twelve—or maybe
thirteen—I'm going to put on long pants and get
myself a job. And the first thing I'll buy will be a
motor-car. A big one, too!"

Yet Hezekiah could never quite decide what
colour his car would be. One day he would choose
a black car. The next day he would be sure that
he wanted a shiny blue car. And the day after the
next, Hezekiah would want a brown one.

12

FIGURE 3.6. Illustration by Oliver Harrington from Ellen Tarry's *Hezekiah Horton* (New York: Viking, 1942).

was patient with my search for an artist whose sketches would meet her ap-proval."[46] In a 1950 profile of Massee, Muriel Fuller described her colleague as "[t]wenty-five years ahead of her time."[47] A decade earlier, Tarry and Massee partnered with Oliver Harrington, a prolific Black illustrator. The first col-laboration among these three was published by Viking in 1942 as *Hezekiah Horton*.[48]

Sponsoring various forms of interracialism in the corporate children's book sector during World War II was the publishing industry's equivalent of the "Double Victory Campaign" led by the Black press. During the war, African Americans were urged to consider fighting the Axis powers abroad as interrelated with a continuing battle for full citizenship, equality, and op-portunities at home. These concepts were not new, but a larger number of white progressives in the publishing world, such as Albert Crone, the direc-tor of Children's Book Week, readily embraced this rhetoric during the war years. In Crone's letter announcing Book Week's slogan for 1943 ("Build the Future with Books"), the educational aims he was promoting for this national celebration couldn't be clearer: "Books about America will develop strong convictions to carry on our democratic tradition. Books about other lands will enable them to regard our allies as individuals and to understand them."[49] To his credit, Crone also made it a point to outline what young readers gained by literary exposure to pluralism in more explicit language: "Reading can prevent the barriers of racial and national prejudices from being raised in the minds of our young people."[50] Prior to World War II, emphasizing the pedagogical values of children's reading was rarely if ever taken this seriously by the white publishing establishment.

Changes in the children's book trade in this era included enormous growth, which dovetailed with new responsibilities directly related to the global con-flict. In 1938, the relatively small number of children's book editors, most of them white women employed by large New York publishers, made it easy for industry insiders to meet "occasionally and very informally" to plan Children's Book Week.[51] Six years later, when Laura Harris assumed control of the 1944 Book Week, her success prompted the establishment of the Children's Book Council. (The group was initially known as the Association of Children's Book Editors.) Muriel Fuller served as the secretary for the organization in 1945 and 1946. Fuller's notes from a meeting in 1946 quote a colleague who explained that it was not until "the war came [that] there were other problems [besides planning Children's Book Week] common to our work that we could discuss together profitably."[52] By the early 1940s, these "problems" included demands from agencies closely affiliated with the federal government calling for the racial and ethnic reform of children's books published by New York's commercial publishers.

The Writers' War Board, the primary domestic propaganda organization during World War II, and the Child Study Association of America (CSA) were the first two organizations to seriously challenge the status quo in the corporate juvenile trade.[53] Beginning in 1943, the CSA offered an annual award for what might best be summarized as "difficult" children's books. That September, *The Brooklyn Daily Eagle* reported, "According to officials of the association, the book must [. . .] be about the contemporary scene, and it must deal with the realities of this scene in a way that will help clarify vexing—perhaps controversial—contemporary problems."[54] The CSA's first award was given to John Tunis, the white author of *Keystone Kids* (1943), a young adult novel that addressed anti-Semitism in professional baseball. Shortly after, the *American Library Association Bulletin* praised Tunis for "courageously handling [. . .] questions of racial and religious prejudice."[55] Growing recognition and institutional support for books like *Keystone Kids* and numerous other racially and culturally progressive juvenile authors and texts heralded real progress during World War II.[56]

Historian Julia Mickenberg has observed: "The Writers' War Board and the Bureau for Intercultural Education developed extensive programs to combat prejudice in children's literature, an issue of paramount concern to writers on the Left, who aggressively pressed for changes in this area."[57] Despite these good intentions, the Writers' War Board and related organizations (e.g., the Council on Books in Wartime, led by white publishing executives) regularly affirmed racial hierarchies they were ostensibly countering. An introduction to one 1943 radio script preserved in the Council on Books in Wartime records at Princeton illustrates how contemporary imbalances were perpetuated. The aim of this fifteen-minute radio program was to promote a canonical Russian folktale. But whoever designed this fictive conversation between an American child and parent advocated for its relevance by situating it alongside the most ubiquitous racist juvenile text of the twentieth century: "Every one of them [Russian children] knows it. [. . .] The way you know LITTLE BLACK SAMBO. [. . .] [J]ust about every American child knows that story."[58] African Americans would not have failed to notice how little some white Americans cared about Black children if articulations of cultural interracialism were this uneven. Fortunately, this script was never broadcast.

The following year, Langston Hughes refused a request from Alan Green, a member of the Writers' War Board, for an endorsement of Ada Claire Darby's *Jump Lively Jeff* (1942). Jeff, the African American child at the center of this story, was named after Jefferson Davis, the president of the Confederate States of America, to cite just one disturbing element of this book. Hughes's response offers a sense of how African American critics frequently responded to outmoded biases promoted by books like *Jump Lively Jeff*: "I think the reason most Negro readers would not like this book is because it seems to perpetuate almost all of the old stereotypes that have been used for many years to caricature the Negro people." Hughes also warned: "It would seem to me the kind of book that would encourage perfectly nice little white children to mistakenly address a perfectly nice little Colored child in broad dialect."[59] Given his own successes working across racial lines in the corporate publishing world, Hughes knew that the Writers' War Board could do better than this if its members tried harder.

The same was true of those who still defended the use of dialect in the white publishing establishment in the early 1940s. In a statement written for *Publishers' Weekly*, a white employee of Tennessee's Chattanooga Public Library complained, "I cannot think of anything worse than a world where people all dress alike, talk alike, and consequently, think alike—a truly standardized set-up."[60] A published response from a collective of Black educators and librarians to this person's opinions and other defenses of "exaggerated characterization[s] of Negro children" warned: "At this time of world strife when children are hearing on every hand the need for unity, tolerance, and democratic ideals, it seems incredible that books strong in racial ridicule should be given such enthusiastic defense."[61] Leslie Pinckney Hill and Beatrice Murphy would have cheered this critique.

College-educated white professionals did indeed require lessons, counsel, and a host of new programming to enact meaningful changes in the children's book sector. By 1946, the Children's Book Council (CBC) had become a formal organization with forty members—thirty-eight of whom were women.[62] Alice Dalgliesh, the CBC's first elected president, was charged with ensuring that her colleagues were aware of the latest social science relevant to childhood reading. Muriel Fuller's CBC notes for the organization's first meeting in 1946 praised Dalgliesh for increasing the group's "awareness of the influence of children's books in cultivating world understanding and friendship. She brought speakers to us and we had several discussions along this line."[63] During World War II, the organization's marketing signaled that the CBC was doing all it could to support more inclusive standards.

FIGURE 3.7. Two posters for Children's Book Week, by Jesse Wilcox Smith in 1919 (left) and Nedda Walker in 1944 (right).

The visual evidence was stunning. In 1944, when women associated with the CBC first assumed control of Children's Book Week, the poster they solicited from Nedda Walker to promote that year's slogan ("United through Books") heralded a sharp break with the iconography that typically represented the corporate juvenile trade.[64] Back in 1919 (and 1930), the poster for Book Week showed two white, blond children in an overflowing home library. The celebration of Children's Book Week in 1944 shifted away from this type of homogeneity: "The theme for this year's Book Week is 'United Through Books,' featuring children's books that will build a solid foundation of understanding among children of all nations, creeds, and races."[65] Statements like these, taken directly from Book Week's organizers, could be found in newspapers across the United States. And they were incredibly popular with parents who wanted a brighter future for their children and for children of all races.[66] (In fact, the "United through Books" theme was so popular that it was reused the following year.) Julia Mickenberg explains: "Book Week, still in existence, typifies the unique status of juvenile publishing among commercial enterprises, as it manages to turn a massive annual sales event into a kind of moral imperative."[67] This assessment is particularly apt for comprehending the transformation of Book Week under the CBC in the mid-1940s.

By 1945, more than twenty American organizations had committed to co-sponsoring the CBC's work. This coalition included several groups dedicated to serving racial, ethnic, and religious minorities, including the Bureau of Inter-cultural Education, the Jewish Education Committee, the National Conference of Christians and Jews, and the National Association of Negro Business and Professional Women.[68] A combination of enthusiasm and contemporary expectations enabled the CBC to aggressively advertise itself as an inclusive, cosmopolitan organization.[69] Indirect mailings to 22,000 American women's clubs, the sale of more than 40,000 posters, widespread radio support, and the distribution of more than 50,000 "free manuals" and 3,400,000 bookmarks aided the public's recognition of the Children's Book Council.[70] CBC meeting notes from December 1945 indicate how surprised several members were by the group's rapid ascent and newfound authority. One member remarked: "Here at home [in the United States] the correspondence to the Children's Book Council has increased tremendously. The letters ask for material, ideas, sugges-tions. They are taking us seriously as an information center. It is staggering!"[71] Steady increases in consumer interest cemented the CBC's reputation as an outlier in the publishing business for the rest of the 1940s.

Discerning and forward-looking families that could finally afford children's books in the 1940s had access to dozens of more dynamic, antiracist Black and interracial children's books than previous generations. During the Depression years, publishers such as Holiday House had a reputation for selling "collectors' items," including children's books such as *Boomba Lives in Africa* (1935), written by Caroline Singer, illustrated by her husband, Cyrus LeRoy Baldridge, and praised by the National Urban League.[72] By 1947, Vernon Ives, the director of Holiday House, claimed in an interview with Muriel Fuller that the juvenile texts his firm published were "less exotic in appearance and far more popular in content and appearance" than *Boomba* had been.[73] This shift dovetailed with a new generation of children's books that were far less primitivist. Between 1940 and 1950, these titles helped establish new and improved standards for the depiction of Black protagonists and interracial narratives.

As other scholars have pointed out, several of these books were distinctive collaborations involving authors, illustrators, editors, and protagonists of different races—intentionally designed as such in various interracial configu-rations.[74] The following are just a sample of the many impressive Black and interracial texts published in the mid-1940s by authors and illustrators hailing

FIGURE 3.8. Carol Singer's *Boomba Lives in Africa*, illustrated by
Cyrus Leroy Baldridge (New York: Holiday House, 1935).

from a variety of backgrounds. In 1944, Julian Messner, Inc. sponsored the
publication of Shirley Graham and George D. Lipscomb's *Dr. George Washington Carver, Scientist*, a biography (for teenage readers) detailing the accomplishments of the preeminent Black inventor. Two years later, another book of
Graham's—aimed at the adult market—*There Was Once a Slave: The Heroic
Story of Frederick Douglass* (1947), won the Julian Messner Award for the Best
Book Combatting Intolerance. Three white authors, Clifton Fadiman, Carl Van
Doren, and Lewis Gannett, selected Graham's book for the $6,500 prize out of an
estimated six hundred manuscripts.[75] Among major publishing houses, Messner
was one of the leaders in diversifying its juvenile list before the mid-1950s.

FIGURE 3.9. (Left) Prizewinning Julian Messner author Shirley Graham, photographed by Carl Van Vechten, 1946. Beinecke Library Collection © Van Vechten Trust. Among white publishers, Messner was an outlier at mid-century in diversifying who was hired to produce children's books for the firm and what was published. (Right) The back cover of Georgene Faulkner's *Melindy's Happy Summer*, illustrated by Elton Fax (New York: Julian Messner, 1949), is an example of how the firm promoted its interracial initiatives and aspirations.

Literary scholar Jodi Melamed has argued that "race novels" for adult readers, written and supported by a variety of cross-racial configurations, "constrained antiracist discourse to forms compatible with the political and economic arrangements emerging out of the Cold War."[76] Similar patterns emerged in the Black and interracial books commissioned and authorized by white editors in the corporate juvenile trade in the decade following World War II. Yet it would be a mistake to minimize or ignore how revolutionary—or inflammatory—some of these texts for younger readers were before the legal dismantling of Jim Crow. One of these books, Lorraine and Jerrold Beim's *Two Is a Team* (Harcourt, 1945) imagined an interracial friendship between a Black child and a white child in an era when this was neither obvious nor obviously acceptable behavior in many white communities. Jerrold Beim's children's book *Swimming Hole* (1951) was a variation on this theme but with more kids in the story. Several years later, *Publishers' Weekly* reported in 1959 that Bobby Shelton, the Ku Klux Klan's "Grand Dragon" of Alabama, had informed the Associated Press that *Two Is a Team* was "one of about a dozen books the Klan will campaign against as pro-integration literature."[77] A similar interracial juvenile text, Black author Jesse Jackson's *Call Me Charley* (Harper, 1945), may have also met opposition from the Klan. Rather than pretending that discrimination against African Americans did not exist, Jackson's narrative traced myriad pressures on Charley, a Black preteen whose family had recently moved to a white, suburban neighborhood.

In 2010, Ann Mulloy Ashmore noted, "*Call Me Charley,* Jackson's first young adult novel, is dedicated to Hans and Margret Rey," a white Jewish couple who fled to the United States from Europe at the beginning of World War II.[78] From 1941, Hans Rey gained fame after the first book in the couple's Curious George juvenile series was published. Ashmore points out that their "relationship" with Jackson "was not one-sided, however. One consequence of their friendship with Jackson was a heightened awareness of racism on and off the page of children's books."[79] According to Muriel Fuller, this cooperative spirit extended to Ursula Nordstrom, Jackson's white editor at Harper.[80] In a 1947 profile of Nordstrom, Fuller credited her as an outlier in supporting diverse children's books: "Like many children's book editors, Miss Nordstrom is not only deeply aware of the vital issues confronting the world today, but of the necessity of doing something constructive about them." In this essay, Fuller also acknowledged Jackson's second children's book, *Anchor Man* (1947), and praised him for writing "the first book to represent not only problems which concern Negroes and whites, but the more subtle ones of Negroes themselves." Nordstrom informed Fuller, "I insist that I do not force my ideas on any author [...] but by a happy coincidence our authors feel as I do, that tolerance is important."[81] It would be a surprise if Fuller did not see how closely Nordstrom's professional relationship with Jackson correlated with her own advocacy on behalf of Black author Frank Yerby's literary promise just a few years earlier.

The Postwar Years

Between 1945 and the Supreme Court's *Brown v. Board of Education* (1954) decision mandating the desegregation of American schools, several editors associated with the wave of new Black and multiracial texts tempered this work or reversed course. Alice Dalgliesh, Muriel Fuller, Vernon Ives, and numerous others retreated in different ways from both real and rhetorical investments in diversifying the children's books (set in the United States) that their firms published in this era. Complaining about what she and her peers now commonly termed "propaganda" in 1947, Fuller remarked, "There's a lot of pressure being brought to bear these days on editors about [sponsoring] books with a message. One would think there never had been any published before!"[82] Fuller's interpretation of "propaganda" two years after the war couldn't be more at odds with Carter G. Woodson's assessment of anti-Black "propaganda" that was so common in American classrooms, libraries, and homes back in the early 1930s.

In the postwar years, Fuller and most of her colleagues disavowed responsibility for implementing racial reforms in the corporate publishing houses they worked for. This included refusing to either monitor or criticize Black and multiracial juvenile books that reinforced white standards of beauty via servile, demeaning illustrations of children of color, who were often unattractive in countless other ways. Julia Mickenberg has argued that while some "radical cultural expressions of the early 1930s did seem to disappear after the war," there were "avenues of cultural production that remained open to leftwingers during the Cold War, [and] children's literature merits special attention."[83] Still, a growing number of white children's book editors resisted calls for a more equitable Black and interracial print culture well before the Cold War ramped up in the late 1940s.

The marked increase in conservative perspectives and business practices dating from early 1945 carried real and long-term consequences for American children's literature. At the same time, there was nothing new about authors and literary professionals disclaiming any relationship between politics and commercial publishing. Responding to one white author's anxieties about rampant xenophobia in 1943, Muriel Fuller's words laid bare her own rejection of tying contemporary racial tensions to either her personal or her professional responsibilities: "Lady, I see eye to eye with you on the situation in our country today. I am not politically or economically minded, but I keep hoping there is some way out of [this] mess. I'm afraid it is going to be a great deal worse before it [gets] better."[84] By this logic, Fuller's own modest contributions to diversifying American print culture, both in and outside of the juvenile trade, were little more than a personal hobby.

Despite racial biases for which Langston Hughes chided the Writers' War Board, the organization's leaders sought to challenge editors like Fuller who wanted to remain "neutral" on racial matters. Rex Stout, a famous author of detective fiction, was the chairman of the board, which included several other well-known intellectuals and literary professionals. Meeting at the Barbizon-Plaza Hotel on Central Park South in January 1945, the board's leaders discussed parallels between domestic and broader interethnic tensions underpinning the global war. Days later, an unidentified female editor employed by a major publisher reported attending the board's meeting on "someone else's ticket," in a personal letter to the nation's preeminent literary critic, Harry Hansen. Shortly after, Hansen forwarded this report to Fuller. The writer of the letter assured Hansen that she had "no intention whatsoever of representing [her firm's] juvenile authors" at the Writers' War Board meeting. "Stout made a point of saying that the people invited were publishers, editors and writers," she noted, "but I didn't recognize too many. They looked like the Same Thing. The Same Thing we had during the Thirties, I mean. In new form."[85] Comments like these casually branded racial reformers as socialists—or even worse, communists—who obviously deserved to be dismissed. Such views were only becoming more common within Fuller's white publishing circles.

The anonymous editor's letter illuminates concerns among those who rebuffed racial reforms in the book business at the end of the war. Stout reportedly informed the board meeting's attendees that "they wanted to call the evening [event] 'How to Avoid Civil War in America,' but thought that a little frightening." Stout was also said to have argued that "this White Anglo-Saxon myth is dynamite, [and] that racial tensions here are the most dangerous in the world, etc." But the editor describing Stout's lecture was deeply skeptical of his assertions and poked fun at the leadership of the board for insisting that "[b]ooks for boys and girls should be slanted to teach them tolerance." The editor justified her annoyance, in part, by detailing what was described as a game called "Education, please" performed at the meeting, which foregrounded scenarios spotlighting cultural prejudices: "All had to do with racial tensions and religious intolerance. A typical one: Name five phrases in our common speech which unintentionally express prejudice. The answers: 'Nigger Heaven,' 'Jew somebody down,' 'Nigger Rich,' 'Injun giver,' 'Very white of you.'"[86] At the beginning of 1945, resistance to consciousness-raising in this vein was growing, especially in the corporate juvenile sector. The timing was not auspicious. Just two months earlier, the immense popularity of the 1944 "United through Books" campaign had been directly responsible for the decision to grant the CBC unchecked authority to direct the nation's childhood reading agenda.

Within a year, a defiant Alice Dalgliesh declared in *Publishers' Weekly*: "We have been reading a good deal about 'stereotypes' in books, stories, the radio, the movies. The War Writers' Board presents research on this to prove that we have certain racial stereotypes—that we have built up a myth of 'Protestant

Anglo-Saxon superiority." If this exists, it has not been especially fostered by children's books."[87] Indeed, tensions flared when affiliates of the Bureau for Intercultural Education rejected a number of children's books submitted by publishers in 1945 that had not met agreed-upon, contemporary, nonracist standards.

At the end of the year, CBC members heatedly discussed a "report of the Intercultural Group," written by academic psychologist Helen Trager, outlining why "they took 253 titles and chose only 61 books."[88] This was an unsettling statistic for almost every editor pressed to ensure that their juvenile departments kept growing. More so than other social scientists, Trager, an administrative head of the Service Bureau for Intercultural Education, was an active threat to literary professionals who did not believe that American children's books were white supremacist.[89] At mid-century, much of Trager's research was dedicated to testing children's racial attitudes.[90] In an essay in *Publishers' Weekly* in 1941, Trager asserted: "Booksellers and businessmen are interested in 'how much' but are fairly indifferent to 'what' children read. From a purely commercial point of view indifference to 'what' children read, I think, is shortsighted business policy, to say the least."[91] But the consensus among white children's book editors shortly after the war was that they and their consumers were tired of thinking about "social tolerance." According to the CBC, the quantity of racially and ethnically progressive books endorsed by academic psychologists (and countless others) during World War II had overwhelmed American consumers. "The market for such books had been ruined (overcrowded) by such 'stimulation'—too many books, produced too fast," Alice Dalgliesh, the former chairperson of the CBC, argued.[92] The language here parallels white opposition to school desegregation over the following three decades.

When this statement was made at the CBC's final meeting of 1945, the majority of its members—who now represented forty influential publishing houses—firmly rejected every proposal to continue formally monitoring racism in juvenile texts: "The feeling of the editors seemed to be against such censorship." One of the frustrations, Dalgliesh suggested, was what she characterized as the "trivial" rejections of children's books by Helen Trager and other social scientists. According to Fuller's notes:

> Dalgliesh [. . .] reported on something she had been asked for [at] various book meetings in the last few weeks, [and especially at] two in particular, the Child Study Association meeting, and the Child Study Reviewers' meeting. In the latter meeting (which came first) the Child Study and the Writers' [War] Board, called together the reviewers of juvenile books—May

FIGURE 3.10. An illustration by Else McKean, a white educational psychologist, for *Our Negro Brother* (New York: Shady Hill Press, 1945), written by McKean's mother, Edith H. Mayer. This image offers a sense of the biracial democratic ideals some children's books promoted in the 1940s.

Lamberton Becker, Lockie Parker, Ellen Lewis Buell, Mary Gould Davis, etc.—and suggested a foundation be set up or backed to see whether truth is presented in juveniles. The general opinion seemed to be there should be no such study. The reviewers were asked to write down any derogatory remarks about minorities and report them. This the six reviewers refused to do. [...] The other question was that when any editor had a book about a minority group that she should send it to that [minority] group to go over. Miss Dalgliesh said she wouldn't do it either as an editor or author (she is both, as well as a reviewer). [...] She said her thesis is simple and obvious: in dealing with books about racial subjects, handled by people with creative ability, that they shouldn't be hurried. [...] There was more discussion. It developed into more than informal censorship, to which the reviewers were opposed.[93]

Under Dalgliesh's guidance, CBC members were asked to remind their critics that juvenile texts have "the same rights as adult ones."[94] Women at the top of the children's book business were essentially adopting a "many sides" philosophy on the value of challenging racial biases.

The following month, in January 1946, Dalgliesh stated that "an editor can really only say, if asked how the [CBC] stands in relation to books dealing with social problems: 'We have discussed these freely in the [CBC], and are well-informed about them, but how this carries over into publishing is a matter for the individual point of view.'" In Dalgliesh's words, children were shaped "by all types of experiences" and "all types of books." In a record of a general discussion at this meeting, Fuller noted that another member suggested that the CBC needed to recommit to "fun" as the fundamental element of consumer sales and other professional work in the sector: "All-inclusive, yet bring it back to the fun of reading, and understanding for pleasure and entertainment."[95] This hands-off policy certainly came back to haunt those editors still working in commercial publishing just a few years later during the Civil Rights Movement.

Children's Literature at Mid-century

Though difficult to quantify, growing resistance to coordinated, institutional racial reforms during and after the mid-1940s was arguably a major setback for America's young readers. Groundbreaking Black and interracial children's book collaborations continued during the early Cold War years. But many white editors, publishing houses, and media outlets were ill-prepared to re-spond to renewed calls for diversifying their cultural programming and prod-ucts on the eve of the Supreme Court's landmark school desegregation ruling in 1954. Nevertheless, there was another dramatic transformation across the juvenile trade over the next twenty years, as editors were pressured to publish a much larger number of African American writers or books with Black themes.[96] Most of this cultural momentum can indeed be attributed to the *Brown* decision and, later, the legal and legislative civil rights victories that followed. A few editors, however, including May Massee and Ursula Nord-strom, had already established successful working relationships with Black authors and literary professionals, well before others were forced to. Or as Nordstrom herself explained in one 1963 letter, during her decades-long career at Harper, under her direction, the firm had published several children's books "by and about" African Americans. Nordstrom also outlined collaborations with Black authors and illustrators such as Jesse Jackson and Richard Lewis. At the same time, she listed several white professionals who had either written or illustrated Black and interracial juvenile texts for Harper.[97] Regardless of how contemporary readers might assess her record, Nordstrom was one of the trailblazers in forging these cross-racial partnerships in the 1940s.

Beginning in 1954, many leaders of major publishing houses strongly encouraged their children's book editors to solicit new Black juvenile books and to reprint older titles. For two decades, the juvenile trade did both in unprecedented numbers. But by the mid-1960s, the children's book business in the United States was so large that this growth represented only a tiny fraction of the juvenile market. In 1966, Fuller reported that in the previous year alone, close to three thousand children's books had been published in the United States. Fuller also noted that "publishers are increasingly aware of the enlarged market for books about minority groups."[98] Still, after several decades of relative—though not exclusive or uniform—neglect, it was now virtually impossible for white editors in the corporate trade to publish a proportional number of Black and multicultural children's books.

Such inequities in this sector did not go unnoticed by dissatisfied contemporaries. In a talk delivered on the first evening of a 1966 conference, "Children and Books in a Changing World," one junior scholar cautioned: "There is a danger that books with interracial characters will be used in urban schools, while elsewhere the old materials prevail. If this comes to pass, it will be a tragedy."[99] The relatively smaller scale of Black children's book publishing helps explain why large publishers came under congressional scrutiny in the 1960s, but only to a degree. Commercial firms were also criticized for a lack of minority representation in this era. Equally important, if not more pressing, was establishing whether publishers knew what constituted a good multiracial children's book. A representative critique published by two Black women cautioned: "Too many of the integrated books or books for 'interracial harmony' tend to reinforce the very attitudes they are trying to dispel. In too many of these books the white child dominates the story. He is the controlling factor, the active character. The focus of the story is on his character development." In contrast, "the black child is then necessarily placed in a subservient role. He is the passive character. [. . .] He literally and figuratively waits for the white child to invite him in, to figure things out, to be enlightened. In short, the black child is the problem; the white child has the problem."[100] White writers, critics, and editors were flummoxed by reactions like these to myriad imbalances enabled by interracial juvenile texts published in the 1960s and early 1970s.

In 1966, one of Houghton Mifflin's vice presidents, George Manuel Fenollosa, testified in front of Congress's Ad Hoc Subcommittee on De Facto School Segregation of the Committee on Education and Labor. Fenollosa claimed, "I am aware of no problem in the past few years in connection with the failure of our publications to gain listings or to be purchased because of our treatment of integration." Fenollosa offered a similar account of related books, testifying that Houghton had "received few demands from school personnel for revisions of our texts to correct inadequate treatment of minority groups."[101] The long history of intransigence in the corporate trade on these matters made it difficult to take editors and publishing executives like Fenollosa at their word. Some firms did, in fact, have much better records in diversifying the children's books they published and avoiding offensive racial stereotypes. At other firms, Black children's books were little more than a series of jokes that could turn a profit.

E. P. Dutton, for example, continued to reprint white author Inez Hogan's juvenile texts that purported to represent African American life. Hogan's *Mule Twins* (1939), a book that was ostensibly about twin mules, featured Sim, a young African American child who was barely distinguishable from these animals. In a profile of "junior authors" published by Muriel Fuller in 1963, Hogan proudly stated that writing children's books was her "sole means of support. I can think of no happier way to make a living."[102] Historian Joseph Boskin has characterized Hogan's renderings of Black children at mid-century as "unmistakably in the Sambo pattern," yet still "stocked in school libraries and often used as standard classroom fare."[103] Though Hogan published more than sixty children's books, it was her twelve-volume Nicodemus series, which began with *Nicodemus and His Little Sister* (1932), that was enormously popular with white readers.

In 1941, white author Christine Noble Govan, an "author of many books about Negro children," boasted in a letter published by *Publishers' Weekly*: "Inez Hogan, writing from New York, knows that books in dialect sell, as her annual doings of 'Nicodemus' show."[104] Close to two decades later, in 1958, *Publishers' Weekly* reported that "the total sales figure for all of her books [was now] over the 1 million copy mark. All but 4 of the 44 children's books Miss Hogan has written and illustrated for Dutton in the past 25 years are still in print."[105] At the end of the 1930s, future children's book activist Augusta Baker was embarrassed and deeply unsettled by Hogan's newly released *Mule Twins*. Baker, a young African American schoolteacher in New York City, had the misfortune of starting to read Hogan's *Mule Twins* aloud to an audience of Black students on one of her first days in the classroom, before verifying its content. The fact that Dutton published *Mule Twins* in 1939 suggests that the firm consulted few, if any, Black educators during the interwar period. "Oh, my goodness, what a book to read to these little children," Baker recalled. "They were looking up at me, trusting me. Should I stop and say to the children, 'This is a terrible book and I'm not going to read this anymore?' Should I just try to struggle through to the end and ignore the whole thing[?]"[106] Baker made a split-second decision to keep reading the book but quickly regretted it.

Hogan's renderings of Black children also puzzled Baker's young audience: "[O]ne little boy went off with [*Mule Twins*] and spent a great deal of time looking at it. Then he brought it up to me and gave it to me, and without any bitterness at all, he said to me respectfully that the Mule Twins were cuter than the [Black] boys."[107] In the end, Baker's accidental encounter with Hogan's *Mule Twins* was a catalyst for literary activism in Harlem. After sharing this story, with support from Black friends and colleagues, Baker cofounded the 135th Street Library's James Weldon Johnson Memorial Collection of Children's Books. In 1944, *Publishers' Weekly* reported that this collective had recently published "the first printed bibliography of [its] collection and it has been brought out at this time to further interracial understanding. The books in the collection have been carefully selected by Negro librarians as giving a fair, truthful, and human picture of the Negro."[108] Hogan dedicated *Mule Twins* to John Macrae, the president of E. P. Dutton until his death in 1944, "because he wants a book about mules."[109] He got it. But it was Black teachers and children who paid the price.

Decades later, parsing through the particulars of these genealogies mattered less as white editors became more comfortable admitting racial problems in the juvenile trade. A draft of a lecture delivered in 1971 by Viking's editor-in-chief of children's books, Velma Varner, offers a glimpse of how decades of divergent practices and distinctive records were increasingly flattened for public consumption. In the early 1970s, Varner was a veteran of the juvenile trade. In a profile of Varner by Muriel Fuller published in 1959, a quote from the Viking editor summarized her precocity: "I wanted to be an editor of children's books while I was still in my teens."[110] After serving in World War II, Varner was offered a position at Harcourt in 1946 and quickly rose up the ranks. In addition to directing and establishing several children's book departments for major firms in New York City, Varner was elected president of the Children's Book Council in 1960 and still served on the CBC's executive board in the 1970s. Shortly before her death from cancer at the age of fifty-six, Varner discussed historical deficits in the juvenile trade at a colloquium held at the State University of New York at Albany.

In her talk, Varner readily conceded that new organizations such as the Council on Interracial Books for Children (CIBC), a nonprofit organization established in 1965, were "right" about numerous contemporary deficiencies in juvenile letters:"[W]e must have black writers, good black writers, for I do agree with them [the CIBC] that a white person cannot possibly write meaningfully of the black experience."[111] Here it bears remembering how different this declaration was from the interracialist perspectives of prior generations of literary professionals: authors, illustrators, editors, and publishing houses closely associated with this tradition before the mid-1960s who eluded discrete Black and white racial boundaries and who produced children's books that featured protagonists of different races and ethnicities.[112]

Calls and acknowledgments similar to Varner's, prompted by growing demands from the CIBC and other constituents, encouraged publishing firms to hire more Black authors, illustrators, and intellectuals than ever before. One white editor later recalled: "Sometimes they [the CIBC] made us feel bad about what we had published. But if they hadn't forced us to look, we never would have found these artists and writers [of color]."[113] Sharing much in common with earlier cross-racial collaborations, this pressure was not sustained.

Varner maintained that prior to the 1940s, "the white, Anglo-Saxon, Protestant ethic prevailed and it was taken for granted by most people."[114] She summarized the shift away from this myth with a quote: "'Then came World War II to kill it,' Gertrude Stein said, and of course she was right."[115] Some of Varner's assessments are reminiscent of Ellen Tarry's recollections of the corporate trade before World War II: "There were practically no stories about city children and certainly none about the inner city. We didn't know that phrase. Blacks rarely appeared at all except in stories set in the South, and then they were 'darkies.'"[116] Acknowledgments of these historical imbalances were surely important. On the other hand, narratives of the book business like Varner's elided tributes to the men and women who had challenged racial stereotypes in juvenile texts for several decades.[117] Nor should it be forgotten that it was women like Virginia Kirkus who cheered subpar books about "plantation children," assuring white adults that children would "love" poorly rendered protagonists—whom she characterized as "darkies."

———

Building scholarly and commercial interest in the history of Black children's literature necessarily requires a deeper engagement with institutional, professional, and financial structures that remain poorly understood.[118] On both sides of the color line, the pursuit of interracialism in the production of children's literature in the United States led to fewer racist (and racially exclusive) books for young readers by the late 1940s. Over the first half of the twentieth century, Black cultural activism in this sector ranged from publicly and privately criticizing white literary professionals to seeking and accepting cross-racial collaborations on juvenile texts. Though inadequate, especially from a quantitative perspective, increased interest in and support for better Black and interracial children's books, produced during and after World War II, laid a foundation for a longer epoch of forward-looking, racially inclusive juvenile literature. Perhaps more so than any other genre of American publishing, the children's book trade was transformed by progressive Black and multiracial books that could and did displace *Little Black Sambo*. Too often, the trials and triumphs of the people who enabled these shifts are taken for granted.

In 1968, when Black author Kristin Hunter accepted the first Council on Interracial Books for Children award for her book *The Soul Brothers and Sister Lou* (1968), she claimed: "My book is only a beginning. I hope many, many more will be written to help minority children build positive images of themselves and to help *all* children grow in their awareness of the world as it really is."[119] Before the 1960s, the corporate history of producing Black, cosmopolitan, and multiracial children's books was filled with, and defined by, compromises. However imperfect, these artistic breakthroughs and commercial successes at mid-century were crucial precursors to a range of comparable Black-authored texts published in the years that followed.[120]

The next chapter investigates authors and cultural professionals on both sides of the color line who joined Black women like Ellen Tarry in foregrounding their American—rather than "hyphenated"—identities after World War II. Overall, the books, plays, and projects they wrote and produced were far more popular, socially conscious, and avant-garde than exasperated critics of this epoch of "Americanization" have typically accounted for.

4

What Was Postwar American Culture?

MANY OF THE SAME PREJUDICES tempering the growth of Black and inter-racial children's books at the onset of the Cold War persisted in the broader publishing trade. On the other hand, the rise of paperback publishing enabled the production of more Black-authored books, and texts with Black themes, than the world had ever seen. Beyond paperbacks, the sheer number of books by Black writers published during the postwar decades suggests just how intent these writers were to be published, against all odds.[1] To be sure, the climate of censorship in the United States imposed real limits on Black author-ship after World War II. But neither were Black writers, or books about Black life, as poorly represented as some critics alleged. In these years, cultural progressives on both sides of the color line mentored and advised aspiring Black authors, promoted capacious reading habits, sponsored integrated book fairs, and welcomed the paperback revolution.[2] One outcome was that attempts to address, resolve, or overlook social prejudices blurred racial identities and culture. For some, these shifts were contentious.

As civil rights activist Bayard Rustin later recalled, African Americans in this era were forced to contend with both race and nationality: "I tell you, brother [in this case, Black children's book illustrator Elton C. Fax], I fought against it for years—against being American—in my speech, my manner, everything. It's a hard thing for a Negro to accept, being American, but you can't escape it."[3] By the mid-1950s, another prominent intellectual, Blyden Jackson, was just one of several Black critics to mourn either the death, "dearth," or "pitiful trickle" of "Negro Literature," as various attempts to pro-mote cultural interracialism gained more supporters.[4] Jackson knew that there

was little agreement on what counted as African American literature, but for
him, these were books "produced by" Black Americans.

In this spirit, Jackson acknowledged the time and effort Langston Hughes
and Arna Bontemps were devoting to "writing respectable juveniles"
(children's books), also noting that "Frank Yerby has written a juvenile also,
along with his ninth novel." Signaling his deference to this cohort's diverse
literary pursuits, Jackson wrote, "[T]he most encouraging single phenomenon
is that some of the old hands keep writing, and writing well."[5] Moreover, Jackson was particularly upbeat about the fact that Yerby's long-standing publisher,
Dial Press, had just published John Oliver Killens's first novel, *Youngblood*
(1954), the story of a Black family navigating racism in a town in Georgia after
the turn of the century.

The cover design of the paperback edition of *Youngblood* was characterized
by *Publishers' Weekly* as "treat[ing] an interracial theme with restraint and dig-
nity, yet with powerful visual impact."[6] Killens, who later moonlighted as a
judge for the annual award granted by the Council on Interracial Books for
Children, praised this image, which featured two shirtless male teenagers (one
Black and one white) lying across from one another, as "a thing of beauty and
significance."[7] On the paperback cover of *Youngblood*, these two young men
were connected to each other via an intravenous line. This illustration was
both revolutionary and incendiary in an era when Southern hospitals still kept
blood donations racially segregated, if they accepted Black blood donations at
all. Five years later, at a champagne-fueled New Year's Eve party ringing in
1960, Killens raised a glass—or several—to the "quality and profundity" of
African American writing over the 1950s.[8] According to literary scholar Keith
Gilyard, Killens was certain that Black authorship between World War II and
1960 had exceeded both the quantity and the caliber of comparable work produced during the Harlem Renaissance. Killens was certain, Gilyard writes,
"that the 1950s had been the most fruitful and important decade for African
American writers."[9] These estimates, and their divergence from Blyden Jackson's concerns about the status of "Negro Literature," are emblematic of wider
uncertainties that once existed over how to appreciate, categorize, and distin-
guish American versus African American cultural achievements.

American writers and cultural professionals across the color line attempted
to elevate a range of Black narratives and perspectives after World War II,
despite uneven popular support for these reforms. James Baldwin and Ralph
Ellison are the best-known Black authors who emerged during these years.
But it is only in recent years that scholars have documented how these

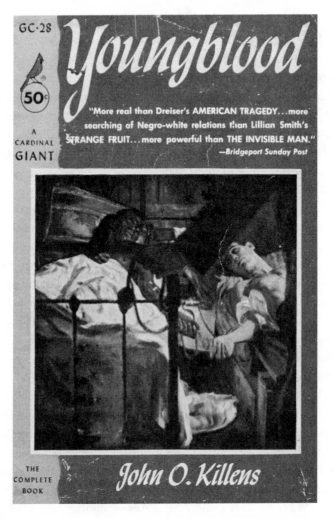

FIGURE 4.1. The paperback edition of John Oliver Killens's novel *Youngblood* featured an illustration by Tom Dunn (New York: Pocket Books, 1955 [1954]).

now-canonical writers were part of a much larger network of Black books and culture.[10] At the same time, the sheer quantity, scope, production, and distribution of lesser-known Black books and culture in the Cold War years remain poorly understood. Between 1947 and 1959, numerous African Americans won recognition as trailblazing American authors who were not easily bound by racial categories. Their critical and commercial successes complemented Black cultural contributions in other sectors.[11] This unwieldy cohort of writers were

perceived as universalizing African American authorship. As such, their published stories, plays, film adaptations, nonfictional studies, and cross-racial
collaborations were often framed as operating from within—rather than outside or independent of—mainstream American culture.

This chapter examines the breadth of related transformations in book publishing, literary criticism, retail sales, and consumer expectations and assumptions about African American writing and cultural productions. The popularity
of interracial aesthetics in the publishing world was a key reason that numerous critics applauded or lamented the death of "Negro literature"—books that
could be easily identified as written by African American authors—by the late
1940s.[12] Yet these were inadequate, often offensive, characterizations of the
state of African American literature at mid-century. More accurately, in this
period, dozens of Black authors managed to defy popular conceptions of how
expansive African American cultural interests were. With support from white
interlocutors, professionally successful Black writers became exceptionally
adept at navigating within and between various media sectors such as the theater and, by the end of the 1950s, television. Or as Langston Hughes explained
in this era, writing—irrespective of racial heritage—had become "adjacent"
to other ascendant entertainment businesses.[13] Older and newer forms of
American culture were reshaped by this trend.[14]

While their strategies, experiences, and perspectives varied, interracialists
of this generation saw the dismantling of Jim Crow norms in and beyond the
publishing sector as a widely shared goal. Black authors and creatives were
particularly entrepreneurial in their pursuit of work in Broadway and off-
Broadway plays. New technologies after the war supported new markets,
higher print runs, and lower production costs, especially for large publishing
houses. Whenever they could, African Americans took full advantage of these
developments.[15] Their achievements, including those that were not clearly
marked or regarded as Black, were important symbols for African Americans
seeking access to white-dominated industries and professions.

In a column published in the African American *Atlanta Daily World* at the
end of 1952, an unidentified journalist observed that "[p]robably 95 percent of
Negro novelists write 'Negro' novels or documentaries protesting segregation
and reiterating the social ills of the world." The critic acknowledged a "sore
need" for such books but argued that "there is also [a] need for additional
Frank Yerbys, who make it possible at times to visit a neighborhood theatre
and see a picture produced by a major motion picture studio, written by a Negro."
In time, "perhaps," one of these films might even be "directed by a Negro."[16]

American culture, this Black commentator suggests, should not be the exclusive purview of white writers and cultural professionals.

Offering an explanation of Yerby's starring role in bridging the nation's literary traditions in an essay titled "Surmounting Barriers," with "Yerby in [the] Lead," in 1954, another Black critic asserted: "A second death in Negro literature took place during the Second World War." Dissimilar from Blyden Jackson's summary of Black writing published the same year, here the "second death" of African American literature was characterized as a positive development. Arguing that "old racial barriers and taboos" had crumbled as a consequence of the global conflict, this commentator noted, "[W]ith the rebirth of a new world came a forceful new [Black] literati with new ideas, new characters, and new techniques."[17] Or as Atlanta University's Thomas Jarrett commented, also in 1954: "Indeed, it might be argued that [Black writers] ha[ve] now entered into the mainstream of American fiction. He [the Black writer] has a higher regard for literary values, and he evinces a growing social consciousness and a universality in the treatment of a greater variety of themes."[18] Attempts like those above to amplify, and make sense of, the "universal" character of African American writing heralded yet another foundational shift in reimagining Black contributions to American culture and society.

Efforts to update American print culture after World War II did not lead to racial parity in the publishing world. Black writers in particular had to grapple with the confusing, frustrating, and often infuriating nature of racialized literary categories during and after the McCarthy era, when scores of artists, intellectuals, and other cultural producers were surveilled and blacklisted. Worse, poor compensation, arbitrary rejections, and Black-authored texts designed for a predominantly white customer base went hand in hand with assumptions that Black culture and thought were synonymous with "protest."[19] Despite tenacious obstacles and racial stereotyping, scores of Americans of all backgrounds never relented in their drive to diversify American literature and entertainment.[20]

Worlds of Print

In 1966, Langston Hughes boasted, "[T]oday the sun is always rising somewhere on books by American Negro writers whose works in English and in translations are being read around the world. [Richard] Wright, [Ralph] Ellison, [James] Baldwin, [Chester] Himes, Hughes, and Yerby have all been translated into at least a dozen major languages and are to be found in the libraries and bookshops of most of the earth's large cities."[21] Arguably more so than any other development, exponential growth in the production of paperbacks enabled cheap access to a whole new world of ideas—including those pitched by Black authors.

In the commercial publishing sector, it would be difficult to overstate how the emergence of paperback publishing enabled larger print runs and sales for Black-authored books than were possible before World War II. African Americans benefited from demographic and industrial transformations in hardcover publishing as well. In 1946, *Ebony* boasted that the white president of Cleveland's World Publishing Company "tossed out antique lily-white theories on plant labor relations" and "gave employment to many Negroes. Today 143 out of World's 500 employees are Negro."[22] By 1953, New American Library had sold more than a million paperback copies of Willard Motley's *Knock on Any Door* (1947). That same year, total sales of the New American Library reprint of Ann Petry's novel *Country Place* (1947) were an estimated 972,500 copies.[23] By comparison, the novel Petry remains famous for, *The Street* (1946), had sold fifty thousand copies in hardcover by 1955.[24] As literary scholar Paula Rabinowitz has observed: "Paperback books opened worlds for readers and writers alike—providing access to literature thought to be beyond the capacities of most readers, on the one hand, and enabling audiences larger than most writers expected, on the other."[25] In 1949, 538 titles were published in the United States, netting total sales of more than 180 million books.[26] Back in 1940, American publishers had sold only about six million paperbacks. By 1953, figures for total sales that year included more than one thousand paperback titles.

In this twelve-month period alone, publishing houses in the United States sold more than 250 million books—or over forty times more than sales in 1940, a stunning transformation. In the 1950s, researchers and trade professionals explained that most paperbacks printed in the United States were exported to Europe. In 1958, one industry observer, Frank Schick, described paperbacks as "the only books which Europeans could afford to buy in quantity."[27] With the technological improvements that enabled faster and cheaper manufacture of softcover books, production networks and facilities shifted accordingly. Previously, publishers had relied on printers specializing in mail-order catalogs, magazines, and other mass-market publications. Following World War II, a number of book manufacturers expanded their printing facilities in the Midwest and Northeast to produce paperback books for both national and international markets.[28] At mid-century, Black readers, critics, and professionals

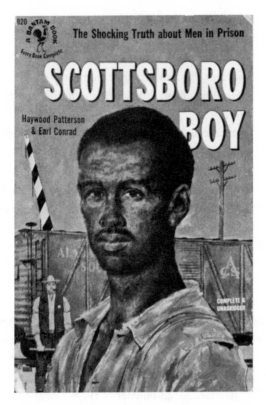

FIGURE 4.2. Haywood Patterson and Earl Conrad's
Scottsboro Boy (New York: Bantam Books, 1951 [1950]),
with paperback cover art by Joseph Hirsch.

were occasional contributors to—and always close monitors of—related transformations in the publishing trade.

In 1948, *Publishers' Weekly* (*PW*) announced that Black children's book author Ellen Tarry had "been appointed special consultant in publicity and promotion at the New American Library," a firm that specialized in paperback reprints. According to *PW*, Tarry was hired to "direct a project to develop new channels through which books may be more widely distributed to Negro communities in which they are not generally available in large quantities."[29] Three years later, when Gertrude Martin reported in her *Chicago Defender* "Book Reviews" column that another leading paperback firm, Avon Publishing, was expanding its operation of "mechanical book dispensers" (a coin-operated vending machine called the VendAvon) to airports, hospitals, and transportation terminals, her Black readers were likely just as happy as she was.[30] Like other large firms, Avon published several popular African American authors and also reprinted Black classics in the early 1950s. Better still, most of these books cost only a quarter, if not less.[31] When Martin's column appeared, Black New Yorkers were already benefiting from the VendAvon installed on the 125th Street railway platform in Harlem.[32]

Even with the extraordinary number of paperback titles published, including cheap editions of popular Black and interracial titles, access to books remained highly uneven after World War II. And this was especially true for African Americans. As paperbacks went on sale in vending machines, at drugstores, and in other commercial outlets, actual bookstores remained scarce in most Black communities. In 1949, a *PW* profile of the Hugh Gordon Book Shop, "very far downtown in Los Angeles, in the center of the Negro section," effectively branded the neighborhood as a book desert. "It is the only bookstore serving this community of 148,000 people," the *PW* journalist reported.[33] Yet, as *PW*'s coverage of this Black bookstore reminded industry professionals, the staff at Hugh Gordon's organized and collaborated with schools, churches, and other neighborhood groups to strengthen local interest in books, and the store was thriving. The shop opened in June 1948 at 1109 East 42nd Place, in South Central Los Angeles.

Adele Young, the manager and owner of Hugh Gordon's, expressed optimism about the future of her bookstore. Despite threats to her business that included Black unemployment and mail-order book retailers, Hugh Gordon's was both "needed and wanted," *PW* concluded after interviewing Young. Moreover, according to the magazine, Young was "assured by the enthusiasm about [Hugh Gordon's] opening and by the numbers who attend autographing parties and other events in the store." *PW* reported that Young had held book launches for a diverse range of titles, including Hollister Noble's *Woman with a Sword* (1948), a biographical novel about Anna Ella Carroll, an antislavery lobbyist who advised Abraham Lincoln's presidential Cabinet, and Beatrice Griffith's *American Me* (1948), a sociological narrative of Mexican Americans in California.[34]

References to books like these, either from Young or the journalist profiling Hugh Gordon's in 1949, signaled an eagerness in this Black community to work and read across racial lines. One contemporary Marxist estimated that this bookstore would "help to bring closer together all minorities, the Negroes, Mexican-Americans and Jews."[35] In a 1954 interview with the *Pittsburgh Courier*, Young described Hugh Gordon's patrons as "all those who want the truth

FIGURE 4.3. Buddy Green and Steve Murdock's *The Jerry Newson Story* (Berkeley, CA: East Bay Civil Rights Congress, 1950).

about the Negro people to be told."[36] Building a robust literary institution certainly wasn't easy in a Black neighborhood that had only one bookstore for 150,000 people. But local resources like the Hugh Gordon Book Shop played a crucial role in building cultural support for the Civil Rights Movement in the 1950s.[37] Indeed, the shop gave readers unrestricted access to numerous new and recently published Black books.

According to *PW*, Hugh Gordon's also carried "pamphlets, periodicals, victrola records, children's books and records," in addition to "specializing in books about the Negro, labor and economics."[38] Before the mid-1950s, this corpus probably included such regionally published titles as Deaderick Jenkins's *It Was Not My World: A Novel to End All Novels* (1942), African American architect Paul Williams's *The Small Home of Tomorrow* (1945) and *New Homes for Today* (1946), Deaderick Jenkins's *Letters to My Son* (1947), and Buddy Green and Steve Murdock's *The Jerry Newson Story* (1950).[39]

Green and Murdock, two white journalists based in San Francisco, were unapologetic advocates for press freedom in the early 1950s. For them, this work extended to writing the life story of Jerry Newson, a twenty-year-old Black man falsely convicted of murder and sentenced to death in 1949.[40] When these authors wrote and published another pamphlet in 1951 on a different unjustly incarcerated Black man from Los Angeles who had been in prison since he was eight years old, Black newspapers such as the *Pittsburgh Courier* readily credited their efforts.[41]

On the other side of the country, Hampton University, a historically Black college in Virginia, hosted a racially integrated book fair cosponsored by the Children's Book Council in 1956. A summary of an accompanying report published by *PW* described the event as "an illuminating account of inter-group cooperation in which the college extended its services to the whole community." Written by Minnie Redmond Bowles, an African American librarian employed by Hampton and an alumna of the library science graduate program at the University of Chicago, the report framed the fair as an experiment in integration and a response to an urgent need for books in the local community for Blacks and whites alike.[42] Bowles stated that because Hampton had always welcomed the white community, "the transition to a fair planned for the general public was a natural one since the Library has served the public of the area—white and Negro—through the years without restrictions of any kind."[43] Months before this detailed account appeared, *PW* had only reported that Hampton's fair "was inter-racial."[44] Bowles wasn't sure this event would be profitable for publishers seeking to broker new distribution networks. But she was certain that the access it provided to up-to-date texts paled in comparison to relatively abundant literary resources in major metropolitan areas.

Prior to the 1960s, New York City was the undisputed publishing center for Black-authored books, as well as books with Black and interracial themes. East Coast cities such as Boston, Washington, D.C., and Philadelphia relied upon an older network of so-called vanity presses to publish a wide variety of Black books, but on a much smaller scale.[45] In New York, publishing opportunities for Black writers were not limited to major commercial publishers. Indeed, several smaller New York–based firms built or maintained a strong reputation for publishing new and established Black writers in the 1950s.[46] The most prominent cooperative publisher in New York for Black writers in the early Cold War years was Exposition Press, founded in 1936 by Edward Uhlan; fees to publish with Uhlan's firm typically ranged from $900 to $5,000 for their largest volumes in the mid-1950s.

In a popular 1956 memoir outlining the importance of "subsidy publishers" as alternatives to "trade publishers," Uhlan explained that at Exposition, "[t]he more books we can sell, the more money we, as well as our authors, will make, and I know that shoddy-looking books don't sell."[47] The same year, one of these books, white author Samuel Warner's novel *Madam President-Elect: A Novel* (1956), imagined the hidden Black ancestry of the first woman to be elected president of the United States. Shortly before her inauguration, she survives an assassination attempt by a white supremacist. A tepid endorsement—reasonably so—from the African American *Pittsburgh Courier* simply advertised that *Madam President-Elect* was a "good book."[48] According to Uhlan, "Americans are a large-hearted race," yet it was "the merchandizers functioning as custodians of our culture who have betrayed us. They have betrayed Americans from the very level at which they learned to read."[49] Uhlan wanted the books his firm accepted to establish cultural patterns that were less racist. For example, a review of Black artist Arthur Diggs's short novel *Black Woman* (1954), published by Exposition, noted that this book had been "[w]ritten against the background of the 'much-discussed' Negro-white problem in America." The reviewer noted that those who read this novel would be "likely to agree that the author has hit upon a potent topic, perhaps dangerously so, because of the uniquely-different role the Negro woman has traditionally played in American life."[50] New York publishers like Exposition ensured that readers could find narratives like these when many larger firms avoided the risks associated with sponsoring Black books.

For those who were lucky and strategic enough, the small number of Black authors supported by New York City's white publishing establishment could gain access to an international audience. Frank Yerby was a conspicuous outlier in benefiting from this precarious business model during the early Cold War years. Contemporaries described Yerby, much like his forebear W. S. Braithwaite, as sitting at the very top of the publishing business, on both sides of the Atlantic.[51] By 1952, the African American press could report with pride that Yerby was the "second most popular American author" in France and the "most popular author" in the United States in the same year.[52] Regardless of how he actually felt, Yerby made modesty an art. Responding to recent reports about his stature in France, the *New York Times* quoted Yerby as declaring: "The reputation of the French for sophistication is highly overrated."[53] Several other enormously popular African American authors also capitalized on the

European market for their books in these years, including Chester Himes and Richard Wright, whom Yerby considered "a splendid writer and a very fine man."[54] Like both of these men, Himes became one of the most popular Black authors in France during the 1950s. Himes's second novel, *Lonely Crusade* (1947), was a hit with French critics. The dust jacket illustration for the French translation of *Lonely Crusade* published in 1952 highlighted its author's meditations on a poisonous interracial affair between a white Communist and the Black union organizer at the center of the novel.

Unlike Wright and Yerby, Himes was strapped for cash. And it was his poor finances that led Marcel Duhamel, an influential French editor, to encourage Himes in 1956 to start writing detective novels. Himes recalled initially rebuffing the suggestion: "I didn't believe I could do it, but I was flat broke."[55] Summarizing this transition to writing in this genre, a Black critic later noted: "Once American literature's angry young man, Chester Himes has pulled a Frank Yerby and now, a French resident, he is a successful mystery writer, with some six or seven books to his credit in this genre."[56] Himes, threatened by the U.S. government's House Un-American Activities Committee, wanted nothing to do with his birth country in the 1950s. In a letter to Duhamel written in 1955, Himes declared: "Needless to say, I am very anxious to get back to Paris. I am more anxious, however, to get out of the U.S. In fact, I am so anxious I would follow Rimbaud's example and spend a season in hell, if I wasn't afraid I might get stuck there. Although, to be frank, I'd probably prefer being stuck there than here."[57] Around the same time Himes pivoted to detective fiction, James Baldwin similarly turned to the European market to bypass white American editors and publishers who were resistant to publishing his work.

When Baldwin approached Knopf about publishing *Giovanni's Room* (1956), his contact at the firm claimed that they were protecting Baldwin by rejecting this queer manuscript. In Baldwin's novel, a white American male in Europe becomes involved with an Italian counterpart of the same sex, but who is much poorer and much less ashamed about his sexuality. On his own, Baldwin secured a small British publisher for the book before Dial Press, Frank Yerby's publisher, agreed to publish it in the United States.[58] Dial pitched *Giovanni's Room* to booksellers as the story "of what happens to the intense relationship between the two young men when the [American's] fiancée returns to Paris from her travels in Spain."[59] Overall, Baldwin's partnerships with major American publishers had never been especially lucrative prior to the 1960s. In 1952, when Knopf agreed to publish *Go Tell It on the Mountain* (1953), the firm offered Baldwin a meager advance of $250, with an additional guarantee of only $750 after the novel was published.[60] The same year Baldwin received his first payment from Knopf, which was approximately $2,500 in today's dollars, a white publishing trade insider commented: "In the intense competition for material, the [paperback] reprint houses can, without any trouble at all, jockey themselves up to an advance of, say, $30,000 for a first novel."[61] Baldwin had many white friends. But he never forgot the white editors and publishers who shortchanged him in these years.

In addition to Dial Press, Baldwin and Yerby also shared a literary agent: Helen Strauss. Like Knopf, Strauss also discouraged Baldwin from publishing *Giovanni's Room*. In fact, Baldwin later

FIGURE 4.4. The French translation of Chester Himes's *Lonely Crusade* (Paris: Correa, 1952).

accused Strauss of instructing him to burn the manuscript. Denying Baldwin's claim years later, Strauss recalled that she had been skeptical of this novel, but simply because she "just thought he could do better."[62] Baldwin never forgave these rejections of *Giovanni's Room* by New York's white publishing establishment. "I was a Negro writer," he said, and white interlocutors warned Baldwin that he would "alienate" his core audience if he published a gay novel: "That, in effect, nobody would accept that book—coming from me."[63]

Commodifying Universalism

In an essay published in 1950 titled "No Kafka in the South," the African American scholar L. D. Reddick cautioned that Black Americans should not be too optimistic about reforms in the white publishing world: "[E]veryone knows that writing in America, more than anywhere else on earth, is a commodity. What do readers expect of 'Negro literature?' Or better, what do publishers expect readers to expect? Something wild, sensational, filled out with muscle and bone action." Reddick also argued that best sellers such as Harriet Beecher Stowe's *Uncle Tom's Cabin* (1852), Carl Van Vechten's *Nigger Heaven* (1926), Lillian Smith's *Strange Fruit* (1944), and Richard Wright's *Native Son* (1940) helped explain why the white reading public expected lurid portraits of Black life from white publishers. For Reddick, the only recent exceptions to these authors and novels, "who have done best-sellers," were those who had "deserted the Negro theme (vide: Frank Yerby and Willard Motley)."[64] These two Black

FIGURE 4.5. Gwendolyn Brooks and Langston Hughes at the George Cleveland Hall Branch of the Chicago Public Library, 1949.

authors, Reddick's observations imply, were unusually savvy in producing what he effectively labeled distinctively "American" commodities.

At the same time, the imaginative novels Motley and Yerby excelled at producing were far more diverse than Reddick's criticism suggests. In the 1950s, Black commentators rarely agreed on how to assess various gains and losses in their discussions of contemporary African American writing. By comparison, white commentators were generally far more optimistic about the commercial and critical successes of Yerby, Baldwin, Ralph Ellison, and Gwendolyn Brooks. These authors' books, essays, professional collaborations, and international readerships were regularly cited as evidence that African Americans were gaining ground in the literary field.

Indeed, some white boosters even claimed that this cohort's achievements were unprecedented. In a doctoral thesis entitled "Trends of Negro Thought" (1952), Joseph Henry, a student in the Department of English at the University of Ottawa, described the contemporary transformation of African American writing: "No longer a freakish phenomenon, as he was in the days of Jupiter Hammon [1711–1806; the first published Black American writer], the colored writer has finally come to the point where he expects to be viewed as a writer first, then as colored, and not in reversed order." According to Henry, the latest generation of Black authors had managed to "merge" themselves with "the mainstream of American life and letters."[65] Black authors and critics would have agreed, even if their opinions differed on the importance of this "mainstreaming."

Yerby and Ellison in particular would have welcomed this interpretation of African American writing. For their part, the Black writers who were leaders in gaining respect from white readers and critics as "writer[s] first, then as colored" often felt battered by debates ranging from disagreements over universalism to the status of "Negro literature." Not infrequently, those Black authors who were most frequently cited, credited, and disparaged responded with humor as one coping mechanism. In 1953, after he won the National Book Award for Invisible Man (1952), Ellison joked about how unwelcome Black authors still were in the publishing establishment.[66] The morning before the award ceremony in New York, Ellison had an unexpected run-in with William Faulkner at Random House, the publisher the two men shared. In an odd exchange, Ellison remarked, referring to himself as Faulkner's figurative son: "[Y]ou have children all around. You won't be proud of all of them, [but] just the same they're around."[67]

In his National Book Award speech later that day, Ellison reported that his own literary standards had enabled him to "see America with an awareness of its rich diversity and its almost magical fluidity and freedom." Ellison then explained that *Invisible Man* was intentionally designed to avoid the fictional trope of "unrelieved despair" that "marked so much of our current fiction."[68] Ellison's commentary didn't qualify that "our" fiction was "Negro fiction," but many contemporaries probably assumed that this declaration was a reference to Richard Wright's *Native Son* (1940).[69] Like many Americans, Ellison was preoccupied with universalism after World War II. "One ironic witness to the beauty and the universality of this era is the fact that the descendants of the very men who enslaved us can now sing the spirituals and find in the singing an exaltation of their own humanity," he stated in an interview for the *Paris Review*. Ellison also asserted that "slave songs, blues, [and] folk ballads" were "infinitely suggestive," leading him to conclude "that a whole corps of writers could not exhaust their universality."[70]

In this era, Frank Yerby discussed his sense and vision of universality as well. Dissimilar from Ellison, Yerby never publicly linked this term to African American culture or his own racial heritage. In one letter, Ellison later estimated that if a Black author "over contains his emotions, he becomes a white Negro writer, in the long gray line from Phillis Wheatley to Frank Yerby."[71] Yet in one of his rare appearances in the media, Yerby implied that he did, in fact, have an irrepressible passion during the early Cold War years: working long hours to captivate and entertain readers from all walks of life. In an interview published in the *New York Times* in 1951, Yerby said that he labored "as much as eighteen hours a day" on his novels. "Not only that; I rewrite," Yerby stated. "And not only that: I do a lot of research." At work on his seventh book "at the ripe age of not quite 35," Yerby was reportedly "spending as much as six hours a day in the library" scouring for background materials for his latest book project. More significant, however, are Yerby's comments on his philosophy of writing, which assured *New York Times* readers that he was on board with literate America's latest craze: "The novelist must try to write with a universality of appeal so that it hits all segments of the people. To do that, a novel must have characters that are alive and a story that is interesting."[72]

A few years earlier, with help from Elizabeth Lawrence, her longtime editor at Harper, Gwendolyn Brooks joined Yerby, Ellison, and scores of others who were preoccupied, albeit in different ways, with universalizing Black books and African American writing. In a 1946 letter, Lawrence encouraged Brooks to focus her writing on African Americans who were "reaching for something better (superficial refinements, standards, comforts)." She also encouraged Brooks to feature Black protagonists who were adept at navigating both sides of the color line: "He (or she) is in the position of having to straddle two cultures to achieve a satisfactory personal compromise. This is inevitable but it does not make for easy going." Lawrence acknowledged how difficult it was to pivot between Black and white communities. Despite this, she insisted that Brooks's protagonists be "comfortable to have around." If Brooks managed to succeed in following this advice, Lawrence maintained, she would produce a "first-rate drama because [the protagonist] posed a conflict that is universal. The discriminating person in any culture [would be] familiar with it."[73] Brooks was not opposed to Lawrence's advice, but this was not the type of narrative that could be written in a short time. The book in question, *Maud Martha* (1953), took Brooks seven years to develop after she received Lawrence's recommendations.

The willingness of ambitious Black authors like Brooks to accept such advice, however excruciating it might strike readers today, enabled greater access to the commercial literary market. Nine months before *Maud Martha* was available for purchase, Lawrence wrote Brooks that it would be "hard to guess" how the editors of *Reader's Digest* would react to the poet's first and only novel. She nevertheless seemed confident enough to inform Brooks that the publisher retained "a good alert woman" at *Reader's Digest*, "who will surely do everything to increase your (and Harper's) store of pennies."[74] For close to twenty years, Lawrence worked hard to guarantee that Brooks and Harper profited as much as possible from their partnership.

Lawrence was diligent in placing and promoting Brooks's writing whenever and wherever she could. Brooks noticed how hard Lawrence worked on her behalf and responded in kind. By the summer of 1964, the women addressed each other as longtime friends. When Lawrence retired in June of that year, a letter from Brooks recognized how important their decades-long dialogue had been for her career. "What a wonderful friend and editor you have been to me," Brooks noted. "You have been loyal to me and have maintained faith in my potential ability. You have made each of my books a little work of art, with I believe, not a single error." Though poetic, it is telling that Brooks informed Lawrence: "I regard your departure with bleakness."[75] Brooks, of course, knew that Lawrence wasn't perfect; nor did Brooks miss the racial biases that occasionally seeped into their professional exchanges. But Brooks chose to offer a remarkably affectionate tribute to her white friend and colleague. Literary historian Jacqueline Goldsby observes: "The baseline of trust that Brooks and Lawrence established not only allowed them a remarkable personal intimacy but also discloses that Brooks's 'integrationist' outlook offered a more tough-minded critique of racial liberalism than she herself recalled in retrospect."[76] Moreover, numerous critics noticed that this iconic, mutually beneficial relationship had indeed answered what Frank Yerby characterized in 1951 as the need for contemporary books with "a universality of appeal." But arguably more so than Yerby, Brooks's prominence at mid-century, and her abiding literary engagement with African American themes, signaled a new direction for distinguished Black writing and cultural contributions. After Brooks became the first African American to win the Pulitzer Prize in 1950 for her collection of poems *Annie Allen* (1949), white newspapers, periodicals, and presses regularly approached her for book reviews, new publications, and other work.[77]

But at the beginning of the new decade, Brooks had little money or income, and her financial problems were much deeper than her white interlocutors could have guessed. When a photographer showed up at her home to take her picture following the announcement that she had won the Pulitzer Prize, Brooks didn't even have electricity. Describing this moment decades later in *Ebony Jr.*, her daughter recalled, "Gwendolyn stiffened. She couldn't tell them about the lights being cut off. What kind of story would that make?"[78] In the years that followed, Brooks became a paramount figurehead of racially inclusive American culture. And for the rest of her career, Brooks's reputation and professional opportunities only grew.

In a letter to Brooks in 1958, the public relations director for the *Chicago Daily News* thanked her for serving as a judge for the newspaper's Silver Knight Award in Language Arts. Acknowledging her "conscientious attention to each entry," Arthur Youngberg wrote: "The whole project is enjoying considerable respect because of the prestige and experience you have contributed to it." Inviting Brooks to the presentation ceremony at Chicago's Orchestra Hall, Youngberg assured her that if she agreed to attend, she would of course "be seated in the center of the stage with the other judges."[79] In the late 1950s, it was still unusual for Black and white Americans to fraternize in public, on equal terms. (In fact, it would take nearly half of a century before the Chicago Symphony, the primary occupant of Orchestra Hall, hired its first Black musician.[80]) Youngberg's desire to see Brooks on this platform alongside her white colleagues at mid-century paralleled a broader interest in championing Black expertise—at the pinnacle of the nation's leading cultural establishments.[81]

Symbolic interracialism was laudable but unsustainable. Much the same can be said about preoccupations with universality, which were often far more subjective than white authors, readers, critics, editors, and publishers were willing to admit. For some, universal literature and culture required avoiding almost all racial themes in, or removing them from, African American writing, irrespective of genre. Other commentators insisted that only working-class Black culture and experiences qualified as "universal" African American literature.

Regardless of what they wrote, or how hard they tried, every established Black writer who published a book in the early Cold War years was subject to harsh criticisms from both Black and white readers at some point. With insensitive critics such as John S. Lash, the chair of Southern University's English department, African Americans couldn't even find support for a racially distinctive literary tradition from a professor at a historically Black institution. Lash's 1947 essay "What Is 'Negro Literature'?" is a venomous diatribe against scholars and scholarship dedicated to this genre. "Literature must remain the study of belles-lettres and must not be allowed to be prostituted to the cause of social justice for any group," Lash warned. "The study of literature must properly concern itself with major authors, and Negro authors do not measure up to this demand."[82] This scorn for African American writers, and academics who studied them, offers important context for better understanding Chester Himes's reaction to a talk he gave at the University of Chicago seven months after Lash's essay was published.

In early 1948, during his residency at Yaddo, the prestigious writers' colony in Saratoga Springs, New York, Himes took a short break to give a lecture in Chicago titled "Dilemma of the Negro Writer." The *Chicago Tribune* reported that Himes's intention was to "discuss his work as a novelist dealing with the theme of Negro race consciousness."[83] The topic did not go over well. Decades later, Himes could still vividly recount the profound silence from his audience at the university: "When I finished reading that paper nobody moved, nobody applauded, nobody ever said anything else to me. I was shocked. I stayed in Chicago a few days drinking, and then I was half-drunk all the rest of the time I was in Yaddo." Himes was already an alcoholic, but he later remembered this period as the moment when he "started getting blackouts" because he "was drinking so much."[84] Himes's personal problems did not stem from one poorly received presentation. But it would be a mistake to ignore how stressful the Cold War years were for Black writers in particular.[85]

African American critics could be just as tough on Black authors in this era. From the late 1940s, as laudatory coverage of their commercial and critical

FIGURE 4.6. Chester Himes, photographed by Carl Van Vechten, 1946.
Beinecke Library Collection © Van Vechten Trust.

achievements in the Black press waned, criticism of their professional choices
and literary themes increased exponentially. Black critics were particularly
irked by any signs or evidence of racial abandonment. James Baldwin's first novel,
Go Tell It on the Mountain (1953), was widely lauded by white New Critics. On its
own, this wasn't enough to signal that Baldwin was what some critics would consider a race traitor. But it did prompt criticism, reminding Black readers that these
endorsements from some white critics had come with a steep cost.

Reporting on the novel for *The Crisis* in 1953, Henry Winslow observed, "Mr. Baldwin has been urging as an anti-protest novelist critic, a thesis which is being warmly endorsed by the clique of critic-patrons who sponsor this notion through publications like the *Partisan Review* and *The Reporter*." While concluding that there was "much truth" in *Go Tell It on the Mountain*, Winslow informed his readers that "there is less art [in the novel], for there is nothing new."[86] An unsigned review of *Go Tell It on the Mountain* published in *Jet* magazine a few months earlier was similarly hostile: "Such *avant garde* publications as the Partisan Review have reveled in pieces like his 'Everybody's Protest Novel.' [...] Baldwin insisted it was time colored novelists grew up and started writing about Negroes as 'people first, Negroes almost incidentally.'" While Baldwin was credited for writing "a provocative as well as a well-written book," *Jet's* critic concluded, "[W]hether Baldwin himself has fulfilled his literary injunction to others [against protest fiction] is questionable. Baldwin is telling the by-now-overworked story of the migration of a Negro family from the South to Harlem. [...] [H]e has not attained his goal of writing a raceless book."[87] If the white literary world was willing to ignore Baldwin's shortcomings, in the early 1950s, influential African American publications refused to.

At the same time, mainstream publications controlled by white writers and editors were typically far less empathetic and self-aware in their coverage of Black writers. As just one conspicuous example, *Time* magazine published an unusually negative profile of Frank Yerby in 1954, despite the lengths he had gone to position himself as a racially ambiguous author with a "universality of appeal." In a salacious description of Yerby's work, an unidentified journalist for the magazine noted: "Few of the Southern housewives who buy Yerby's slick melodramas of sex, sadism and violence, know that their favorite author is a Negro."[88] The literary scholar Thadious Davis has commented that this *Time* "article drips sarcasm, even labeling Yerby's unpublished novel 'a Richard Wrighteous novel.'" Davis adds: "Despite dismissive treatment in the white press, Yerby was well known as a successful black author, [and as] a storyteller."[89] Muriel Fuller, Yerby's first literary agent, was mortified by this profile of an African American man she considered her friend. Writing to a white friend, Fuller remarked: "<u>Time</u> has its [write-up] of Frank this week. Yow! It could be a lot worse, but it's snide enough. They called me two weeks ago; just pulled me out of the phone book, and from that sweet tribute Frank gave me in 'Current Biography'—1945, I think. I was alarmed and angry."[90] Not surprisingly, Black readers were much wearier of the banality of racist attacks in American mass media.

FIGURE 4.7. James Baldwin, photographed by Carl Van Vechten, 1955.
Beinecke Library Collection © Van Vechten Trust.

Alain Locke characterized the casual mistreatment of, and disrespect for,
Black authors as "the high price of integration." He used this phrase as the title
of his annual book summary published at the beginning of 1952.[91] As the
preeminent authority on African American letters for close to three decades,
Locke candidly reflected on the many costs associated with the recent mainstreaming of Black authors. Nevertheless, in the years leading up to his death, the
man who gave America *The New Negro: An Interpretation* (1925) still insisted

that aspiring and established Black writers should not be segregated from their white peers.

The year after Locke outlined literary integration's shortcomings, he credited Ellison's *Invisible Man* as "one of the best integrated accounts of interactions between whites and Negroes in American society that has yet been presented, with all characters portrayed in the same balance and perspective."[92] In the same review essay, Locke also praised Yerby's little-remembered *Saracen Blade* (1952) as one of the novelist's "best and most elaborate historical romances." Locke then argued that Yerby's novel "vindicate[d] once more the right of the Negro as artist to any theme and province he chooses as a freeman of the world of letters." As such, Yerby's "cumulative maturity" and "general success with the public will be an incentive to younger Negro writers that may spread our creative production over wider subject-matter fields than usual."[93] Here it bears remembering how important a statement like this would have been as an older generation of African Americans considered new possibilities for Black youth on the eve of the Supreme Court's school desegregation mandates.

Less than two years after this essay was published, Locke died at New York City's Mount Sinai Hospital. He was sixty-eight at the time of his death in 1954. Locke's dear friend William Stanley Braithwaite, born in 1878, was still alive and healthy enough to deliver a eulogy. A year later, *Jet* reported that "Braithwaite, 76-year-old New York poet, editor and literary critic, was commissioned to write a biography of the late Dr. Alain Locke," explaining that the publishing veteran "received the assignment from executors of Locke's estate."[94] Despite plans for a quick turnaround, this book was never completed. In 1955, Braithwaite argued before Locke's Memorial Committee in Manhattan that it wasn't "Negro literature" that best represented "the spirit of Alain Locke"—it was "Negro authorship" in "American literature."[95] Braithwaite recalled that Locke "had been tutored in the universal law of humanity—that law of 'unity of diversity,' as Locke called it." According to Braithwaite: "This was the demand that Locke made of Negro authorship, and along with it, the concomitant demand for its recognition by the white world."[96] Few serious observers in 1955 would have disagreed that African American writing had been elevated in the decades since Locke published *The New Negro* back in 1925. Locke's final study, *The Negro in American Culture* (1956), finished shortly after his death by Margaret Just Butcher, simply affirms Braithwaite's descriptions of Locke's belief in the deep interconnections between Black artistic genius and "American culture."

FIGURE 4.8. The 1957 paperback edition of *The Negro in American Culture* (New York: New American Library, 1956) was Alain Locke's final study, funded by the Rockefeller Foundation in 1951 and completed by Margaret Just Butcher after Locke's death.

After summarizing how Locke had led Black writers "to the promised land of literary fulfillment," Braithwaite exclaimed that he had done this so "that we may add a new glory to American culture!"[97] Before the end of the decade, there would be countless signs that Locke's aspirations for Black authors, artists, and cultural professionals were closer than ever.

Supporting Black Professionals

Between 1945 and 1960, African American writers lived and traveled all over the world.[98] Black movement and settlement in this period were prompted by a mix of personal desire and practical concerns.[99] In 1958, African American author Richard Gibson published a biting critique reminding American readers why a conspicuous number of Black men and women still remained abroad.[100] Gibson explained: "The bright young white boys, after the end of their Fulbrights, are able to return with reasonably light hearts to the dens of Madison Avenue or the provincial Ph.D. factories. It is still impossible for an American Negro to return to the land of his birth in the same spirit."[101] Gibson's critique anticipates what one scholar has termed the "possessive investment in whiteness" in the postwar United States.[102]

Prior to the 1960s, Black writers, intellectuals, and countless other professionals were much more dispersed, geographically and socially, in comparison to their predecessors.[103] Cold War politics were an outsized factor in this development. Nevertheless, New York City was once again becoming a major site of Black and interracial cultural productions.[104] Indeed, over the course of the 1950s, Black-authored plays and theatrical productions flourished there. Arguably the crowning achievement of this intertwined cultural momentum was the Broadway debut and outstanding reception of Lorraine Hansberry's canonical *Raisin in the Sun* (1959).[105]

Scholars and other commentators have painstakingly documented how Cold War hysteria in this period decimated Black cultural organizations, including formidable groups such as the New York–based Committee for the Negro in the Arts (CNA).[106] In 1952, visual artist Ernest Crichlow, the group's Black chairperson, informed Shirley Graham and W.E.B. Du Bois, early members of the group, that the CNA nurtured an active "campaign for the full integration of Negro artist[s] in all forms of American culture."[107] When the CNA was founded in 1947, the organization was just the latest of several ad hoc groups that had sought to "build a legitimate Theatre in Harlem" in the 1940s.[108] The early CNA shared much in common with later manifestations of cultural activism in Harlem, including Amiri Baraka's Organization of Young Men, which, at least initially, was also a multiracial group.

Close to two decades before Baraka moved uptown in the mid-1960s, the CNA was established by a small group of Black and white professionals thoroughly committed to cultural pluralism. Paul Robeson and two white friends and colleagues, Margaret Webster and Carl Van Doren, organized on behalf of the CNA, beginning in January 1948. At the end of that month, a Black newspaper in Alabama described these three, "along with their sponsors," as throwing "a cocktail party" as one of several initiatives "to support the serious musician and other artists in their efforts to apply themselves to their arts."[109] Less than seven days after the founding of the CNA was announced to the American public, it was branded a "Communist front."[110] In the months that followed, white journalists regularly slandered the organization. As a consequence, the literate public would have never guessed that the CNA's leadership was intent on forging more, rather than less, social cohesion by advocating for cultural desegregation. In a letter written in 1949, members of the CNA promoted the organization's attempts "to stimulate the broadest possible action on the part of both white and Negro toward a solution of the problem which faces the Negro artist in all cultural media."[111] More so than their white counterparts, the Black press did cover the CNA's objectives.[112]

Announcing the CNA's sponsorship of two well-trained and highly ac-claimed classical musicians to perform during New York's Negro History Week in 1948, *The Pittsburgh Courier* made its appreciation for this initiative explicit: "This presentation marks the third in a series of concerts to introduce outstanding musicians who are ready to take their place in the musical life in America." In a line printed directly below this commentary on the CNA's two Black audition winners, the *Courier* stated in bold letters: "END JIM CROW IN WASHINGTON."[113] (At the beginning of 1948, legal desegregation in Washing-ton, D.C., was still half a decade away.) The cultural group's assets in its earliest years included the renowned Harlem Writers Guild, which was among the collectives briefly under the CNA umbrella.[114]

On the eve of the CNA's establishment of its writers' workshop in 1950, Ruth Jett, the executive secretary for the collective, stated the group's aims in an announcement published by *The New York Age*: "Negro Writers must con-stantly shape their writings with an eye as to whether or not they will be read by the lily-white publishers. Not only must we end this practice, but Negroes must actually work in the publishing and newspaper industries so that we, too, can have a word about what honestly speaks for us."[115] In a groundbreaking study of this period, literary scholar Mary Helen Washington has com-mented, "[T]he CNA was a militantly black, politically Marxist, socially bour-geois, interracial cultural organization that was, perhaps, the most successful black/Left collaboration of New York's Black Popular Front."[116] John Oliver Killens's memories of the group accord with this description.

Describing his memory of the CNA writing group's "first meeting in the very late Forties, or the early Fifties," Killens recalled "eight young men and women" in attendance: "We got together over a store front on 125th Street in Harlem. I read, in a very shaky, trembly voice, the very first chapter of a novel that came to be known as *Youngblood*. None of us had been published before, except John Henrik Clarke."[117] Shortly thereafter, this suborganization began promoting itself as the Harlem Writers' Workshop of the YMCA.[118] In 1953, the year that racial segregation in the nation's capital was outlawed, the blacklisted CNA formally disbanded. Despite the government's efforts to censor the group, members of this collective continued producing Black and interracial productions.[119]

A mix of stress, infighting, racial prejudices, and inadequate financial compensation made cultural work in the 1950s enormously difficult for African Americans, yet many formed deep personal and professional ties. The critical acclaim of several writers, creatives, and sponsors affiliated with the CNA before the 1960s, including Jacob Lawrence, James Earl Jones, Harry Belafonte, Lorraine Hansberry, Alice Childress, Sidney Poitier, and Julian Mayfield, suggests just how productive and spectacular this period in New York City was.[120]

Mayfield, who was also an actor, was an outsized figure in New York's Black and interracial literary circles in these years. He directed the CNA until he was accused of being a Communist sympathizer in 1953.[121] The following year, Mayfield approached several presses, fairly confident that his "novel in preparation" might be useful to publishers either as a paperback or as a book that could be published in hardcover at the same time. "Information has reached me that Farrar, Straus & Young is interested in a novel of this type as a possible dual publication in hard cover and paperback as a cooperative venture with Ballantine," Mayfield noted in a letter to John Farrar.[122] It would not be surprising if one of his Black peers had encouraged Mayfield to reach out to Farrar, Straus.[123] According to Mayfield, collaboration was a hallmark of this era in New York. "As actors and writers, we worked on Broadway and off, way downtown and way uptown, wherever we could find work and get training in our crafts," Mayfield recalled.[124]

In the early 1950s, there was confusion surrounding how to classify Mayfield's cultural work. At the time, Black readers and audiences questioned whether an African American–directed project such as *417*, his one-act play on the numbers game in Harlem, was a remarkable contribution to "American Literature." Or as other viewers of *417* "very angrily exclaim[ed]," according to

Mayfield in a 1953 letter, was his play a representation of one of the "worst pieces of anti-Negro literature in existence"?[125] Detractors did not stop Mayfield and other early members of the CNA from creating or from teaching and mentoring a younger generation of Black artists and intellectuals in New York's metropolitan area. Before disbanding as a formal organization, the CNA was on track to become the region's preeminent institutional resource supporting the cultural development of working-class Black youth.

As an organization, the CNA certainly had its problems, and its efforts at cohesion were thwarted by dissent from Black intellectuals such as Harold Cruse, who chafed at the group's white directors.[126] According to one historian, "What ultimately underlined the black cultural front [e.g., the CNA] was not political infighting or white domination, but the destructive power of the anticommunist crusade."[127] As working across racial lines became more common, skeptics struggled to believe or appreciate how subversive doing so was in the early to mid-1950s. Rebuking Cruse's criticisms of interracialism within the CNA and elsewhere, Mayfield stated in 1968: "Backing the cause of racial integration and the correction of social injustice (whether the victim is white or black) may be unfashionable and uncle tomish now, but there was a time not so long ago when it was downright dangerous."[128] Correspondence between CNA members suggests that the group's commitments to cross-racial fraternity were indeed powerful, positively influencing diverse audiences that were otherwise separated from one another as a general rule—and in some cases, by law.

After reading Lorraine Hansberry's glowing review for *Freedom* magazine of William Branch's play *A Medal for Willie* (1951), one white Southerner was curious enough to travel from North Carolina to New York City with her son to see it. In a letter to Branch, the woman observed that "being a white woman from the South[, she] 'knew' many of the characters practically as next-door neighbors!"[129] Branch and Hansberry would have cheered this woman's courage, but the fact that she was white would not have surprised either of them. Less than a month later, in early 1952, one Black CNA patron published a letter questioning why whites "outnumbered the colored patrons almost 3 to 1" at one of the group's recent theatrical productions.[130] The provocation was intended as a reminder that the CNA needed support from African Americans to ensure the group's longevity.

While the CNA was not able to sustain itself as a New York–based cultural resource, members such as William Branch and Alice Childress were far nimbler. Suggesting as much, fans of CNA productions continued discussing their plays for several years after they were first produced. In 1954, a columnist for the *New York Age* had nothing but fond memories of Branch's *A Medal for Willie* after running into one of the play's actors, Clarice Taylor, at a supermarket. Taylor informed this journalist that she had recently become a playwright herself. And it was this update that prompted an announcement that Childress was working on a new script: "This trend to writing by experienced theatre craftsmen is a good sign. We'll be able to open those doors one way or the other."[131] Critically acclaimed plays by this cohort of former CNA affiliates would soon make it possible for Black communities around the country to "open new doors" by adopting and adapting their racially inclusive and empowering narratives.[132]

In 1955, rather than performing *A Man Called Peter*, a play adapted from a 1951 biography about a Scottish immigrant's experience in the United States, the faculty at Allen University, a historically Black university in South Carolina, considered performing Childress's *Trouble in Mind* (1955), although they ultimately chose a play by Branch.[133] The theater director at Talladega College, Alabama's oldest private, historically Black college, posed a similar request for the *Trouble in Mind* script. But he was bolder in describing his interest in Childress's work than Allen's theater faculty: "Each year I like to give at least one play that does not represent the usual Broadway play. Also I am interested in scripts by Negro authors."[134] Childress's play checked both of these boxes. It also pushed the limits of respectability by poking fun at the Cold War and some of the shortcomings Childress associated with cultural interracialism.

Trouble in Mind was a comedic meta-drama about social and professional tensions between a white director and a set of Black actors caused by stereotypical portrayals of Black female characters, combined with only slightly veiled references to McCarthy's blacklist. Articulating her frustrations with the tenacity of racial inequities in the United States years later, Childress commented: "This society tells us they would rather support us as charity cases than to open the doors and let us win or fail, live or die, as full citizens of this country."[135] Contemporaries regularly noted that the quality of Childress's writing made her plays valuable for Black creatives. Or as another fan claimed, in Childress's plays, "[t]here is a glorious not-taking sides value in them. In this sits your greatness, I swear, not in judgment, but in making us judge."[136]

By 1956, a growing number of Black actors were being trained in Los Angeles, but largely without the support of commensurate Black plays to perform and draw inspiration from. That year, Childress received a letter from a new organization, Negro Actors Associated (NAA), which the business manager described as "a small group of actors, directors, technicians, and writers" dedicated to "training our people in the field" because of the "lack of opportunities for Negroes" in theater. Though smaller, the configuration of this group paralleled the configuration of the CNA, which predated the establishment of the NAA by several years. The goal of the NAA was to provide "opportunities for these same people to display their talents, [and] show Hollywood, and the movie industry that we are ready for better roles, and better jobs behind the scenes, in Hollywood."[137] Childress's literary work made it possible for groups like the NAA to perform widely respected plays that matched these goals.[138]

————

Less than four years after *Trouble in Mind* captivated a national fan base, the premier of Hansberry's *A Raisin in the Sun* attenuated Broadway's color line for Black playwrights. When *Raisin* was adapted as a film two years later, many industry insiders praised it for maintaining the quality and character of the play. For those who agreed with this assessment, these attributes distinguished the film version of *Raisin* from earlier Hollywood adaptations of Black-authored texts—for example, Yerby's *Foxes of Harrow* in 1947 and Motley's *Knock on Any Door* in 1949. Two months before *Raisin*'s public debut in 1961, a white commercial photographer wrote Hansberry after attending a private screening of the film at Columbia University. He reported: "Unashamedly, I cried. And so did 90% of the audience. And these are all hard-bitten show biz folk 'in-the-know.'"[139] Decades later, interest has only increased in Hansberry's civic and intellectual contributions, which clearly transcended *Raisin*'s impressive 530 initial performances on Broadway.[140]

It would be difficult to overstate the impact of *Raisin*'s many successes on the eve of the 1960s and into the new decade. The wide array of offers and requests Hansberry received after *Raisin*'s debut included opportunities ranging from an invitation to produce a television series to interest in a Southern tour of *Raisin*. And much like Childress, Hansberry received dozens of requests from professional and amateur acting ensembles for rights and permissions to perform *Raisin*. David Swerdlow, the director of New York's Elbee Audio Players, described his group of blind actors as grateful that a play like *Raisin* existed to facilitate cultural interracialism: "We expect to produce 'Raisin' this fall. As for the cast—our present plan is to use a mixed group of Negro and white players. I am now looking for qualified Negro men and women who are competent braille readers and who have a strong interest in the theater."[141] A publisher's 1959 solicitation for a book by Hansberry was one of several letters to acknowledge how overwhelmed she must have been: "As the author of a smash Broadway hit, you have surely, I would imagine, been flooded by all kinds of offers and proposals. I feel sure that any number of highly respectable, highly successful commercial publishers have already approached you with book offers galore."[142] Particulars aside, this guess was fairly accurate.

A surprising number of Hansberry's fans went out of their way to avoid imposing racial categories on either *Raisin* or Hansberry. This tendency merged an older conception of raceless universality with Hansberry's play, which is still regarded as an exceptional rendering of a Black family seeking a better home for themselves in Jim Crow Chicago. One Black fan even apologized for identifying herself as African American in a letter to the playwright in 1959: "This is incidental, but I think I might mention that I am a Negro. Please understand that my response would have been the same even if we did not have this very basic fact, not of our choice, in common."[143] In another letter to Hansberry, gay author Lonnie Coleman poked fun at the nation's critics for "their self-congratulation at liking 'the first play to be produced on Broadway by a woman Negro dramatist'— a phrase that must have bored [Hansberry] as it did [Coleman]." Casting himself as an outlier among the nation's white racial progressives, Coleman assured Hansberry, "I admire your work simply because it's fine work."[144] As both letters illustrate, fans on both sides of the color line struggled to reconcile *Raisin*'s universal acclaim and Hansberry's own unapologetic Blackness.

Worse still, Hansberry's popularity was treated as nothing short of a serious threat to the United States, at least in the eyes of the federal government. The FBI was deeply suspicious of Hansberry, as it had been of the CNA, Alice Childress, and numerous other Black cultural professionals. As literary scholar William Maxwell has pointed out, the FBI's file on Hansberry, held in conjunction with *Raisin*, is 1,020 pages, "far longer, then, than any book ever published" on the play. By comparison, W.E.B. Du Bois, whose career as an activist spanned over seventy-five years, had an FBI file of 756 pages.[145] The FBI kept close tabs on Hansberry for several years after *Raisin* opened on Broadway, even though the only threat she posed to the government was her willingness to offer perceptive commentaries on racism, civil rights, and international politics.

In the end, most African Americans were simply proud of Hansberry's commercial successes. Willard Moore, a Black poet and photographer based in New York, and a former member of the CNA, was just one of dozens if not hundreds of fans to send her a personally crafted gift. Moore's offering was a poem that probably resonated deeply with Hansberry, especially given their mutual interest in ensuring that American culture didn't exclude African Americans.[146] Humorously, Moore's poem foregrounds the significance of

Raisin attracting so many white entertainment-seekers to Hansberry's Broadway debut:

SEEING ME

(To Lorraine)
By Willard Moore.

Oh it's so good to see
White folks paying
To see me.
I said, it's sure is good
To see
White folks paying
To see me
Being ME!

On that GREAT WHITE WAY!

Where I've been caged
In a servant's uniform
On stage;
And never, never being me.

Now my roots are sunk
Deep
On that GREAT WHITE WAY!
From now on,
Where
I'll stage my say.

'Cause it's so good to see
Folks, white, paying me
To see me
At last being ME![147]

In his letter of praise to Hansberry in 1959, Julian Mayfield offered a remarkably similar account of *Raisin*'s importance: "I take a selfish pleasure in all this, and I'm sure the other writers of our group [former CNA affiliates] feel the same way. [. . .] With *Raisin*, you have blasted a hole that will make things better for the rest of us." If Black audiences had been divided over his CNA play, *417*, years earlier, *Raisin* was "something of which, for a change, THE FOLKS can be thoroughly proud,"

Mayfield wrote.[148] But in the years that followed, a growing number of Black critics would come to see Hansberry as a "sellout" instead.

———

Hansberry's achievements would have been impossible without friends, peers, and forebears associated with the Committee for the Negro in the Arts. In what is likely the most famous issue of the Black scholarly journal *Phylon*, Charles Nichols argued in 1950: "The racial pride, the Quixotic radicalisms, the propaganda [. . .] the bizarre aspects of the 'New Negro Renaissance' have given way to a deeper, subtler tone, a more universal quality, and a more impressive technique in the literature written by the group."[149] For the majority of Black authors whose books and productions were praised as "more universal" in the late 1940s and 1950s, cultivating white readers, audiences, and other interlocutors was virtually a necessity. These interracial partnerships, collaborations, and consumption patterns were remarkably varied, as were the cultural genres they influenced. Because of these efforts to work and reach audiences across racial lines, African Americans were better represented in hardcover and softcover paperback books, plays, and print journalism; on television; and in Hollywood films. When analyzed together, these attempts at forging connections across the color line illuminate the various strategies Black authors, thinkers, and artistic professionals frequently used to seek space within (rather than outside of) American culture after World War II.

If celebrating racial progress and "integration" shaped the years prior to the Cold War, the following years were indelibly marked by divisions over these cultural milestones. But as the variety of entertainment genres and Black authorship suggests, the expansion of mass media and other cultural commodities in this era was more beneficial than some contemporaries were willing to admit. And the range of social, professional, and artistic interests and opportunities for established and newly prominent Black writers only expanded further—even if remuneration continued to lag for Black writers such as Chester Himes and countless others during this period.

African Americans were forced to contend with numerous precarities as desegregation gained momentum. But as the 1960s Civil Rights Movement gathered steam, friendships and professional collaborations across the color line became increasingly tense in the United States. The final chapter of this study examines how the social turbulence of those years deepened rather than bridged racial divisions between writers, intellectuals, critics, and cultural activists on the eve of the Black Power Movement.

5

Toward Disunion

"FOR SOME TIME NOW it has been apparent that the traditional leadership of the American Negro community—a leadership which has been largely middle class in origin and orientation—is in danger of losing its claim to speak for the masses of Negroes."[1] This was the warning with which Julian Mayfield, a rising star among mainstream Black authors, opened his 1961 essay entitled "Challenge to Negro Leadership: The Case of Robert F. Williams." Williams was a Black civil rights leader from Monroe, North Carolina, who founded the "Black Armed Guard" to protect African Americans in his hometown from the Ku Klux Klan. Mayfield's essay appeared in *Commentary* long before the magazine began describing itself as "the flagship of neoconservatism."[2] Founded in 1945 by the American Jewish Committee, *Commentary* aimed to popularize the idea of a "democratic, pluralistic, and prosperous America."[3] Even in the early 1960s, the magazine's editors and their closest interlocutors were still at least a decade away from formally endorsing right-wing politics in the United States.[4]

In the 1950s, when *Commentary*'s white producers still identified as "liberal," they were arguably in the vanguard—at least among mainstream publishers—in working across racial lines in their coverage of civil rights matters.[5] Black-authored essays were commissioned to help the magazine's white readers better understand life on the other side of the color line. As the Civil Rights Movement gained momentum in this era, there was still a shortage of Black perspectives in mass media. More so than ever before, white readers and cultural professionals wanted to redress this imbalance by reading and hearing from Black commentators like Mayfield. His 1961 article for *Commentary* focused on a set of African Americans in the South who were responding to violent—sometimes murderous—white supremacist threats by taking steps to protect themselves, which included acquiring weapons as a defensive measure. Though Mayfield discussed Williams as his case study, his essay centered on the working-class men and women who had come to form the majority of new NAACP members in Union County, North Carolina.

Mayfield explained that by the beginning of the 1960s, Union County's NAACP had emerged as the first chapter in the United States to shed virtually all of its "respectable," nonviolent, middle-class members: "[It was] the only one of its kind now in existence. Its members and supporters, who are mostly workers and displaced farmers, constitute a well-armed and disciplined fighting unit."[6] Mayfield's essay is an impressive but little-remembered elaboration on how and why life in this region had changed after *Brown v. Board of Education* (1954), when the Supreme Court invalidated the legality of racially segregated schools. According to Mayfield, white aggression in Union County included a revitalized Ku Klux Klan and terrorist strikes on African American homes, as well as boycotts of and arson attacks on Black-owned businesses. *Commentary*'s interest in soliciting dynamic Black writing and analyses represented the magazine's commitment to progressive interracialism at the time. As other white publications and media organizations invested in similar work, the content and quality of these initiatives varied. Mayfield's essay was a good-faith effort to educate and engage white readers who could help shore up and support interracialism. These Americans needed to know how white supremacist threats undermined a racially inclusive vision of the Civil Rights Movement. But by the second half of the 1960s, most newspaper reports, radio programs, magazine essays, and books discussing the state of the movement became more cynical and ambivalent about prospects for racial reconciliation.

This chapter traces the fractious history of cultural interracialism that emerged in the second half of the 1950s. Faltering relations between Black and white literary professionals underpinned calls in this era among Black writers to abandon white publishers, media organizations, and related institutions. Tensions between Black commentators and white interlocutors—for example, peers, politicians, and audiences—anticipated, and later paralleled, the Black Power Movement of the late 1960s. As the historian Nancy Bristow observes, "As many African American activists wearied of persistent white supremacy, ongoing violence, and the inconsistent support of white liberals, the center of gravity" moved toward Black Power. Bristow notes that Black activists who stopped prioritizing desegregation by the late 1960s were "recognizing the place of power in making change, voices calling for self-determination, self-defense, and racial consciousness—for Black Power."[7] In 1966, civil rights activist Stokely Carmichael declared, "I know black power is good because so

An American Negro

views the African Gold Coast

BLACK

POWER

RICHARD WRIGHT

by the author of

NATIVE SON and **BLACK BOY**

FIGURE 5.1. Richard Wright's *Black Power* (New York: Harper & Brothers, 1954).

many white folks came out against it."[8] Carmichael wasn't exaggerating. But when he took credit for popularizing "Black Power" with a series of speeches on shortcomings and failures of the Civil Rights Movement in the 1960s, he obscured the biracial origins of the term.

Indeed, educated readers on both sides of the color line would have recognized the slogan from a 1954 book by Richard Wright, a memoir of the author's visit to Africa's Gold Coast. In April of that year, Wright's literary agent, Paul Reynolds, informed Harper & Brothers that Wright wanted the title of this book to be *Black Nation*.[9] The publisher's response was mixed. Two days earlier, the firm had received Wright's proposal to name the book *Black Power*, in response to his agent's request for a "strong title" that was no more than two words.[10] Soon after receiving Wright's subsequent suggestion of *Black Nation*, his editor and Harper's president, Frank MacGregor, sent a counterproposal. Harper's "salesmen [had] responded very favorably to the book," MacGregor informed Wright, but "[t]hey all feel that BLACK POWER is a good title and if you agree, we'll settle on that."[11] Wright responded with a brief letter, noting, "BLACK POWER suits me fine as a title."[12] For those Americans who read Black authors, Wright was the luminary of his generation. But it was Harper's white "salesmen" who were responsible for marketing the first widely known, pan-African conception of "Black power" in this era.

White progressives made numerous positive contributions to the Civil Rights Movement.[13] Nevertheless, real and imagined relationships between Black and white Americans deteriorated rapidly by the beginning of the 1960s. Writers, intellectuals, and cultural professionals across the political spectrum—on both sides of the color line—contributed more to this development than is commonly understood. Literature and culture shifted in tone under their direction. Intractable racial frictions became a staple of American print and other forms of mass media. Unifying cultural interracialism was much less prominent than it had been in the 1950s. Authors such as Lorraine Hansberry, James Baldwin, and Frank Yerby contributed to the flourishing of Black aesthetics and reportage on Black life in the 1960s. But this seasoned cohort of Black writers held political beliefs and cultural values that were often in tension with calls for racial separatism.

Desegregating Mass Culture

In a 1947 essay entitled "For Whom Does One Write?" the French philosopher Jean-Paul Sartre articulated a double bind facing Richard Wright, the foremost African American author of the early Cold War period. "Each of Wright's works contains what Baudelaire would have called 'a double simultaneous postulation,'" Sartre posited, with "each word refer[ring] to two contexts; two forces are applied simultaneously to each phrase." According to Sartre, Wright's capacity to reach across cultural divides to appeal to both Black and white readers during the Jim Crow era was exceptional by historical standards: "Jeremiah spoke only to the Jews. But Wright, a writer for a [racially] split [American] public, has been able to maintain and go beyond this split. He has made it the pretext for a work of art."[14] The literate public, in the United States and elsewhere, was indeed "split."[15] Prior to the 1960s, most corporate publishers solicited white authors for books on current issues related to civil rights and racial injustice more broadly.

In the United States, before James Baldwin, Lorraine Hansberry, Langston Hughes, and other Black celebrities led much of this work in radio, on television, and elsewhere, white counterparts such as Lillian Smith and Robert Penn Warren were much more prominent. Smith's *Now Is the Time* (1955), which focused on the *Brown* decision, and Warren's *Segregation: The Inner Conflict in the South* (1956) are typical nonfiction contributions to this genre.[16] Smith's book was published in hardcover by the Viking Press and simultaneously printed as a twenty-five-cent "newsstand edition" paperback by Dell. Similarly, Random House sold Warren's book as a hardcover, while Modern Library distributed *Segregation* the same year as a paperback.

Many white readers and critics saw these writers as invaluable contributors to progressive developments commonly associated with the Civil Rights Movement. In an announcement that Smith would be visiting Vassar in the fall of 1955, one of the college's student journalists wrote that it remained "difficult to assay accurately the influence Lillian Smith has wielded upon Southern mores and how she [would] go down in history." More tangible, according to this young commentator, was the respect white progressives held for this author: "Although Miss Smith has been severely criticized as a Southerner for speaking out against traditions and beliefs, she is universally recognized as an honest person with the courage of her convictions and as a talented writer."[17] From a commercial standpoint, book buyers were certainly interested in reading what white authors had to say about civil rights and interracial matters. More than six thousand copies of Robert Penn Warren's *Segregation* were sold after just one month on the market.[18]

Shortly before Warren's book was published in 1956, a short excerpt was published in *Life* magazine.[19] Popular white-authored accounts and reports on race relations like Warren's were direct precursors to Black-authored essays such as James Baldwin's "A Letter from a Region in My Mind," published by the *New Yorker* in 1962. Before the Supreme Court's ruling in *Brown* in 1954, the market for nonfiction books on racial matters was much smaller. But as the Civil Rights Movement gained momentum by the second half of the 1950s, Americans of all backgrounds responded passionately to writing about, and other media coverage of, desegregation. Leading commentators were often inundated with letters about the problems of race and racial injustice. A remarkably wide-ranging response Warren received from a fan in Columbus, Ohio, merits quoting at length:

> I just finished reading your article on [the] "Divided South" and the "integration" subject.—I [also] wrote your magazine [*Life*],—when it published

those grand pictures of the continent of Africa. [. . .] "The MAJORITY rules" has been our slogan, since 1776.—There will be some Southerners who will CONTINUE to obey SATAN and NEVER consider the Ethiopian, their brother,—but will continue their narrow-mindedness, regardless [of] the fact that the "majority" of nations in the U.N. represent people of dark complexion, they [white Southerners] are determined to hate.—But I am sure the "majority" of Southerners will,—after they have been told these historical facts,—be as broad-minded as you,—and honor a person according to their ability, and NOT because of the lack of "pigment" under their skin. Therefore, I suggest, as the "ruling" power, you Gentiles get busy and create a "U.N. Racial board"—that [. . .] will set up rules for our States to follow [. . .] and ANY OTHER country which has trouble getting adjusted.—All States and Countries who will reject the rules laid down by this board should, automatically, be disconnected, financially, and socially, with the rest of the world.[20]

Clearly this reader presumed that Warren's clout held the potential to help dismantle white supremacist norms worldwide.

But what is fascinating about the publication of books and essays like Warren's on desegregation in the 1950s is how easily white authors gained or were granted access to write about Black life in the United States—even if they were ambivalent about civil rights. White American readers readily trusted men and women who looked like them to discuss race relations. But in Warren's case, his outsized presence as a commentator on desegregation bore little relation to his actual cultural interests. The first time Warren had debated the "integration question in Southern schools" was over dinner one night with his brother-in-law, who happened to be an editor at *Life* and who then invited him to publish an essay on the subject. Warren initially declined, only to reconsider a few weeks later when a representative from *Life* approached his agent with another proposal. In a 1958 letter Warren wrote from Italy explaining why he had changed his mind, he recalled wanting to challenge "a lot of stupid or malicious misrepresentation[s] of ["the integration question"] in novels" and "want[ing] to get something said in more unequivocal terms."[21] And yet, opportunities like these (at least in premier outlets) were waning for white writers by the end of the 1950s. Smith and Warren were effectively the last cohort of white authors to avoid stiff competition, and numerous other challenges, from their Black peers.

Between 1954 and 1968, a large cohort of African Americans followed Wright's lead and gained access to major publishing houses, radio stations, theaters, periodicals, and other popular venues. By the late 1950s, a growing number of white editors, booksellers, and media professionals called on Black artists, writers, and academics to contribute their perspectives on race and racial tensions as public intellectuals. Most of these requests were attempts to address the absence of Black voices from the cultural sphere. Over the following decade, demand in this ill-defined sector complemented other calls for more complex portraits of Black life and anti-Black racism in an even larger number of progressive publications. Across the publishing sector, the support of African American literary contributions was often treated or perceived by white cultural professionals as a commitment to civil rights.[22]

By the mid-1960s, Black artists, intellectuals, and writers were collaborating with a broad range of established publishing firms, as well as emerging leaders across the entertainment industry. The interracial format, or forum, became an increasingly popular style employed by many publishing and mass media organizations during this period.[23] An increase in cross-racial collaborations meant that more Black perspectives could be read, heard, and seen in traditionally white-dominated news and cultural outlets. Most of these contributions to print media, radio productions, and filmed commentaries were, in practice, commitments to help facilitate diffuse conceptions of desegregation. At the same time, these efforts introduced Black authors and other voices to vast new audiences, including racially progressive white readers, listeners, and viewers who otherwise had little contact with African Americans.[24] It would be difficult to overstate how diverse this content was.

Progressive interracialists such as Lorraine Hansberry and James Baldwin produced texts signaling that all Americans could and should contribute to upending allegiances to white supremacy. Hansberry's *The Movement: Documentary of a Struggle for Equality* was published in 1964 by Simon & Schuster. California's *Oakland Tribune* described this "large picture-and-text" book as one of the finest offerings on the market: "Miss Hansberry's comments on segregation, the Black Muslim movement, the nature of race relations and the character of the civil rights movement are direct and intelligent. And they are skillfully integrated with excellent photographs, many of which are by Danny Lyon."[25] James Baldwin's collaboration with his friend from high school, the photographer Richard Avedon, *Nothing Personal* (1964), was similarly interracial in character. Before the book was published, the *Philadelphia Inquirer* reported that "James Baldwin and Richard Avedon are collaborating on a book about America."[26] This book was a collection of Avedon's photos of Americans of all backgrounds, divided into four thematic sections, accompanied by Baldwin's commentary.

In Avedon's description of the project, he recalled, "Baldwin had a good idea [of] what I was doing, and actually did see some of the photographs in the process of being organized. We deliberately talked about not illustrating one another, but obliquely worked out of the same sources in different directions."[27] This collaboration effectively proposed what American art and literature could be if cultural and racial conventions were upended. Shortly after the book was published, Manchester's *Guardian* praised their "rare but splendid picture" book as an attempt to overcome divisions between Black and white Americans in particular: "The authors indeed, lifelong friends, have long wished to do this study together, to ram home in picture and word the pain and anguish of racialism and the colour bar." The *Guardian* noted that while "Baldwin's road has been harder" than Avedon's, their artistic effort to counter white supremacist customs, together, was unmistakable.[28]

White responses to these books, and Black and interracial cultural activism more generally, remained divided in this era. Some Black writers and critics, including Julian Mayfield, later argued that institutional support for related media and texts was more superficial than many contemporaries realized. In an interview published in 1973, Mayfield commented: "Blacks are not being published as widely as it appears. It is simply that there were so few published before now, and the appearance of *two* in the *New York Times* on a Sunday, where only one had been before, makes it look like a flood. As with television."[29] Sharing much in common with Hansberry and Baldwin, Mayfield was a candid pragmatist. During the Civil Rights Movement, each of these writers was remarkably consistent in maintaining real and imagined (fictional) dialogues with white Americans to challenge separatist impulses. Recognizing as much, in 1962, Australia's *Sydney Morning Herald* described Mayfield's novel *The Grand Parade* (1961)—republished and retitled as *Nowhere Street* in 1963, with an angry, violated Black woman on its cover—as "uphold[ing] the Negroes and integration."[30]

Numerous other Black writers and celebrities were either tapped or credited for similar contributions during the 1960s. But few if any African Americans could match how often James Baldwin was courted by the nation's political and cultural establishment during the Civil Rights Movement. In an essay published in the mid-1960s, a skeptical Black critic noted: "A romance has ensued. A perverse love affair between white Americans, especially the communications industry, and James Baldwin. It is marvelous, for such a public love affair with a black man is unprecedented. Yet it is hazardous, not only for whites but for Baldwin as well."[31] Baldwin's success with the "communications

75c PAPERBACK LIBRARY 54-589

"POWERFUL...racism and bossism
...are interwoven with sex and violence;
rape, murder and bombings confront
the reader on almost every page."
—The New York Times

Nowhere Street

(original title: *The Grand Parade*)

a novel by Julian Mayfield

FIGURE 5.2. Julian Mayfield's 1961 novel
The Grand Parade was published in paperback
as *Nowhere Street* (New York: Paperback
Library, 1963).

industry" was directly responsible for his meetings with Robert F. Kennedy, the U.S. attorney general, in 1963.[32]

"Integration" in Practice

At the second of these back-to-back meetings, Baldwin was joined by Hansberry and a number of other Black and white writers, activists, and celebrities commonly known as integrationists. Yet in its report on this meeting, Tennessee's *Chattanooga Daily Times* claimed: "Baldwin, Miss Hansberry and several other participants in Friday's discussion with Kennedy are sometimes referred to as members of the school of 'angry young Negroes.'"[33] It was common for white publications in this era to casually misrepresent and malign progressive

Black interracialists this way. Clarifying how racially inclusive his invitations to the Kennedy meeting were, Baldwin later recalled: "There were many more people than I can name here. Let us say that I simply called black or white people whom I trusted." According to Baldwin, the people he invited to Kennedy's penthouse in Manhattan in 1963 "would not feel themselves compelled to be spokesmen for any organization or responsible for espousing any specific point of view."[34] Baldwin wanted Kennedy to see that Americans of all backgrounds, across the political spectrum, had the capacity to support civil rights.

By the time the attorney general proposed his first meeting with Baldwin, school desegregation was already faltering. White Southerners were violently resisting efforts to register Black voters and other attempts to dismantle racist laws and customs. At the same time, the Civil Rights Movement was moving beyond the South in response to racial injustices around the country. The attorney general was struggling to comprehend the exponential rise in Black demonstrations in the weeks after thousands of federal troops were deployed to restore order in Birmingham, Alabama, that May.[35] Days after federal troops reached Birmingham, Baldwin's appearance on the cover of *Time* magazine (May 17, 1963) prompted the attorney general to arrange a one-on-one meeting with the author at his home outside of Washington.

Like other white Americans grasping to understand the Civil Rights Movement, Kennedy assumed that Baldwin was perfectly qualified to help him. Yet Baldwin's demanding role as a racial spokesperson was by no stretch unprecedented. Since the turn of the twentieth century, observers on both sides of the color line had considered Black professionals as stalwarts of "integration" or interracialism.[36] After the turn of the century, variations of this custom stretched all the way back to Booker T. Washington's dinner at the White House with Theodore Roosevelt in 1901. Objecting to the ultimate futility of Roosevelt's gesture, Julius Lester observed: "Theodore Roosevelt was not loved by blacks, even though he had been the first President to invite a black man, Booker T. Washington, to dine at the White House."[37] Roosevelt had invited the race leader to dinner based on his admiration for Washington's recently published autobiography, *Up from Slavery* (1901). Robert Kennedy had a better reputation than Roosevelt among African Americans. But much like the invitation Roosevelt extended six decades earlier, Kennedy's proposal that Baldwin visit him at home in Virginia was poorly planned.[38]

Baldwin interrupted an unusually hectic professional calendar to have breakfast with the attorney general on the morning of May 23, 1963. Baldwin's appearance on the cover of *Time* days earlier was a tribute to the critical and commercial success of his recently published book *The Fire Next Time* (1963), adapted from his recent *New Yorker* essay.[39] An Associated Press review of this book in January described it as a "small package of sociological dynamite" penned by "a novelist and essayist [that] says more for the American Negro than many dusty, academic volumes ever could hope to say."[40] More so than any of his previous titles, *The Fire Next Time* made Baldwin an American celebrity.

When Baldwin arrived at RFK's home after flying in from New York City, he was granted only about twenty minutes to speak with the attorney general. As a modest sign of respect, Kennedy proposed that Baldwin organize a gathering of a larger group of Black celebrities in New York the following day. Kennedy had fewer ties to African Americans than some of his political forebears (e.g., Theodore Roosevelt's niece, First Lady Eleanor Roosevelt).[41] He was politically progressive, but as was the case for his older brother, President John F. Kennedy, his lack of awareness extended well beyond racial matters.[42] Baldwin later remarked that Kennedy's "father had been Ambassador at the Court of St. James—among other quite stunning distinctions—and it goes without saying (nor was it his fault) that he had not the remotest concept of poverty."[43] When the attorney general invited Baldwin to meet in New York after their brief meeting in Virginia, Kennedy didn't know the address for the penthouse his family maintained on Central Park South. As the celebrities who gathered there the following day would complain for years after this episode, the attorney general was conspicuously oblivious to his own wealth and social status. Shortly after the meeting, Baldwin was quoted as concluding: "We were a little shocked at the extent of [Kennedy's] naiveté."[44] For many white Americans, this remark was another reminder that Baldwin was an "angry young Negro."[45]

In a summary of Baldwin's meetings with Kennedy in 1963, Arthur Schlesinger Jr. described the author as "a brilliant, passionate, sensitive, [and] dramatic man" who was "imbued with a conviction of utter hopelessness about the black fate in white society."[46] And yet, this is not how committed and aspiring white interracialists such as Wallace Putnam perceived Baldwin's published writing and broadcasted perspectives in the 1960s. In a 1963 letter to Lorraine Hansberry, Putnam explained, "I am one of many to whom the writings of James Baldwin have been 'an experience'—so that the morning after reading [his] New Yorker article [the essay adapted as *The Fire Next Time*] I began a series of drawings of Negro life on the strength of the impact."[47] Responses like these suggest that Baldwin's work as a public intellectual was less pessimistic than Schlesinger later claimed. Moreover, accusations such as Schlesinger's affirming the "utter hopelessness" Baldwin allegedly spread simply ignored how accommodating he and several others had been in making time to meet with Kennedy on twenty-four hours' notice. Lena Horne's willingness to meet the attorney general was particularly noteworthy. The singer and actress flew across the country from Palm Springs, California, at Baldwin's request. Baldwin later explained that Horne readily did so, despite the fact that she hated flying: "I found her wearing a beige suit, sitting in Bobby Kennedy's lobby and complaining that she had a 'hole' in her shoe from guiding this plane across the continent. She had just driven in from Idlewild—soon to be renamed Kennedy."[48] Schlesinger's biography of the attorney general neglects to acknowledge how flexible and determined Horne and other Black celebrities and civil rights activists were to advise Kennedy.[49]

The cocktail party at Kennedy's penthouse was harmonious at first. The attorney general welcomed his guests and assured them that he was eager to listen to their concerns. And yet, Horne later claimed that astute attendees could sense a pending disaster from the very beginning: "The character of the meeting was symbolized by the seating arrangements. Somehow, all the white people were on one side of the room, [and] all the Negro people on the other."[50] Things quickly went downhill after the gathered group selected Jerome Smith, a celebrated Black activist, to speak first. This was how Horne later characterized this choice:

> It was very simple. [Smith] had been in the South working for voter registration. His wife and children had to be sent away for their own protection. He had been jailed and beaten and he was still physically ill from what had been done to him. You could not encompass his anger, his fury, in a set of statistics, nor could Mr. [Harry] Belafonte and Dr. [Kenneth] Clark and Miss Horne, the fortunate Negroes, who had never been in a Southern jail, keep up the pretense of being the mature, responsible spokesmen for the race any more. [...] That's what I mean about that young man being the soul of the meeting. He took us back to the common dirt of our existence and rubbed our noses in it.[51]

Emphasizing "the compassionate type of attitude on the race question" that "Baldwin, Hansberry, and Lena Horne" represented, the Black sociologist who described Baldwin's relationship with white America as "a romance" complained: "The only Negro at Robert Kennedy's little tryst who represented the actual leadership of the masses was Jerome Smith."[52] Smith, who had previously practiced Gandhian pacifism, was arguably the most famous survivor of the 1961 Freedom Rides. He had likely been beaten more, and spent more time in Southern jails, than any other member of the Congress of Racial Equality, one of the "Big Four" civil rights organizations.[53] In fact, Smith was available to accept Baldwin's invitation to Kennedy's penthouse only because he was in New York City seeking medical treatment for a recent beating that had impaired his ability to speak.

In the end, Smith's speech impairment seems to have exacerbated Kennedy's annoyance. Almost immediately, the attorney general dismissed Smith's comments as far too angry and unpatriotic.[54] Kennedy reportedly turned his back on the activist and said to the celebrities in the room: "I'll talk to *you*, who are civilized. But who is *he*?"[55] Hansberry responded that Smith was "[t]he only man you should be listening to. [. . .] That is the voice of twenty-million people."[56] According to the political scientist Nicholas Buccola, "Kennedy appeared unmoved by Smith's testimony or Hansberry's plea."[57] Nor did Kennedy appear convinced, as every single one of Baldwin's guests were, that desegregation was a "moral" issue.

Baldwin's group proposed that President Kennedy accompany a Black child into a white Southern school to desegregate it. In light of recent events in Birmingham, which included the murder of four Black girls in a terrorist bombing of an African American church, this was not an arbitrary request. The attorney general balked at the idea, rejecting it as a "meaningless moral gesture."[58] This disjuncture led Horne to conclude that Kennedy was clearly unprepared for the meeting he had proposed: "I wondered afterward whether [Kennedy] had read any of James Baldwin's books or been briefed on them. [. . .] What has made the Negro mood of the moment is not logic. You can't think about his condition or his demands these days in a purely logical way. There is no logic in the way the Negro has been treated."[59] Kennedy's insistence on statistics was deeply upsetting to the men and women Baldwin had gathered, and Horne was no exception.

In an artistic summary of this paradox, Baldwin once noted: "In our image of the Negro breathes the past we deny, not dead but living yet and powerful, the beast in our jungle of statistics. It is this which defeats us, which lends to interracial cocktail parties their rattling, genteel, nervously smiling air."[60] It was by no means an accident that Baldwin's reference to Henry James's novel *The Beast in the Jungle* (1903) was later reprinted in his collection of essays *Notes of a Native Son* (1955), a title partially riffing on the second volume of James's autobiography, *Notes of a Son and Brother* (1914).[61] Baldwin never stopped writing, working, and loving across racial lines. His candid reflections on lackluster white liberalism were not separatist. Many of Baldwin's dear friends and professional interlocutors, including Hansberry, had romantic partners who were white. One literary scholar has noted that these two "supported each other's work enthusiastically and fought side by side in the civil rights movement. What united them was their shared understanding of and approach towards race relations in America."[62] Much the same was true in their sentiments regarding contrived interracial fraternizing.

Hansberry never publicly commented on her meeting at Kennedy's home. Privately, however, she reflected on how infuriating it would be for an African American to navigate fraught encounters like these. In an unpublished draft of an essay describing "the North's feeble attempt to be 'cosmopolitan,'" Hansberry noted: "Imagine the indignity which must accompany a Negro sitting at the same table with two representatives of the white upper middle class."[63] Hansberry began treatment for pancreatic cancer a month after Kennedy's cocktail gathering. But Baldwin later suggested that the attorney general's resistance to making a "moral commitment" to the Civil Rights Movement was the reason Hansberry looked ill after leaving his penthouse: "She was walking toward Fifth Avenue—her face twisted, her hands clasped before her belly, eyes darker than any eyes I had ever seen before—walking in an absolutely private place."[64] The depth of Kennedy's racial insensitivity, it seems, had broken Hansberry's heart.

Divisions Writ Large

In the cultural sphere, the mid- to late 1950s likely struck many Black observers in hindsight as close to the apex of cross-racial cooperation. In 1979, discussing Lorraine Hansberry's story of a Black family's spirited attempt to leave the Black Belt of Chicago for a decent home, *Raisin in the Sun* (1959), Julian Mayfield remarked, "I don't suppose anybody today is going to sit down to write a play about the problems of a black family moving from the ghetto into a white, middle-class neighborhood."[65] This form of integration, Mayfield's sentiments suggest, was no longer a priority (or as feasible) for the Black middle class in the late 1970s. Some Blacks managed to escape the ghetto in the 1960s. But these were typically Black families relocating to what increasingly became African American suburbs.[66] Historians and other scholars have described the reemergence of segregation in poorer suburbs (and elsewhere) in this era as "white flight."[67] For most African Americans, the promise and prominence of social and cultural interracialism were distant memories—if that—on the eve

FIGURE 5.3. Leslie Alexander Lacy's *The Rise and Fall of a Proper Negro: An Autobiography* (New York: Macmillan, 1970).

of the Reagan era. "But in the 1950s, black class mobility was as much a burning issue as was the desegregation of schools and other public facilities," Mayfield noted in his reminder of how powerful Hansberry's *Raisin in the Sun* had been for African American strivers.[68] Mayfield's own attempts to strengthen racial liberalism in periodicals like *Commentary* in the 1960s reflected a similar imperative.

In this era, African Americans gained some ground establishing relationships with white-led publishers and other mass media outlets. But the voices and publications in the second half of the 1960s were often designed to accentuate seemingly irreconcilable divides between Black and white Americans. Julius Lester's *Look Out Whitey! Black Power's Gon' Get Your Mama!* (1968), Leslie Alexander Lacy's *The Rise and Fall of a Proper Negro: An Autobiography* (1970), and Calvin Hernton's *Coming Together: Black Power, White Hatred, and Sexual Hang-Ups* (1971) are just three popular texts patterned after the broader decline of social and cultural unity during this period.[69] *Publishers' Weekly* claimed that Lester's book would "jar the ear of the conventional middle class, both white and black, as well as lacerate the spirit," all while "translat[ing] into writing the harsh music of ghetto speech."[70]

Several factors inhibited demand and support for previous Black and interracial cultural standards. Growing cynicism, shortcomings, and failures of seeing and working across racial lines inspired texts that boldly trumpeted discord rather than pluralism. Baldwin, Hansberry, and many other Black writers were chided by some readers and critics for being too angry—and by others for not being angry enough. On both sides of the color line, seasoned Black cultural professionals commonly associated with unifying American entertainment were accused of lacking racial conviction in their professional work. Indeed, ardent Black supporters of desegregation in the literary field were frequently maligned by Blacks and whites alike as wanting to be white. Perhaps worse still, white authors and publications wanted to remain free to interpret Black and interracial life, and the state of the publishing field, as they saw fit.

None of this stopped white Americans in particular from being shocked that African American writers weren't all fully preoccupied with civil rights, Black cultural themes, and stories about their own lives. Racial essentialism dogged a well-meaning exchange in a 1953 letter from Richard Wright's white literary agent to Harper's Jack Fischer concerning plans for his client's book, *Black Power*: "I have been worried for a long while as to what Wright should do. He told his story in fiction in NATIVE SON [1940] and non-fiction in BLACK BOY [1945]. It seemed to me clear that he couldn't live in Paris and write about the Negro problem in America." Wright's agent also noted his awareness that a white author was "writing a book for [Harper's] on Africa, but I don't see why Wright, limited to the Gold Coast, should seriously conflict."[71] The first of these comments assumes that Wright's ability to write about Black life in the United States was impaired by his escape from Jim Crow America, while the second statement suggests that if Wright's *Black Power* was "limited to the Gold Coast," his book wouldn't compete with or detract from a white author's ambitions for a much grander (geographic) narrative of African decolonization.[72] Assumptions such as these help explain why many Black writers resisted white preoccupations with either racial categories or the African diaspora in this period.

Six years after the letter above was written, an editor at *Harper's* magazine requested that Frank Yerby self-identify as "Negro" in an essay clarifying why he specialized in "pulp" rather than "protest" novels: "As the piece has been revised you discuss books on racial themes at various points but never say you are a Negro. I wonder if you would be willing to add [. . .] 'Perhaps, as a Negro, it took me longer than it should have to learn this lesson.'"[73] Yerby responded: "As for your suggestion that I use the phrase, 'As a Negro, etc.—' no. [It] smacks of breast beating and special pleading to me. Besides which, it is irrelevant, both in writing and in life, at least to anyone who has managed to grow up."[74] Yerby was certainly aware that millions of American readers already knew that he was Black. In the years since the publication of *Foxes of Harrow* in 1946, numerous commentators had remarked on his race. While some critics poked fun, others described him as a racial propagandist, as Alabama's *Birmingham News* did in 1957: "Yerby, an accomplished Negro who doesn't spare the pen in describing his loutish Negro characters, nevertheless gets in insidious propaganda for [the] social equality of the races."[75] This was also the year Norman Mailer first published *The White Negro: Superficial Reflections on the Hipster*, foreshadowing a virtual free market for any white intellectual willing to push the boundaries of respectable multiracial discourse.[76]

Years later, Amiri Baraka maintained that his own contributions to the establishment of the Black Arts Movement were inspired by an effort to develop "individual philosophic approaches to these various social (and ethical) problems ["re: race problems in U.S., Colonialism, Hipsters, &c."]."[77] In just one of many chauvinist passages in "The White Negro," Mailer claimed: "I remember once hearing a Negro friend have an intellectual discussion at a party for half an hour with a white girl who was a few years out of college. The Negro literally could not read or write, but he had an extraordinary ear and a fine sense of mimicry."[78] Earlier in the essay, Mailer had already unapologetically informed his readers that the average Black man in urban America "subsisted for his Saturday night kicks, relinquishing the pleasures of the mind for the more obligatory pleasures of the body," in devotion "to his rage and the infinite variations of joy, lust, languor, growl, cramp, pinch, scream and despair of his orgasm." Black jazz, Mailer insisted, was an extension of the African American male's "orgasm, it is the music of orgasm, good orgasm and bad, and so it spoke across a nation."[79] Citing Mailer's fetishization of Black men and vernacular African American music, Hansberry remarked in 1959: "In jazz rhythms, alien

FIGURE 5.4. Norman Mailer's essay *The White Negro: Superficial Reflections on the Hipster* (San Francisco: City Lights Books, 1957).

minds find only symbols for their own confused and mistaken yearnings for a return to primitive abandon."[80] At the time "The White Negro" was published, Mailer knew that the claims he was making about African Americans were controversial.

But many white authors and cultural professionals were less aware of how their commentaries and publications distorted Black lives. Literary and cultural opportunities to do so, it seems, were endless. Though difficult to

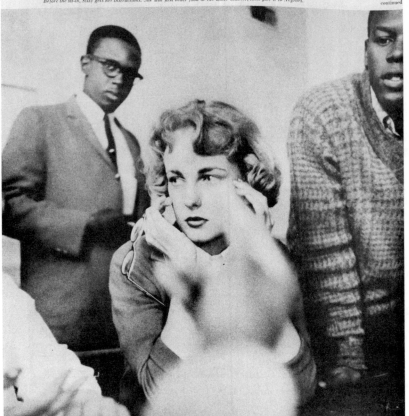

EXPLOSIVE YOUTH

INTRODUCTION TO A SIT-IN

MARGARET (SISSY) LEONARD is a native-born Southern girl who believes strongly that racial discrimination is cruel and unjust. An increasing number of young white Southerners feel the same way. Sissy is one of those who are putting their beliefs to the test of action. As a sophomore on full scholarship at Sophie Newcomb College in New Orleans, she has much to lose by public avowal of beliefs rigidly opposed by most of the adult community. In spite of this, Sissy recently went to a meeting of the local chapter of CORE (Congress on Racial Equality) and offered to take part in any kind of demonstration protesting segregation. Her offer was accepted, and she was given an important role in a lunch-counter sit-in planned for an afternoon in October. On the following page, she reports what happened.

Before the sit-in, Sissy gets her instructions. She will first order food at the white counter, then give it to Negroes.

continued

FIGURE 5.5. "Explosive Youth: Introduction to a Sit-In," *Look*, January 3, 1961.

measure, older and newer forms of white biases were ubiquitous in American popular culture during the 1960s. A relatively innocent example is an interracial profile published by *Look* magazine in 1961. This biweekly periodical could count on more than seven million readers taking notice of its spread "Explosive Youth: Introduction to a Sit-In"; in these years, *Look* was one of the most

FIGURE 5.6. Glenford E. Mitchell and William H. Peace III, eds.,
The Angry Black South: Southern Negroes Tell Their Own Story
(New York: Corinth Books, 1962).

popular periodicals in the United States.[81] The feature in question centered on
a young, attractive white woman sitting between two handsome African
American student activists. More than delineating contemporary politics, this
photo essay accentuating the biracial character of the sit-in movement evoked
the book covers of contemporary romance novels selling illicit sex. Of course,
selling the specter of interracial relationships in the United States stretched
back decades. Yet, in the 1960s, this was compounded by marketing narratives
emphasizing Black resentment, as evidenced by such titles as *The Angry Black
South: Southern Negroes Tell Their Own Story* (1962), published by Corinth

Books, a small publisher run by the white owners of the Eighth Street Book Shop in New York.[82]

The booksellers who sponsored the publication of this essay collection maintained that the book would offer an unprecedented Black perspective on the South. Theodore Wilentz, one of the publishers, pitched the project to Lorraine Hansberry in 1961: "The six contributors and the young editors were all active participants in the various non-violent movements for desegregation. We believe this is the first book of its kind written entirely by Southern Negroes, and that, as such, it has a unique validity and importance."[83] Wilentz, a friend and colleague of Amiri Baraka's, was hoping that Hansberry would contribute a "brief preface" to *The Angry Black South*. Hansberry's response is not preserved in her manuscript collection, but it is not surprising that she did not contribute to a volume marketed with such a divisive title.

In the 1960s, Hansberry was perennially irked by contemporaries like Norman Podhoretz who amplified various tensions associated with the Civil Rights Movement or who devalued social activism. Trivial invitations were a staple in Hansberry's mailbox, especially in the years leading up to her premature death at the age of thirty-five in 1965. In 1960, a white theater critic stated that he would be thrilled if Hansberry would commit to being one of his key "assets" at a cocktail party given by the Committee for a Sane Nuclear Policy.[84] One can only imagine what her reaction was upon receiving a telegram from *Playboy* publisher Hugh Hefner in 1962, requesting "the pleasure of [her] company at a party in [his] home" that would not end until midnight or, perhaps, much later.[85] In 1963, Hansberry received a request that she chair a "Fashions for Peace" luncheon for five hundred women at New York's Plaza Hotel, hosted by the *National Guardian* and described as a fashion show "featur[ing] such spring firsts as, 'what to wear as a H.U.A.C. witness' or 'how to appear on a peace picket line' or 'a spring bonnet, the latest in fall-out head-gear.'" Hansberry instructed her assistant to decline the invitation on her behalf and to respond that she would be "out of town" if prodded.[86]

Many white interlocutors fumed when Black celebrities chafed at their invitations and standards. When James Baldwin chose to publish "Letter from a Region in My Mind" in *The New Yorker* instead of in *Commentary*, Norman Podhoretz quickly responded by outlining the "twisted feelings" he harbored "about Negroes" in "My New Problem—and Ours." In the February 1963 issue of *Commentary*, Podhoretz declared: "We have it on the authority of James Baldwin that all Negroes hate whites. I am trying to suggest that on their side all whites—all American whites, that is—are sick in their feelings about Negroes."

For Hansberry, Baldwin, and many others, Podhoretz's fallacious assertions were deeply insulting and arbitrarily divisive: "[W]hen I think about the Negroes in America and about the image of integration as a state in which the Negroes would take their rightful place as another of the protected minorities in a pluralistic society, I wonder whether they really believe in their hearts that such a state can actually be attained."[87] Several decades later, Podhoretz defended his 1963 diatribe against interracialism. In 2013, he commented that "contrary to a widely held suspicion," he was not trying to "offend everyone" with these sentiments.[88]

True to her fashion, Hansberry was Podhoretz's most vociferous critic following the publication of "My Negro Problem—and Ours." In a lengthy draft of her rebuttal written shortly thereafter, Hansberry lambasted Podhoretz's essay: "Mr. Podhoretz is agitated because it is so apparent that the liberal ought to be saying and doing something: that he ought to be stepping into the street to join the parade but that, as always, His Majesty has discovered that he hasn't got a stitch on." And as Hansberry's incisive critique makes plain, Podhoretz was sowing further divisions between Black and white Americans: "[M]ost painfully of all, I charge [Podhoretz] with something I know that he cannot presently appreciate the seriousness of: of having given those impassioned young black folk who have 'given up [on whites like him]' a document [. . .] to heighten their ever-deepening [. . .] contempt." As a political and cultural activist who characterized her own work as "trying to maintain the chain" between Black and white Americans, Hansberry relayed to Podhoretz that she had "been handed a body blow" after reading "My Negro Problem—and Ours."[89]

Many white Americans of Podhoretz's class and generation did not see a fundamental problem with how the Civil Rights Movement was discussed in the mainstream press. As Black critics and observers frequently noted, many "white liberals" simply prioritized their own interests and perspectives on race and interracialism. In 1964, Hansberry began corresponding with John Anderson, a white Harvard alumnus who lived in the suburbs. Responding to a public statement Hansberry made proposing that *Time* be banned, Anderson wrote to say that he admired her but did not understand why she was so incensed by *Time*: "Why? What are the unforgivable sins? You have succeeded in making me feel stupid for not knowing already." Hansberry sent Anderson a diplomatic, detailed response on her issues with *Time*'s lackluster coverage of civil unrest in America's crumbling cities, which prompted a lengthy and somewhat sheepish response. "This is kind of silly," Anderson admitted, "my being out here on this limb for Time, which is less important to me right now than is the wild cat that I see at this moment, stalking through the annoying inconvenience of the snow outside my window, gorgeously alive and attentive." Anderson's poetic response to Hansberry's "wonderful, long letter" was genuinely sympathetic and conciliatory. At the same time, it was easy for him to backtrack from defending *Time*, "in spite of its imperfections," from the comfort of a bucolic white suburb.[90]

Many well-intentioned white liberals in this era rarely considered how much they were asking of Black friends, colleagues, authors, and other correspondents. Even Frank Yerby, who had gone out of his way to avoid contending with American racism head-on, was urged to do so in the mid-1960s by Helen Strauss, his long-standing literary agent based in New York City. In a letter sent to Yerby's home in Spain in 1964, Strauss warned: "You cannot ignore the entire civil rights question. Newspaper reporters will be in touch with you, also the various civil rights groups, and no matter how adroit you may be on the subject you'll definitely have to participate in some way."[91] In his response, Yerby rejected Strauss's assertion that he had any responsibility whatsoever to address the "civil rights question" for a nation still thoroughly committed to a segregationist regime: "I am not patriotic. Why the hell should I be? I regard it as rather sad that in Franco's Spain, I can and do belong to the Country Club, while in Johnson's U.S.A. Ralph Bunche's son can't play tennis on a Long Island Court." Yerby's lack of patriotism was rooted in his own family's encounters with American racism: "[A]s for evading the racial problem, my considered opinion is that any person of noticeably Negro ancestry, who can afford not to, and who voluntarily lives in the Union of South Africa or the United States of America is in serious need of psychiatric care."[92] Yerby had always been polite and deferential in his professional exchanges with Strauss and his other white colleagues in the publishing world. But in 1964, he deeply opposed Strauss's interest in adding civil rights commentaries to his portfolio just because it was the popular thing to do.

Here it also bears remembering that by the mid-1960s, it was becoming far more common for white liberals to blame Black people for contemporary racial schisms. Just a few months after Hansberry began corresponding with Anderson, in 1964, she received a litany of complaints from Blanche Dorsky, a white woman from Milburn, New Jersey, who described herself as "actively, morally and financially" concerned with African American causes for several years. According to Dorsky, Hansberry's appearance on a recent panel discussion—"The Black Revolution and the White Backlash: A Town Hall Forum"—broadcast on WBAI, a listener-supported radio station, did not reflect her own interracial virtues: "It was heartbreaking for me to hear a group of prominent and respected Negro artists play traitor to their fellow American Negro. At a time like this, when we need the support of every American in this national crisis [. . .] I hear irresponsible rabble rousing." Dorsky then accused the playwright of being too hot-tempered: "You have the right to your anger; I have the right to mine; The kind of good heated argument that one carries on in one's living room but not in a Town Hall Forum."[93] It is unclear whether Hansberry responded to Dorsky. But given her scarring encounter with Robert F. Kennedy thirteen months earlier (which she never discussed publicly), it is unlikely that Hansberry was sympathetic with this last piece of advice.

At the beginning of the broadcast of "Black Revolution and the White Backlash," another Black panelist, Amiri Baraka, claimed to be far less interested in explaining the Civil Rights Movement to "white liberals." Offering his own interpretation of the forum's theme, Baraka questioned whether there was really "a necessity for new honest dialogue between" Black and white Americans. Baraka then posited: "The 'new' part doesn't seem right, but for an honest dialogue, I think if there's going to be one, it would have to be new because I don't think there's ever really been an honest dialogue between white Americans and Black Americans."[94] During and after the 1960s, Baraka chastised anyone who questioned his assertion that American society and culture were profoundly inauthentic—and anti-Black.

Varieties of Resistance

Baraka is widely credited as one of the founders of the Black Arts Movement of the 1960s and 1970s. Cultural products and offerings associated with this movement were intended, first and foremost, for African-descended individuals and communities. While the white cultural establishment wasn't forgotten, preoccupations with interracialism were much less important for many Black writers and artists. In 1968, Larry Neal argued: "Black Art is the aesthetic and spiritual sister of the Black Power concept. As such, it envisions an art that speaks directly to the needs and aspirations of Black America."[95] In practice, the early years of the Black Arts Movement in New York City were masculinist by design. As one of the foremost architects of this movement, Amiri Baraka prioritized the education and mentorship of "young men." In a letter to Lorraine Hansberry in 1961, he explained, "I have recently gotten together an organization of young men (most of whom are black, and in the arts in one way or another) and we need monies to further some of our projects." The promotional material he sent Hansberry for his recently established Organization of Young Men offers a clear sense of Baraka's political goals: "This letter goes out as a call to young Negro men. A call to form some highly militant organization in the United States to combat the rise of Uncle Tomism, shallow minded white liberalism, racism, and ignorance. It is a call to form some kind of formal resistance."[96] By the early 1960s, Hansberry had been forced to contend with male chauvinists of all backgrounds in New York's intellectual circles for close to a decade.

The stationery Baraka used in his request for money for the Organization of Young Men had been designed for the Totem Press, which he had founded in 1957 with his white wife, Hettie Jones (née Cohen). Decades later, Baraka's ex-wife recalled a growing "pressure on all black people to end their interracial relationships" by the mid-1960s. Summarizing how neatly this trend squared with the demise of her own marriage in this era, Hettie remembered: "So there was a scandal downtown: LeRoi Jones Has Left His White Wife. It fit right in with dissolving black-white political alliances."[97] When Baraka wrote Hansberry back in 1961, his name was still LeRoi Jones, and he was still living in Greenwich Village with Hettie and their two-year-old daughter; the couple's second daughter was born two months later.

Given the many contradictions between Baraka's personal life and his professional aspirations, it is not surprising that Hansberry rejected his request for support. In a remarkably angry response to Hansberry's rejection, Baraka wrote: "To my mind, the position you have made for yourself (or which the society has marked for you) is significant, if only because it represents the thinking of a great many Americans [. . .] black as well as white." This was not meant as a compliment. In telling Hansberry that her "writing comes out of and speaks for the American middle class," and insisting that "critics, etc., were joyous about Raisin [her prizewinning play A Raisin in the Sun] for exactly that reason," Baraka argued that Hansberry should see the world as he did: "And as an articulate voice of an entire class you certainly do become a 'leader,' like it or not."[98] Hansberry already was a leader, however, and it pained her that men like Podhoretz and Baraka, by accentuating racial animosities and other differences, casually undermined her long-standing commitments to reaching across these divides.

Baraka also became increasingly alienated from some of his white friends and colleagues. Eventually he moved to Harlem, leaving Hettie and their children in 1965. According to Theodore Wilentz, who published Totem Press's books as well as The Angry Black South, "After 1964 [Baraka] began to drift away from the [Greenwich Village literary] scene and grew more and more involved with the black movement. [...] We all felt a great loss as he moved away. The better I knew [Baraka] the more I had respected him and liked him personally. [But] his new politics and racism shocked and saddened me."[99] As Baraka drifted away from his white friends, colleagues, and family, he criticized commercially successful Black authors harshly. In one of a series of essays published during the mid-1960s, Baraka claimed: "You can be Frank Yerby, speaking from the vantage point of raceless historical sex fantasy, and make all the loot you want—but then you have to be an American." As in his 1961 letter to Hansberry, Baraka was using "American" as an insult. "Though Yerby is cooler than that and has moved out," Baraka qualified, referring to Yerby's decision to live abroad, "his books are always good for at least one hard-on, as I remember."[100] In different ways, Baraka, Yerby, and Hansberry all helped establish the groundwork for the 1960s Black Arts Movement. But when Baraka mockingly referred to his African American literary peers and elders as "American," he contributed to a broader disavowal of the importance— or significance—of this pathbreaking work, which Yerby never completely abandoned.

Yerby had struggled for decades to find interest from white editors, agents, and publishers in Black literary themes. Memories of those rejections added to his other frustrations with the white publishing establishment in the 1960s. In 1963, Yerby tried to publish a novel, drawn from his own experience, about an African American family integrating a white neighborhood, entitled *The Tents of Shem*. This was a personal theme for Yerby, since his family had been driven out of their home on Long Island when white neighbors realized he was a newly famous Black author.[101] The novel was never published, and Yerby acknowledged that interracialism and "integration" were no longer in vogue. His preface to *Tents of Shem*, written in 1969, noted: "This novel will seem curiously out of date to the average reader. The reason for this is very simple: It was written in the early part of 1963. At that time, John and Robert Kennedy, and Martin Luther King were still alive."[102] By 1969, cultural support for desegregation seemed hopelessly optimistic. Even in 1966, after an interview with Yerby appeared in *Ebony*, one letter to the magazine denounced the novelist: "Yerby ran out on us when our backs were to the wall. But as for his being interested in our plight now, will someone in the audience please stand and tell Brother Yerby we don't need him now."[103] Powerful—or at the very least, empowered—messages like these, which echoed Baraka's critiques, were a hallmark of the period.

Commercially successful Black writers from the previous generation, including those who remain central to the Black canon to this day, were simply
no longer seen as Black enough in some African American circles.[104] In a 1971
letter, Ralph Ellison complained: "Imagine, some of the young black radicals
who know nothing about me treat me as though I was brought up rich and safe
and know nothing of the harsh aspects of Negro life. But then I forget that <u>they</u>
are a new people, the <u>Blacks</u>, born only a few years ago out of the mouth of a
Malcolm X!"[105] Two years earlier, in 1969, the scholar and writer Charles R.
Johnson recalled that on a visit to the offices of a Black Studies program at
Southern Illinois University, he asked the program's librarian where he could
find Ralph Ellison's novel *Invisible Man* (1952) and was informed that Ellison's
title did not merit inclusion in a Black Studies collection "[b]ecause Ralph
Ellison is not a black writer."[106]

While many African Americans continued reading, discussing, teaching,
and celebrating an older generation of internationally renowned Black writers
and cultural professionals, it became more common for African Americans
suspicious of working and reaching across racial lines to publicly or privately
reject some of these figures. From their perspective, emphasizing or privileg-
ing "integration" as a civil rights strategy was increasingly conflated with either
whiteness or futility. Books, whether fiction or nonfiction, that were not leg-
ibly or easily identifiable as "Black" were frequently labeled and dismissed as
"white" writing. Other African Americans were criticized simply because they
had achieved critical and mainstream success with white readers.

Only a handful of seasoned Black authors avoided a backlash against their
work during and after this period. Gwendolyn Brooks was one of them. In
1968, Brooks left her long-standing publisher, Harper, and initiated partnerships with smaller, African American publishing houses. This trajectory was
complex. Brooks was a supportive yet cautious figurehead of a longer African
American literary tradition. Arguably one of the best examples was her defense
of Langston Hughes, whose credentials as an African American writer were
sometimes questioned in the 1960s. Brooks was unapologetic in honoring his
legacy when he died in 1967. She characterized his work, collaborations, and
friendships that year as "rooted in kindness." Brooks credited Hughes for these
attributes in an obituary published shortly after his death, which opened with
an elegy for the camaraderie of a bygone era: "THE AGE OF KINDNESS is
not now. This is the Age of Detachment, a time of cold. The world has never
contained so bright-minded a population. And articulate, articulate, articulate!" In this celebration of Hughes's legacy, Brooks also emphasized that he

had opened doors for successive generations, which included support for her own literary career when she was still a teenager: "Langston held high and kept warm the weapons until the youngsters could cut the caul, could wipe away the webs of birth and get to work. He, himself, preceded them with a couple of chores, a couple of bleedings." This last point reminded readers how much more difficult professional conditions once were for African American authors.[107]

Between the mid-1960s and the early 1970s, African Americans developed an unprecedented number of new arts organizations, magazines, publishing houses, and other resources. Francis and Val Gray Ward, reflecting on the "newest Black Consciousness stage" in a 1971 issue of *The Black Scholar*, noted that artists "had [recently] made the most significant break with the past of any generation of Afro-Americans." For them, "[w]hatever the effectiveness or motivation of their participation, it's no doubt that their presence makes it difficult, if not impossible, for black artists to maintain the fiction that their art was not related to real-life struggles for equality and freedom."[108] This abundance of beautiful, emboldened African American and Afrodiasporic culture, written and produced by Blacks, put new initiatives and institutions in direct competition with white corporate publishers. But the cutthroat business of print fueled by Black and white firms competing in an already saturated market for "Black" culture was unsustainable. Most Black publishing houses founded during the second half of the 1960s would shutter before the end of the decade. American literary culture was undoubtedly richer during the Black Arts Movement, and yet funding for Black-directed publications, publishing houses, films, and other cultural projects remained scarce. This dynamic created real dilemmas for Black artists, writers, and professionals who accepted time-consuming work outside of Black communities and organizations.

———

A decade after his 1961 *Commentary* essay, Julian Mayfield followed Black dissidents who called for moving away from work for predominantly white institutions. For Mayfield and other acclaimed African Americans of his generation, however, clean breaks in either direction were rare: many established Black intellectuals, artists, and cultural professionals continued to work across racial lines and cultivate new audiences, despite burgeoning rhetoric that suggested otherwise. After receiving a contract faculty position at Cornell University in 1967, Mayfield stayed in this Black Studies position for close to four years. In a letter to a friend, Sandra Drake, the daughter of the preeminent Black scholar St. Clair Drake, Mayfield explained how tenuous this work was: "One college near here [Cornell] has been through 4 black studies directors in one year."[109] As the historian Martha Biondi explains: "Even after commitments to create Black studies had been won, another round of conflict often ensued over precisely what form it would take and who would be calling the shots. Similarly, an intellectual battle over the character of Black studies developed over time."[110] Personal income mattered for Black intellectuals who directed these programs as well. When Mayfield resigned from Cornell in 1971, he was still torn over whether to accept a comparable position at a higher salary nearby: "Because with $22,000 a [year] I could perhaps pay off a few debts. But I thought at the time you ought to have a better reason than that for taking such a job."[111]

When St. Clair Drake was appointed the first academic chair of the African and African American Studies program at Stanford in 1969, his daughter Sandra was certain that his esteemed position would be enormously difficult: "My father's got a real hot seat—head of the Afro-American Studies Program. The Administration wants him to put out the fires[,] so his job is to keep it while not doing what they want him to."[112] In other words, St. Claire Drake's position at Stanford required a delicate balancing act: resolving racial conflicts at the university as directed by the administration, while maintaining allegiances with activists who were demanding change. While Mayfield estimated that St. Clair Drake was "indisputably, the greatest teacher I have ever seen or heard of," he didn't think that any Black scholar could survive this juggling act: "Everyone I know, even young deans, [are] getting out because of the impossibility of serving several gods at once. This is the year for getting back to teaching or writing and research."[113] For Mayfield and other Black writers and intellectuals, returning to their own projects rather than pursuing administrative positions at elite white universities was urgent. And Mayfield was particularly worried about what he perceived as a precipitous drop in demand for Black books by the early 1970s. After years of struggling to find a publisher for an Afrocentric biographical novel of Alexander Pushkin's life, Black novelist John Oliver Killens complained: "When blacks stopped being in the streets, publishers stopped publishing black writers."[114] Killens died two years before *Great Black Russian: A Novel on the Life and Times of Alexander Pushkin* (1989) was finally published.

Two decades earlier, in 1970, Julian Mayfield advised W.E.B. Du Bois's stepson, David Du Bois, on how to navigate this weakening market for Black books.

David was working on a book about African Americans in contemporary Egypt and was planning to seek a U.S.-based publisher. Mayfield warned him that federal funding that had recently supported a broad range of Black books was drying up under Richard Nixon's administration: "One reason publishers could afford to try to meet the demand for Black books was that schools and poverty programs were receiving large chunks of dough from the government, and they were expected to buy a lot of the books which would be published." Worse still, one of Mayfield's friends, "who happen[ed] to be a communist," was predicting that a major economic recession would likely hit the United States around the autumn of 1970.[115]

Mayfield urged David to act quickly if he hoped to publish his book on Africa. In his opinion, in addition to fiscal changes, white America's interest in African and African American literature was waning rapidly:

[Federal funds have] been slashed almost in half, and may be slashed further. Thus publishers will no longer be able to experiment very much with black material. [. . .] Large numbers of whites, especially among the liberal sections who buy books, are losing interest in racial questions because, firstly, they can't or won't do anything about it, and secondly, they have been rejected by the blacks with whom they would like to work (as leaders, as always), and thirdly, there are other causes to interest them now. There is not only the continuing war [Vietnam], but [also] THE ENVIRONMENT, which is all the rage now. I suspect it will be the "In" thing in the next year or so. If they must stick to people, they'll take the American Indian Cause or the Mexican American Cause. My last reason you should hurry may be the most important for you: There is practically no general interest in Africa now.[116]

Despite the inhibiting factors Mayfield outlined, David Du Bois did manage to publish a novel with Palo Alto's Rampart Press on African American expatriates, *And Bid Him Sing* (1975). After returning to the United States in 1972, he also joined the Black Panther Party and accepted a lecturing position at Berkeley's School of Criminology.

Still, Mayfield's interpretation of the American scene in 1970 was accurate. A letter to the literary agent Muriel Fuller from a white friend in New Haven, Connecticut, expressed no sympathy for either Black activists or activism. Fuller had fought her own mother's deep-seated racism decades earlier. But by the second half of the 1960s, she and her white friends blamed African Americans, and especially the Black Power Movement, for the nation's divisions and social disorder. In 1966, Stokely Carmichael complained: "White people associate Black Power with violence because of their own inability to deal with blackness."[117] Four years later, early in the spring of 1970, Fuller's friend Ginny was incensed by a recent "rally in support of the Black Panthers" organized by Yale students: "I'd like to see all of them go to the electric chair, so the world would be well rid of the barbarians. The Panthers have a dangerous and tragic hold on the young black people." What made these students even more insufferable, Ginny insisted, was how little they cared about the movement now occasionally termed Green Power. Ginny complained: "[N]one of these young people made any attempt to help clean up their environment. We live in a crazy era. [. . .] I'm off to clean up my environment by raking the yard."[118] These comments suggest that when Julian Mayfield informed David Du Bois that white Americans had lost "interest in racial questions," and were focusing on the environment instead, he wasn't exaggerating. Hope was dimming for a functional multiracial democracy in the United States. But a general failure to get Americans to appreciate and maintain faith in a common humanity did not occur overnight.

Coda

IN 1964, a white newspaper quoted educator and civil rights activist Mary McLeod Bethune (1875–1955) as stating, toward the end of her life, "Our aim must be to create a world of fellowship and justice where no man's skin, color or relation is held against him. Loving your neighbor means being interracial."[1] But "color blindness" was no longer feasible during the 1960s Civil Rights Movement. During and after this period, tensions between white and Black intellectuals and cultural professionals paralleled a revitalized, violent, white supremacist movement.[2] This history recalls a similar uptick in violence, tensions, and cultural essentialism that inhibited progressive interracialism in the late 1910s and 1920s. In a sense, these and related developments might be considered provocations for deepening cultural understandings of the "fractures" the historian Daniel T. Rodgers has characterized as central to the post-1960s United States.[3] In a 1973 interview, Julian Mayfield commented: "It is difficult to talk about how integration has been used, because—except for public facilities in many places—it has not been achieved in many meaningful areas. And now there is a growing opinion among both blacks and whites that it is not desirable. (I'm speaking here of social integration.)"[4] There was a cultural dimension to these divisions as well.

Countless African Americans encouraged Black-centered social and cultural agendas. They did so, in part, because the sympathies of white liberals for fairer representation in the publishing sector had been uneven and insufficient. Social and political changes affirming the utility of Black Power were deeply interconnected with broader literary and other cultural trends. Most notably in relation to this study, decades of activism did not create sustained support for equitable, inclusive publishing networks. Nor were enough white publishers in the 1960s seriously challenging biases that were—and continue to be—perpetuated by authors of all backgrounds. Over the preceding decades, the gains of some Black authors, and some Black and interracial books, were not nearly enough to stem growing disillusionment with the lofty promises of racial "integration" in other areas of American life.

None of this is meant to suggest that progressive interracial publishing simply died in the 1970s. Many commercial presses either started or continued to publish African American and Afrodiasporic authors. Racially progressive white readers also continued reading Black authors, including those who were sponsored by smaller publishers directed by people of color. To name just a handful of writers, intellectuals, and cultural professionals, Toni Cade Bambara, Octavia Butler, Lucille Clifton, Jayne Cortez, Angela Davis, Shirley Graham Du Bois, Nikki Giovanni, Virginia Hamilton, Kristin Elaine Hunter, Esther Cooper Jackson, Gayl Jones, Audre Lorde, Gloria Oden, Carlene Hatcher Polite, Rose Robinson, Carolyn Rodgers, Sonia Sanchez, Ntozake Shange, Alice Walker, and Sarah E. Wright all gained (or maintained) wide readerships during and after the 1960s, if not earlier. Readers, critics, and teachers can and should do more to enrich themselves with this feminist epoch of African American and Afrodiasporic writing.[5]

Moreover, as scholars continue examining the interrelationship between Black activism and white supremacist ideologies, analyses of books and literary texts that affirmed the power of African American womanhood in the post–Black Power era deserve far more attention. In her edited collection *Midnight Birds: Stories of Contemporary Black Women Writers* (1980), literary scholar Mary Helen Washington stated that "white men have always held this power, a power in evidence everywhere in the world. In all the great capitals—I am thinking particularly of Washington and London—there are hundreds of monuments to them."[6] Decades before the current national furor over grandiose public monuments to white supremacists erupted, Mary Helen Washington was calling attention to what many white Americans continue defending. But the stories collected in *Midnight Birds* were about Black women, written by Black women. Outlining a distinguished genealogy these stories were building upon, Washington observed: "It is unique that black women have consistently given us a heroic image of the black woman. Not the conquering hero of daring exploits but women like Zora Hurston's Janie Crawford, Nella Larsen's Helga Crane, Ann Petry's Lutie Johnson, Gwendolyn Brooks' Maud Martha, Paule Marshall's Reena, Alice Walker's Meridian, Toni Morrison's Sula. These are women who struggled to forge an identity larger than the one society would force upon them. They are aware and conscious, and that very consciousness is potent. In searching out their own truths, they are rebellious and risk-taking, and they are not defined by men."[7] When Toni Morrison became the first African American fiction editor at Random House just a few years earlier, she also helped elevate a successive generation of writers who continued this tradition of venerable Black authorship.

Like Mary Helen Washington and numerous other African American peers of this generation, Morrison also taught. This stellar, sizable cohort's contributions to building Black Studies departments and institutional archives, publishing anthologies of Black writing, and mentoring younger generations of scholars and students still deeply inform the present.[8] *Impermanent Blackness* would not have been possible without their strength, their efforts, and the white interlocutors who supported and encouraged their work. To take just one example of how powerful this cultural activism remains, these Black intellectuals led and advocated for the archiving of hundreds of years of Afrodiasporic history and literature during and after the 1960s. In 1976, the year Henry Louis Gates Jr. became a lecturer at Yale, he informed Chester Himes: "We are very, very interested in purchasing your collected papers, Mr. Himes. We regard you as an important figure in the Afro-American literary tradition; in fact, I shall be teaching one of your books next year in my black novel course."[9] In the twenty-first century, it has become relatively easier to honor the most famous Black authors who have contributed to diversifying the publishing landscape in particular and American culture more broadly.

Others have faced a much more complex task, especially writers and scholars who have produced biographies and critical studies that illuminate the stories of African American authors such as W. S. Braithwaite, Juanita Harrison, Ellen Tarry, Frank Yerby, Alice Childress, and Julian Mayfield over the past few decades. During their careers, some of these Black authors minimized their racial identity or helped ensure that it was ambiguous. They made these choices for different reasons, ranging from allegiances with contemporary tastes to attempts to elude Jim Crow–styled literary customs. In 1969, Mary Helen Washington reminded readers: "For the last 50 years Langston Hughes, J. Saunders Redding, [and] William Stanley Braithwaite—to name only a few—have been condemning the traditions in American literature which exploit and degrade the image of Black people."[10] What unites the professional experiences of these Black cultural producers is that they wanted to write during an epoch when African Americans were summarily denied the privilege to publish any text that signaled racial parity. After all, legal segregation in the United States was built on the fiction of Black inferiority. Historians and literary scholars cannot understand the so-called racelessness of most African

American cultural contributions in the first three-quarters of the twentieth century without remembering the ubiquity of denigrating racial essentialism, including dialect poems, minstrelsy, "pickaninny" children's books, racist cartoons, and racially offensive book titles and illustrations—all of which catered to, and were designed for, white audiences. This history, and its implications for our collective memory, still haunts and undermines an ascendant progressive agenda across American print and mass media.

Regardless of their backgrounds, writers, intellectuals, editors, and publishers associated with innovative literary interracialism wanted to create an American culture that enabled readers to come together and find common ground. Before the 1960s, Yerby's supporters (on both sides of the color line) regularly credited him for "surg[ing] beyond the race barrier and [. . .] becom[ing] a leading American novelist," despite "experienc[ing] the limitation of being black."[11] Yerby's international popularity was incredibly lucrative for Dial Press, the novelist's long-standing publisher. By 1959, Dial was boasting to booksellers that "Frank Yerby's novels are known throughout the world. His books have appeared in nearly a dozen foreign languages including French (in France he and Hemingway are the most popular American writers)[,] German, Italian, Finnish, Spanish, Danish, Portuguese and Norwegian."[12] With thirty-three novels and global book sales topping fifty-five million copies by the last quarter of the twentieth century, Yerby is still one of the best-selling American authors of all time. In many ways, the poetry of Amanda Gorman, the novels of Zadie Smith, the reportage of Malcolm Gladwell, Michelle Obama's best-selling autobiography, and the media empire of Oprah Winfrey are all newer variations on this older tradition of Black literary celebrity.

A century ago, while Black literary entrepreneurs like W. S. Braithwaite were exceptionally deferential in their engagements with both white interlocutors and the public, they believed that this was necessary to build support for an equitable, future-oriented American literary culture. When Braithwaite died in 1962, *Negro Digest* credited him for a literary career that was "broad and varied" and which "transcended the limits of race."[13] Braithwaite's Blackness, the racism he encountered, and his work on behalf of white modernists and African American writers alike are no longer common knowledge. Worse still, his disappearance from the canon was all but guaranteed by racist white critics such as Ezra Pound and Alice Corbin Henderson—who both insisted on erasing Braithwaite's support for creative writers in the United States in the opening decades of the twentieth century. Their campaign was successful.

Given the tenor of race relations in 2022, it is difficult to imagine political activists championing another polymath like Braithwaite or his commercially acclaimed successor, Frank Yerby. But overall, our collective ambivalence toward some Black authors who were enormously popular during the Jim Crow era is a symptom of a broader separatist drift, rooted in decades of social fractures following the Civil Rights Movement. In 1968, Prince Wilson, a University of Chicago–trained Black academic on the executive committee of the Association for the Study of Negro Life and History, expressed hope that America's leading Black writers would one day be granted the respect they were so frequently denied. "Perhaps the future will give 'white' recognition to such highly accomplished black American writers as Ralph Ellison, Frank Yerby, W.E.B. Du Bois, and Richard Wright or James Baldwin," Prince wrote in a short essay reprinted in newspapers across the country.[14] Each of these authors fostered interracial partnerships that, at their best, nurtured loosely connected ecosystems that countered racial chauvinism.

The literary agent Helen Strauss, whose *New York Times* obituary described her as a "major influence in the worlds of books, motion pictures and the theater," represented several preeminent Black authors from the beginning of her career in the early 1940s. While few of Strauss's professional relationships were without cross-racial tensions, she regularly named Ellison, Baldwin, and Yerby among her esteemed clients. Strauss observed in her 1979 autobiography, *A Talent for Luck,* that at mid-century, she "represented black writers before it was 'in.'" This pithy yet important declaration refers to the publishing and cultural industry's vogue for Black authors and commentators from the beginning of the 1960s. Strauss considered Yerby a "friend, scholar, and great storyteller," indicating how far ahead of American society some white editors were in forging meaningful connections across racial lines.[15] Indeed, she claimed that Yerby "suffer[ed] a great deal of abuse" in his "white neighborhood on Long Island" before *Foxes of Harrow* was even published in 1946. "His children's toys were broken," she recalled, and "'Nigger!' was scrawled across a fence. The Welcome Wagon didn't call."[16] Nor would it ever call for Yerby and his family in this white community.

Attending to the elusive character of cultural interracialism offers a new perspective on the reversals and discontinuities that still hinder and inhibit racial cosmopolitanism in the United States. Doing so also helps render lesser-known people and artifacts associated with related pursuits more legible. While the reputations of these men and women were often conflated with taboo labels ranging from cultural conservatism to authors of "pulp," this broad, diverse cohort played an important role in subverting conflations of literary excellence with whiteness. The shortcomings, failures, and discrimination these Black writers faced reflect how difficult it was—and remains—to work across racial lines.

In the twenty-first century, Barack Obama is perhaps the best example of what it means to "integrate" a Black voice into both national politics and a national discourse on race. After Obama's election to the U.S. presidency, an awed nation celebrated what many viewed as a triumphant end to the nation's legacies of slavery and segregation. Present, but less powerful, was a reckoning in both Black and white communities over what it meant for the U.S. president to be a multiracial American, a reality that was—and often still is—sidestepped for the sake of simplicity. As novelist, critic, and literary scholar Jesse McCarthy has pointed out, "Obama did his best on a near-impossible tightrope, as he tried to normalize, but not completely efface, his blackness. He did his best to calibrate and mediate, to explain (with increasingly evident weariness and strain) the two warring sides of his country to each other."[17] In many ways, Obama's many gestures of social, political, and racial conciliation are reminiscent of what Eleanor Roosevelt desired when she endorsed Willard Motley's queer novel, *Knock on Any Door* (1946), after World War II. However naive, each of these public intellectuals wanted Americans to read beyond their particular identities and to challenge various forms of prejudice.

Arguments and debates over who has the right to represent Black people are far from over. Moreover, many readers and audiences now assume that literature and culture representing multiracial America should be clearly marked by our racial inequities, divisions, and violent conflicts. In the publishing realm, it might be more productive to put more weight on expecting, if not demanding, that Black writers have the same intellectual freedoms, and access to institutional resources, as their white peers. The same might be said for the value of building appreciation and respect for an array of Black perspectives. And finally, Americans of all races need to continue advocating for more professional scrutiny of narratives that claim to be culturally progressive while perpetuating racial inequities and stereotypes.

ACKNOWLEDGMENTS

THERE IS ARGUABLY NO BETTER PLACE to write a book about modern interracialism than a Catholic university, and the University of Notre Dame must be one of the best. It would have been impossible to visit and revisit archives, and acquire dozens of rare books featured in this study, without generous financial backing and support from the College of Arts and Letters; Rachel Bohlmann, Notre Dame's American History Librarian and Curator of North Americana; the Office of the Provost's Resilience and Recovery Grant Program; and various grants administered by the Institute for Scholarship in the Liberal Arts. A short visiting professorship awarded by the University of Florida's Baldwin Library of Historical Children's Literature was crucial to the development of the book's chapter on this topic.

My editor at Princeton University Press, Anne Savarese, recognized the significance of this book and firmly supported the development of every single chapter in the manuscript. Over the past two years, Anne's enthusiasm, encouragement, help polishing prose, keen advice, and wealth of experience made this project immeasurably stronger. I cannot thank her enough for guiding me through the arduous process of completing my first book. Anne's colleague James Collier went above and beyond in helping me put everything together at the final stages.

Over the years, countless people, places, and organizations have shaped this book and contributed in other ways. Warren Kaari, my cross-country coach in high school, was also an exceptional history teacher. I credit my decision to pursue academic work to outstanding mentorship from four historians who taught and advised me as an undergraduate: Anna Clark, Kevin Murphy, Lary May, and Michael Fitzgerald. My dissertation committee at the University of Chicago deserves special thanks. Kenneth Warren's literary expertise was vital in developing this project. Thomas Holt inspired me to ground my ideas within the traditions of the historical discipline, while never asking me to abandon my focus on either writers or fiction. Before I even arrived as a student in the Department of History, Adam Green's brilliant scholarship provided a model for my own research agenda.

It is highly unlikely that I could have found better roommates in Hyde Park than Patrick Dexter and Gautham Reddy. Gautham's friendship and his knowledge of literary history are unparalleled. Patrick taught me how to have more fun traveling (or just hanging around the house) than I thought was humanly possible. At the tail end of graduate school, with Morgan Ng's expert matchmaking, Tomashi Jackson and Nia Evans opened their home in Cambridge to me, which took the archival research for this project to a new level. A number of new and old friends and colleagues have remained steady interlocutors in and far away from Chicago and Minneapolis, my hometown. Special thanks go to Michael Pierson, Elena Comay del Junco, Diana Schwartz Francisco, Tessa Murphy, Chris Dingwall, Ricardo Rivera, Haakon Bratli Sheffield, Audun Hellemo, Hilde Reinertsen, Thor Indseth, Kamini Balakrishnan, Phillip Henry, Emma Broder, Kate Wulfson, Kai Parker, Ashley Finigan, Darryl Heller, Oliver Cussen, Keith Hernandez, Jon Reid, Sarah Miller-Davenport, Corey Rateau, Ben Shepard, Tobi Haslett, Angelica Baldwin, Chad Kampe, Matt Felt, Peter Crandall, Joey Heinen, James Andrew, Ryan Murphy, Ariel Dumas, Maren Bush, Robert Carr, David Parkes, Swathi Reddy, Peter Tomka, and Jonathan Kornman.

In South Bend, Ashlee Bird, Jaimie Bleck, Peter Cajka, Katlyn Carter, Annie Coleman, Kathleen Sprows Cummings, Nilesh Fernando, Ben Giamo, Randy Goldstein, Dan Graff, Perin Gürel, Spencer Hawkins, Richard Herbst, Bridget Hoyt, Richard Jones, Jake Lundberg, Chanté Mouton Kinyon, Sara Marcus, Kate Marshall, Rebecca McKenna, Brandon Menke, Nikhil Menon, Julie Morrissy, Ian Newman, Emily Remus, Francisco Robles, Roy Scranton, James Searl, Sarah Shortall, Idrissa Sidibe, Victoria St. Martin, Bob Walls, and Sophie White have made life in northern Indiana more entertaining and intellectually stimulating than I could have ever imagined. My faculty writing group, Tarryn Chun, Jennifer Huynh, Sonja Stojanovic, Emily Wang, and Xian Wang, banded together to finish our first books, frequently balancing our professional work with celebrations. Over the past few years, Josh Specht was willing to read every word of this manuscript, suggesting and discussing invaluable revisions both on and off the tennis court. No one knows the ins and outs of this book better than John Fisher, who has cared deeply about this project since our time together at the University of Chicago. This study would not be the same without John's friendship, writing advice, criticism, honesty, and boundless passion for research, books, and reading for pleasure. I look forward to our future plans and pacts.

Mark Sanders, Dianne Pinderhughes, José E. Limón, Renata Limón, Timothy Stewart-Winter, Nicholas Forster, Jarvis McInnis, Koritha Mitchell, Mary Helen Washington, Aaron Lecklider, Kevin Mumford, Kinohi Nishikawa, Lindsay Waters, and Werner Sollors offered feedback and encouragement at key moments of this project. My colleagues in the Department of American Studies at the University of Notre Dame have been exceptionally generous with their time and intellectual engagements with my work. Nothing in our department, including this book, would be possible without Katie Schlotfeldt's unstinting support. Our department chair, Jason Ruiz, has been one of my dearest friends since my days as an undergraduate in Minnesota. As a colleague, he has offered incisive feedback on this project. Two senior colleagues, Tom Tweed and Erika Doss, played outsized roles in sharpening the manuscript and, most importantly, the stakes of this project; after workshopping an early draft of the book with Laura Dassow Walls after my first year at Notre Dame, Tom and Erika have continued to be invaluable interlocutors. Over the past five years, Erika has spent more time in the office with me on weekends discussing a mix of art, monuments, and scholarship than either of us could possibly quantify; without question, her friendship has given this book more substance.

While finishing this project, my family in New Orleans and Minneapolis has been more patient with me than I deserve. I owe my dad a special thanks for ensuring that I took more vacations than I can remember. My paternal family's commitments to education are truly exceptional, and it is doubtful that I would have become an academic without their ideals and outstanding tradition of service. My older sister introduced me to Slavic literature, showed me St. Petersburg, and inspired me to take Russian at a pivotal moment in college. No one in the world has given me more books, money, love, and time than my mom. I dedicate this book to her, for teaching me how to read and for always answering when I call.

NOTES

Introduction

1. See, for example, "Georgia Wins High Rank on Race Relations Schomburg Honor Roll," *Alabama Tribune* [Montgomery, AL], February 14, 1947, 1; "Race Relations Honor Roll," *The Capital Times* [Madison, WI], February 17, 1947, 18; "Race Relations Honor Roll of 1946 Lists 18 Leaders," *The Pittsburgh Courier*, February 15, 1947, 23.

2. For an overview of the film adaptation of *Foxes of Harrow*, and Black-authored precursors to this film, see Charlene Regester, "African-American Writers and Pre-1950 Cinema," *Literature/Film Quarterly* 29, no. 3 (2001): 210–225.

3. "Does Hollywood See the Light? New Pictures to Stick Closer to Facts," *Chicago Defender*, March 19, 1949, 18.

4. Review: "*The Vixens*. By Frank Yerby," *The Washington Post*, April 27, 1947, S11.

5. "WSCS Meeting Held at Home in New Paris," *Palladium-Item* [Richmond, IN], February 26, 1948, 9.

6. For an important sample of some of the recently published scholarship on Yerby, see James L. Hill, "An Interview with Frank Gavin Yerby," *Resources for American Literary Study* 21, no. 1 (1995): 206–239; Gene Andrew Jarrett, "The Race Problem Was *Not* a Theme for Me," in *Deans and Truants: Race and Realism in African American Literature* (Philadelphia: University of Pennsylvania Press, 2006), 143–166; Stephanie Brown, "Frank Yerby and the 'Costume Drama' of Southern Historiography," in *The Postwar African American Novel: Protest and Discontent, 1945–1950* (Jackson: University Press of Mississippi, 2011), 67–98; John C. Charles, "Sympathy for the Master: Reforming Southern White Manhood in Frank Yerby's *The Foxes of Harrow*," in *Abandoning the Black Hero: Sympathy and Privacy in the Postwar African American White-Life Novel* (New Brunswick, NJ: Rutgers University Press, 2012), 130–157; Mark A. Jerng, "Reconstruction of Racial Perception: Margaret Mitchell's and Frank Yerby's Plantation Romances," in James A. Crank, ed., *New Approaches to "Gone with the Wind"* (Baton Rouge: Louisiana State University Press, 2015), 38–65; Matthew Teutsch, "'Our Women . . . Are Ladies': Frank Yerby's Deconstruction of White Southern Womanhood in *Speak Now*," *College Language Association Journal* 60, no. 3 (2018): 334–347.

7. W.E.B. Du Bois, *Mansart Builds a School* (New York: Mainstream Publishers, 1959), 144.

8. James Baldwin to Lorraine Hansberry, no date, Box 63, Folder 15, Lorraine Hansberry Papers, Schomburg Center for Research in Black Culture, New York Public Library.

9. Broadus N. Butler, "The Detroit Reality: A Revolt against Alienation," *Negro Digest* 17, no. 1 (November 1967): 37.

10. Werner Sollors, ed., *An Anthology of Interracial Literature: Black-White Contacts in the Old World and the New* (New York: New York University Press, 2004), 165.

11. Jessie Fauset, "A Good Fight: How a Negro Lad Overcame Poverty and Prejudice and Won Success," *Everyland: A Magazine of World Friendship for Boys and Girls* 11, no. 7 (July 1920): 199.

12. "William Stanley Braithwaite," *The Crisis* 69, no. 6 (June–July 1962): 343.

13. W. S. Braithwaite, "Some Contemporary Poets of the Negro Race," *The Crisis*, April 1919, 277.

14. Claude McKay, *A Long Way from Home*, ed. Gene Andrew Jarrett (New Brunswick, NJ: Rutgers University Press, 2007 [1937]), 26–27.

15. See, for example, Dudley Randall's profile of W. S. Braithwaite, "White Poet, Black Critic," *Negro Digest* 14, no. 4 (February 1965): 46–48.

16. George Hutchinson's meticulous survey of the publishing world in the 1910s, and his painstaking documentation of the critical recognition of Black literature and culture over the 1920s, remains the most thorough investigation of the movement's biracial character. Hutchinson's scholarship on this era explicitly countered popular and scholarly attacks on early twentieth-century interracialism, which underpinned many important achievements of the Harlem Renaissance period. See Hutchinson, *The Harlem Renaissance in Black and White* (Cambridge, MA: Harvard University Press, 1995), 1–7. There are dozens of excellent scholarly works on the Harlem Renaissance. A small sample of canonical scholarship on the Harlem Renaissance includes Nathan Irvin Huggins, *Harlem Renaissance* (Oxford: Oxford University Press, 1971); David Levering Lewis, *When Harlem Was in Vogue* (New York: Penguin Books, 1980); Charles R. Larson, *Invisible Darkness: Nella Larsen and Jean Toomer* (Iowa City: University of Iowa Press, 1993).

17. For three important recent works on the interracial and transnational dimensions of the Harlem Renaissance, see, for example, Carla Kaplan, *Miss Anne in Harlem: The White Women of the Black Renaissance* (New York: HarperCollins, 2013); Brent Hayes Edwards, *The Practice of Diaspora: Literature, Translation, and the Rise of Black Internationalism* (Cambridge, MA: Harvard University Press, 2003); Fionnghuala Sweeney, *Afromodernisms: Paris, Harlem and the Avant-Garde* (Edinburgh: Edinburgh University Press, 2013).

18. Important and illuminating exceptions include A Yẹmisi Jimoh, "Mapping the Terrain of Black Writing during the Early New Negro Era," *College Literature* 42, no. 3 (Summer 2015): 488–524; Trudier Harris, ed., *Afro-American Writers before the Harlem Renaissance* (Detroit, MI: Gale Research, 1986); Harold Bloom, *Black American Prose Writers before the Harlem Renaissance* (New York: Chelsea House, 1994); Ernest Allen Jr., "'The New Negro': Explorations in Identity and Social Consciousness, 1910–1922," in Adele Heller and Louis Rudnick, eds., *1915: The Cultural Moment* (New Brunswick, NJ: Rutgers University Press, 1991), 48–68; William J. Moses, "The Lost World of the Negro, 1895–1919: Black Literary and Intellectual Life before the 'Renaissance,'" *Black American Literature Forum* 21, nos. 1/2 (Spring–Summer 1987): 61–84.

19. Daylanne K. English, "Selecting the Harlem Renaissance," *Critical Inquiry* 25, no. 4 (Summer 1999): 808. Other recent scholarship questioning how scholars and general commentators memorialize the Harlem Renaissance includes Gene Jarrett, "The Harlem Renaissance and Its Indignant Aftermath: Rethinking Literary History and Political Action after Black Studies," *American Literary History* 24, no. 4 (Winter 2012): 775–795.

20. "To Contributors," *The Champion* 1, no. 1 (September 1916): 37.

21. Fenton Johnson, "The Braithwaite Anthology," *The Champion* 1, no. 7 (March 1917): 367.

22. Workers of the Writers' Program of the Works Progress Administration in the State of Illinois, *Cavalcade of the American Negro* (Chicago: Diamond Jubilee Exposition, 1940), 10.

23. Liesl Olson, *Chicago Renaissance: Literature and Art in the Midwest Metropolis* (New Haven, CT: Yale University Press, 2017), 290.

24. Workers of the Writers' Program of the Works Progress Administration in the State of Illinois, *Cavalcade of the American Negro*, 43.

25. Werner Sollors, ed., *Neither Black nor White yet Both: Thematic Explorations of Interracial Literature* (Cambridge, MA: Harvard University Press, 1997), 1.

26. "The Courier Salutes," *The Pittsburgh Courier*, September 18, 1948, 7.

27. Alice P. Hackett qtd. in Gertrude Martin, "Bookshelf," *The Chicago Defender*, March 8, 1947, 13.

28. Alfred Smith, "Adventures in Race Relations," *The Chicago Defender*, February 15, 1947.

29. Harry Keelan, "Voice in the Wilderness," *Afro-American* [Baltimore, MD], October 18, 1947, 4.

30. Langston Hughes, *New Pittsburgh Courier*, October 23, 1965, 9.

31. Frank Yerby, "Health Card," in Langston Hughes, ed., *The Best Short Stories by Negro Writers: Anthology from 1899 to the Present* (Boston: Little, Brown and Company, 1967), 192–201.

32. Imamu Amiri Baraka, "In the Midst of Chaos," *Black World* 22, no. 7 (May 1973): 42.

33. Kathleen Collins, "Whatever Happened to Interracial Love?" in *Whatever Happened to Interracial Love?* (London: Granta, 2017), 57.

34. See, for example, Alex Lubin, ed., *Revising the Blueprint: Ann Petry and the Literary Left* (Jackson: University of Mississippi, 2007); Lawrence Jackson, *The Indignant Generation: A Narrative History of African American Writers and Critics, 1934–1960* (Princeton, NJ: Princeton University Press, 2011); Mary Helen Washington, *The Other Blacklist: The African American Literary and Cultural Left of the 1950s* (New York: Columbia University Press, 2014); Jeffrey C. Stewart, *The New Negro: The Life of Alain Locke* (Oxford: Oxford University Press, 2017); George Hutchinson, *Facing the Abyss: American Literature and Culture in the 1940s* (New York: Columbia University Press, 2018); Saidiya Hartman, *Wayward Lives, Beautiful Experiments: Intimate Histories of Riotous Black Girls, Troublesome Women and Queer Radicals* (New York: W. W. Norton, 2019).

35. See, for example, Jean-Christophe Cloutier, *Shadow Archives: The Lifecycles of African American Literature* (New York: Columbia University Press, 2019). For an overview of the uptick and reemergence of archival research in scholarship on African American literature, see Britt Rusert, "From Black Lit to Black Print: The Return to the Archive in African American Literary Studies," *American Quarterly* 68, no. 4 (December 2016): 993–1005.

36. Chester Himes, unidentified essay draft, no date, Box 22, Folder 225, Chester Himes Papers, Beinecke Rare Book and Manuscript Library, Collection of American Literature, Yale University.

37. William Rose Benét, *Poems for Youth: An American Anthology* (New York: E. P. Dutton, 1925), xxxii.

38. W. S. Braithwaite to W.E.B. Du Bois, July 4, 1934, W.E.B. Du Bois Papers (MS 312), Special Collections and University Archives, University of Massachusetts Amherst Libraries.

39. See, for example, Mia Bay, *The White Image in the Black Mind: African-American Ideas about White People* (Oxford: Oxford University Press, 2000); Charles, *Abandoning the Black Hero*; Stephanie Li, *Playing in the White: Black Writers, White Subjects* (Oxford: Oxford University Press, 2014).

40. William Maxwell, *F.B. Eyes: How J. Edgar Hoover's Ghostreaders Framed African American Literature* (Princeton, NJ: Princeton University Press, 2015).

41. On Braithwaite's life and career, see Lisa Szefel, "Encouraging Verse: William S. Braithwaite and the Poetics of Race," *The New England Quarterly* 74, no. 1 (March 2001): 32–61; Lisa Szefel, "Beauty and William Braithwaite," *Callaloo* 29, no. 2 (Spring 2006): 560–586; Kenny J. Williams, "William Stanley Braithwaite," in Harris, *Afro-American Writers before the Harlem Renaissance*, 7–18; Kenny J. Williams, "An Invisible Partnership and an Unlikely Relationship: William Stanley Braithwaite and Harriet Monroe," *Callaloo* 32 (Summer 1987): 516–550; Craig S. Abbott, "Magazine Verse and Modernism: Braithwaite's Anthologies," *Journal of Modern Literature* 19, no. 1 (Summer 1994): 151–159; Philip Butcher, "W. S. Braithwaite's Southern Exposure: Rescue and Revelation," *The Southern Literary Journal* 2, no. 2 (Spring 1971): 49–61; Philip Butcher, "William Stanley Braithwaite and the College Language Association," *CLA Journal* 15, no. 2 (December 1971): 117–125; Philip Butcher, ed., *The William Stanley Braithwaite Reader* (Ann Arbor: University of Michigan Press, 1972); Glenn Clairmonte, "The Cup-Bearer: William Stanley Braithwaite of Boston," *CLA Journal* 17, no. 1 (September 1973): 101–108. In addition to these sources and my own archival research, my examination of Braithwaite's career in this study is indebted to George Hutchinson's *The Harlem Renaissance in Black and White*, which traces this poet's legacy with both primary and secondary sources, including the editor's manuscript collection preserved at Harvard's Houghton Library. See Hutchinson, *Harlem Renaissance in Black and White*, 40, 112, 149–152, 349–360.

42. Robert Goldfarb qtd. in "Minority Manpower in Publishing," *Publishers' Weekly* 195, no. 5 (February 3, 1969): 34–35.

43. James Baldwin, "Letter from a Region in My Mind," *The New Yorker*, November 17, 1962, 108.

44. Allyson Hobbs, *A Chosen Exile: A History of Racial Passing in American Life* (Cambridge, MA: Harvard University Press, 2014), 5–9.

Chapter 1. How to Segregate a Renaissance

1. "Honor to a Negro Poet-Critic," *Reedy's Mirror* 27, no. 19 (May 10, 1918): 275.

2. Carter G. Woodson, *The Negro in Our History* (Washington, DC: Associated Publishers, 1922), 304.

3. Robert Alden Sanborn, "The All-America Ten Poets," *The Poetry Journal* 4, no. 2 (October 1915): 66.

4. Caroline Giltinan to W. S. Braithwaite, October 31, 1914, bMS Am 1444 (414), William Stanley Braithwaite Papers, Houghton Library, Harvard University (hereafter WSB).

5. W.E.B. Du Bois, *Mansart Builds a School* (New York: Mainstream Publishers, 1959), 77.

6. Alain Locke, "The Negro Poets of the United States," in W. S. Braithwaite, ed., *Anthology of Magazine Verse for 1926 and Yearbook of American Poetry* (Boston: B. J. Brimmer and Company, 1925), 149.

7. Du Bois, *Mansart Builds a School*, 77, 82.

8. Between the mid-1910s and the mid-1920s, Braithwaite was widely recognized as the preeminent Black cultural professional in the literary field, especially by African American peers. In 1925, one Black journalist identified Braithwaite as the "first American Negro to break away from this momentous issue of race, and writing on lofty themes," which this commentator described as one of "the essentials of good literature." Three years earlier, Woodson asserted that Braithwaite's "literary production and criticism won much consideration for the Negroes [...] by demonstrating that the Negro intellect is capable of the same achievements as that of the whites. In his poems, his annual publications, the *Anthology of Magazine Verse*, and his numerous literary criticisms appearing from time to time in the leading publications of this country, Mr. Braithwaite, although a man of African blood, is accepted as one of the foremost literary critics of our day." The range of Braithwaite's literary contributions Woodson outlines is helpful for understanding how expansive the "poetic renaissance" before the 1920s was. Zenobia A. Alexander, "Views and Reviews," *The Buffalo American*, March 26, 1925, 3; Woodson, *Negro in Our History*, 304.

9. W. S. Braithwaite, "Autobiography and Reminiscence," in Philip Butcher, ed., *The William Stanley Braithwaite Reader* (Ann Arbor: University of Michigan Press, 1972), 163.

10. Ibid., 162, 159–166.

11. Ibid., 178.

12. W.E.B. Du Bois to Rufus Clement, memorandum, June 13, 1938, W.E.B. Du Bois Papers (MS 312), Special Collections and University Archives, University of Massachusetts Amherst Libraries (hereafter DBP).

13. For the data and factors influencing book production in these years, see "Book Production in 1906 in the United States," in *The Annual American Catalog* (New York: Office of the *Publishers' Weekly*, 1907), vii. For the figure for 1910, and what librarian William Warner Bishop echoed contemporaries in terming "our literary deluge," see Bishop, "Training in the Use of Books," *Sewanee Review* 20, no. 3 (July 1912): 268.

14. "The Books of 1912," *Publishers' Weekly*, January 25, 1913, 249. On the cultural shift from Victorianism to modernism in the United States before World War I, see, for example, Henry May, *The End of American Innocence: A Study of First Years of Our Own Time, 1912–1917* (New York: Knopf, 1959); Thomas Tweed, *The American Encounter with Buddhism, 1844–1912: Victorian Culture and the Limits of Dissent* (Chapel Hill: University of North Carolina, 2000).

15. Jane Heap, "Lost: A Renaissance," *The Little Review* 21, no. 2 (May 1929): 5.

16. William Stanley Braithwaite, "Poetry of the Years—12th Annual Review," *Boston Transcript*, October 30, 1915, 6–7.

17. Lisa Szefel, "Encouraging Verse: William S. Braithwaite and the Poetics of Race," *The New England Quarterly* 74, no. 1 (March 2001): 33.

18. Georgia Douglas Johnson to W.E.B. Du Bois, January 16, 1924, DBP. Georgia Douglas Johnson, *The Heart of a Woman and Other Poems*, intro. by William Stanley Braithwaite (Boston: Cornhill Company, 1918). For the Jean Toomer references to Johnson referred to in her letter

to Du Bois, see W. S. Braithwaite, *Anthology of Magazine Verse for 1923 and Yearbook of American Poetry* (Boston: B. J. Brimmer, 1923), 94–95.

19. See, for example, W. S. Braithwaite, "The Negro in American Literature," in the now-canonical Alain Locke, ed., *The New Negro: An Interpretation* (New York: Albert and Charles Boni, 1925), 29–46.

20. Chestyn Everett, "'Tradition' in Afro-American Literature," *Black World* 25, no. 2 (December 1975): 25.

21. W. S. Braithwaite, *Anthology of Magazine Verse for 1917* (Boston: Small, Maynard & Company, 1917), x. Braithwaite's commentary circulated elsewhere. See Braithwaite, "The Year in Poetry [1916]," *The Bookman: A Magazine of Literature and Life* 45 (May 1917): 278–282. In a short unattributed essay, *Publishers' Weekly* also reprinted Braithwaite's comments: "Mr. Braithwaite on the Poetry of 1917," *Publishers' Weekly* 93, no. 1 (January 5, 1918): 12–13.

22. Walter Neale to Major John R. Lynch, January 13, 1913, in Darlene Clark Hine and John McCluskey, eds., *The Black Chicago Renaissance* (Urbana: University of Illinois Press, 2012), 7. The book Neale and Lynch were discussing was published as John R. Lynch, *The Facts of Reconstruction* (New York: Neale, 1913).

23. C. E. Bechhofer, *The Literary Renaissance in America* (London: William Heinemann, 1923), viii. Despite his awareness of an "interplay" of "various cultural and racial forces" facilitating America's nascent renaissance, numerous omissions—but arguably none more so than Black authorship—haunt Bechhofer's tentative overview of the movement.

24. Ezra Pound qtd. in Aldon Lynn Nielsen, "Ezra Pound and 'the Best-Known Colored Man in United States,'" *Paideuma: Modern and Contemporary Poetry and Poetics* 29, nos. 1/2 (Spring and Fall 2000): 152.

25. Ezra Pound qtd. in Edward Marx, *The Idea of a Colony: Cross-Culturalism in Modern Poetry* (Toronto: University of Toronto Press, 2004), 165.

26. W. S. Braithwaite to Messrs. L. C. Page & Co., April 3, 1899, in Butcher, *William Stanley Braithwaite Reader*, 237.

27. In ibid., 177.

28. Ibid., 182.

29. Kenny J. Williams, "William Stanley Braithwaite," in Trudier Harris, ed., *Afro-American Writers before the Harlem Renaissance* (Detroit, MI: Gale Research, 1986), 9.

30. Herbert B. Turner & Company advertisement accompanying a first edition of W. S. Braithwaite's *Lyrics of Life and Love* (Boston: Herbert B. Turner, 1904). In author's possession.

31. "New of the Book World: A New Negro Poet," *The Minneapolis Journal*, September 15, 1904, 4. See also, for example, contemporary newspaper coverage of Braithwaite's *Lyrics of Life and Love* in a variety of formats: "Forthcoming Books," *The Buffalo Commercial*, September 1, 1904, 5; "Review of the New Books," *The Indianapolis News*, September 3, 1904, 7; "Men, Women and Books: A New Negro Poet, Whose Genius Is Highly Appreciated in Boston—Notes of New Publications," *The Brooklyn Daily Eagle*, September 3, 1904; "Lyrics of Life and Love," *The New York Times*, September 10, 1904, 602; "Books and Authors," *The Washington Post*, September 10, 1904, 11; "Literary Notes and Gossip: Items of Interest from the World of Letters," *The Inter Ocean*, October 1, 1904, 7.

32. Pero Gaglo Dagbovie, "Reflections on Conventional Portrayals of the African American Experience during the Progressive Era or 'the Nadir,'" *Journal of the Gilded Age and Progressive Era* 13, no. 1 (January 2014): 4–27.

33. "New York City News: A New Poet of the Race Looms Up in Boston," *The Broad Ax*, July 15, 1905, 1.

34. "United Daughters of the Confederacy," *The Montgomery Advertiser*, March 26, 1905, 11.

35. Doubleday, Page & Company advertisement for Thomas Dixon, *The Traitor* (New York: Doubleday, Page & Company, 1907), in "The World's Work Advertiser," *The World's Work*, November 1907, 65.

36. See, for example, Rebecca Burns, *Rage in the Gate City: The Story of the 1906 Atlanta Race Riot* (Athens: University of Georgia Press, 2009).

37. "The Chautauqua in Full Swing," *Independence Daily Reporter*, July 14, 1906, 1.

38. "William Stanley Braithwaite," *New York Age*, March 3, 1910, 4.

39. Butcher, *William Stanley Braithwaite Reader*, 3.

40. Szefel, "Encouraging Verse," 42.

41. "Awakened Interest in the Negro Problem," *The Vicksburg American*, January 10, 1907, 4.

42. Ray Stannard Baker to W.E.B. Du Bois, March 29, 1907, DBP.

43. Walter Hines Page to Charles Chesnutt, March 30, 1898, Houghton MS AM 2535, Houghton Library, Harvard University.

44. Roberta Senechal de la Roche, *In Lincoln's Shadow: The 1908 Race Riot in Springfield, Illinois* (Carbondale: Southern Illinois University Press, 2008).

45. James Weldon Johnson to Brander Matthews, ca. November 1908, in Johnson, *The Autobiography of an Ex-Colored Man: Norton Critical Edition*, ed. Jacqueline Goldsby (New York: W. W. Norton, 2015), 221–222.

46. Brander Matthews, "American Character in American Fiction: Three Books Which Depict the Actualities of Present-Day Life," *Munsey's Magazine* 49, no. 5 (August 1913): 798.

47. James Weldon Johnson qtd. in Lawrence J. Oliver, "'Stepping across the Confines of Language and Race': Brander Matthews, James Weldon Johnson, and Racial Cosmopolitanism," in Noelle Morrissette, ed., *New Perspectives on James Weldon Johnson's "The Autobiography of an Ex-Colored Man"* (Athens: University of Georgia Press, 2017), 23–24.

48. Mary White Ovington, *Black and White Sat Down Together: The Reminiscences of an NAACP Founder*, ed. Ralph E. Luker (New York: Feminist Press at City University of New York, 1995), 32.

49. W.E.B. Du Bois, "Harvard and Democracy" (ca. 1925), DBP.

50. W.E.B. Du Bois, "Reconstruction and its Benefits," *American Historical Review* 15, no. 4 (July 1910): 781–799.

51. W.E.B. Du Bois, "Editing 'The Crisis,'" *The Crisis* 58, no. 3 (March 1951): 148.

52. Hilda's October 29, 1911, letter is quoted in Hilda Sail Polacheck, *I Came a Stranger: The Story of a Hull-House Girl*, ed. Dena J. Polacheck Epstein (Urbana: University of Illinois Press, 1989), 214 n. 5.

53. Gertrude Stein, *The Autobiography of Alice B. Toklas* (New York: Harcourt, Brace, 1933), 66.

54. Carl Van Vechten to Gertrude Stein, October 23, 1933, in Edward Burns, ed., *The Letters of Gertrude Stein and Carl Van Vechten, 1913–1946* (New York: Columbia University Press, 1986), 281–282. Van Vechten claimed that this was a direct quote from a letter written by James Weldon Johnson.

55. Georgiana Goddard King, "A Review of Two Worlds: Gertrude Stein," *The International*, June 13, 1913, 157. A clipping of King's essay is preserved in Box 77, Folder 1408, Gertrude Stein

and Alice B. Toklas Papers, Yale Collection of American Literature, Beinecke Rare Book and Manuscript Library, Yale University.

56. F. H. Hitchcock to Gertrude Stein, February 23, 1910, Box 108, Folder 2172, Gertrude Stein and Alice B. Toklas Papers, Yale Collection of American Literature, Beinecke Rare Book and Manuscript Library, Yale University.

57. "What to Read: Archer's Afro-America," *The Crisis* 1, no. 2 (December 1910): 30.

58. William James qtd. in James R. Mellow, *Charmed Circle: Gertrude Stein and Company* (New York: Avon, 1976), 182.

59. Stein, *Autobiography of Alice B. Toklas*, 96–97. Stein maintained several friendships with African Americans, and her help was crucial in Richard Wright's ability to secure a visa—after he was denied—to move his family to France in 1946. See M. Lynn Weiss, *Gertrude Stein and Richard Wright: The Poetics and Politics of Modernism* (Jackson: University Press of Mississippi, 1998), xii.

60. Lennox Strong, "Diary of Alice James," *The Ladder: A Lesbian Review* 10, no. 3 (December 1965): 23–25.

61. Joel Elias Spingarn, *The New Criticism: A Lecture Delivered at Columbia University, March 9, 1910* (New York: Columbia University Press, 1911), 31.

62. See, for example, the advertisement for *The New Criticism* published by Columbia University Press in "The Crisis Advertiser," *The Crisis* 8, no. 4 (August 1914): 205.

63. Edward D. Pickering, "The Roots of New Criticism," *The Southern Literary Journal* 41, no. 1 (Fall 2008): 93–108; John Crowe Ransom, *The New Criticism* (Norfolk, VA: New Directions, 1941); John L. Grigsby, "The Poisonous Snake in the Garden: Racism in the Agrarian Movement," *CLA Journal* 34 (September 1990): 32–43.

64. For a sample of important scholarly texts featuring or discussing Fauset's career amid other Black female contributions to early twentieth-century print culture in the United States, see Gloria Hull, *Color, Sex and Poetry: Three Women Writers of the Harlem Renaissance* (Bloomington: Indiana University Press, 1987); Cheryl A. Wall, *Women of the Harlem Renaissance* (Bloomington: Indiana University Press, 1995); Thadious Davis, *Nella Larsen: Novelist of the Harlem Renaissance: A Woman's Life Unveiled* (Baton Rouge: Louisiana State University Press, 1996); Lorraine Elena Roses and Ruth Elizabeth Randolph, eds., *Harlem's Glory: Black Women Writing, 1900–1950* (Cambridge, MA: Harvard University Press, 1997); Lean'tin L. Bracks and Jessie Carney Smith, eds., *Black Women of the Harlem Renaissance Era* (Lanham, MD: Rowman & Littlefield, 2014); Maureen Honey, *Aphrodite's Daughters: Three Modernist Poets of the Harlem Renaissance* (New Brunswick, NJ: Rutgers University Press, 2016).

65. Jesse Fauset, "What to Read," *The Crisis* 3, no. 5 (March 1912): 211.

66. George Brett qtd. in John Timberman Newcomb, *How Did Poetry Survive? The Making of Modern American Verse* (Urbana: University of Illinois Press, 2012), 20–21.

67. See Macmillan's advertisements for Rabindranath Tagore's *The Gardener: Lyrics of Love and Life* in London's *Guardian*, October 21, 1913, 6; and October 28, 1913, 6. In at least two of the firm's promotions of Tagore's book that month, they borrowed from Braithwaite and subtitled the volume "lyrics of love and life." Given Braithwaite's stature in the early 1910s, references to his book published in these advertisements and in the preface to *The Gardener* were probably not accidental. Tagore's preface to *The Gardener* states: "Most of the lyrics of love and life, the translations of which from Bengali are published in this book, were written much earlier than

the series of religious poems contained in the book named *Gitanjali*." See Tagore, *The Gardener* (London: Macmillan, 1913).

68. Rabindranath Tagore to W.E.B. Du Bois, ca. July 12, 1929, DBP.

69. James Weldon Johnson to W. S. Braithwaite, July 27, 1911, bMS Am 1444, WSB.

70. W. S. Braithwaite, "Introduction," in Edward Smyth Jones, *Sylvan Cabin; A Centenary Ode on the Birth of Lincoln, and Other Verse* (Boston: Sherman, French, 1911), 5.

71. Werner Sollors, Caldwell Titcomb, and Thomas A. Underwood, eds., *Blacks at Harvard: A Documentary History of African-American Experience at Harvard and Radcliffe* (New York: New York University Press, 1993), 153.

72. Charles Alexander, *Battles and Victories of Allen Allensworth* (Boston: Sherman, French & Company, 1914).

73. W. S. Braithwaite to Amy Lowell, August 22, 1915, B MS Lowell 19, Folder 130, Amy Lowell Correspondence, Houghton Library, Harvard University.

74. Frederick J. Hoffman, Charles Allen, and Carolyn F. Ulrich, eds., *The Little Magazine: A History and a Bibliography* (Princeton, NJ: Princeton University Press, 1947), 57.

75. Dorothea Lawrance Mann, "Mr. Braithwaite and a National Poetry," *The Bellman*, January 22, 1916, 100–101.

76. W. S. Braithwaite qtd. in Lorenzo Thomas, "Harriet Monroe: The Heavyweight Poetry Championship," in Aldon Lynn Nielsen, ed., *Reading Race in American Poetry: An Area of Act* (Chicago: University of Illinois Press, 2000), 94.

77. "Honor to a Negro Poet-Critic," 275.

78. "McClurg's Sell Out 'A Little Dreaming,'" *The Broad Ax*, September 20, 1913, 1.

79. E. A. Robinson, *The Kansas City Sun*, July 4, 1914, 1.

80. Claude McKay, *A Long Way from Home*, ed. Gene Andrew Jarrett (New Brunswick, NJ: Rutgers University Press, 2007 [1937]), 99.

81. The October 1916 cover of the *Pullman Porters' Review* declared that it was "A Publication For All The People" and "A National Magazine."

82. See Claire Badaracco, "Writers and Their Public Appeal: Harriet Monroe's Publicity Techniques," *American Literary Realism, 1870–1910* 23, no. 2 (Winter 1991): 35–51. Badaracco does not discuss Monroe's perspectives on interracialism, but she does offer a comprehensive overview of Monroe's extraordinary successes publicizing her work.

83. Harriet Monroe, "Modern American Poetry," *The Poetry Review* 10 (October 1912): 469.

84. Ibid.

85. Monroe was quoted in a short review essay, with no identified author, which summarized her perspectives on poetry in the United States. In addition to several lengthy excerpts of Monroe's "Modern American Poetry," this promotion of Monroe's *Poetry Review* essay appeared in the "Leading Articles of the Month" section of this periodical. "The Poetry of America," *The American Review of Reviews* 46, no. 6 (December 1912): 745.

86. Fenton Johnson's *A Little Dreaming* (Chicago: Standard Company, 1913) is listed among other "Books Received" in *Poetry* 3, no. 3 (December 1913): 114. Five years later, Johnson considered himself one of Monroe's colleagues and a sincere fan of her writing. In a letter to Monroe in 1918, Johnson praised her recently published poem "The Rose-bush." Likening it to one of Monroe's favorite authors, Johnson reported asking himself, "Has Miss Monroe joined the tribe of successors to Paul Laurence Dunbar?" Fenton Johnson to Harriet Monroe, April 8, 1918,

Box 76, Folder 23, *Poetry: A Magazine of Verse*, Records, Special Collections Research Center, University of Chicago Library.

87. Harriet Monroe, "Comments and Reviews: The Audience," *Poetry* 5, no. 1 (October 1914): 31. Also see Harriet Monroe, *A Poet's Life: Seventy Years in a Changing World* (New York: Macmillan, 1938), 366.

88. "Notes and Announcements," *Poetry: A Magazine of Verse* 1, no. 1 (October 1912): 31.

89. Pound stated this in an interview with Edd Johnson published in *The Chicago Sun*, May 9, 1945; also qtd. in Ira Nadel, *Modernism's Second Act: A Cultural Narrative* (New York: Palgrave, 2013), 34.

90. The United States indicted Pound for treason in July 1943. Of the eight persons indicted for broadcasting on "behalf of the Axis war effort," Pound was the only person charged who was not broadcasting from Germany during World War II. "8 Americans Broadcasting for Axis Cited for Treason," *The Minneapolis Star*, July 26, 1943, 16.

91. Excerpted in Marx, *Idea of a Colony*, 165.

92. Marius de Zayas, "Introductory Note," initially printed in the catalog for the *Negro Art Exhibition* at New York's 291 Gallery in November 1914; reprinted in de Zayas, *How, When and Why Modern Art Came to New York* (Cambridge, MA: MIT Press, 1996), 56.

93. "A Poem on the Negro," *The Crisis* 10, no. 1 (May 1915): 18.

94. Lucien Carey, unsigned article on "The Congo" etc., *The Dial* 57, no. 680 (October 16, 1914): 282.

95. Vachel Lindsay to W. B. Yeats, October 6, 1931, in Richard J. Finneran, George Mills Harper, and William M Murphy, eds., *Letters to W. B. Yeats*, vol. 2 (New York: Columbia University Press, 1977), 521–522. For another discussion of Monroe's dinner in Chicago for Yeats, see Ronald Schuchard, *The Last Minstrels: Yeats and the Revival of the Bardic Arts* (New York: Oxford University Press, 2008), 328–329.

96. Vachel Lindsay, *Adventures While Preaching the Gospel of Beauty* (New York: Mitchell Kennerley, 1914), 176.

97. "Poem on the Negro," 18.

98. Ibid.

99. W. S. Braithwaite, *Anthology of Magazine Verse for 1914 and Year Book of American Poetry* (New York: Laurence J. Gomme, 1914), 150.

100. Vachel Lindsay, *The Congo and Other Poems* (New York: Macmillan Company, 1914), 5; W. E. B. Du Bois, "The Looking Glass—Literature," *The Crisis* 12, no. 4 (August 1916): 182.

101. Bessie Graham, "The Home School for Booksellers," *Publishers' Weekly* 95, no. 3 (January 18, 1919): 136.

102. W.E.B. Du Bois, "Insulting Terms," *The Crisis* 7, no. 3 (January 1914): 126–127.

103. See Carl Sandburg, *Collected Poems* (New York: Harcourt, Brace and Company, 1950), 23–24.

104. Thomas, "Harriet Monroe," 93.

105. Carl Sandburg qtd. in Lisa Szefel, "Beauty and William Braithwaite," *Callaloo* 29, no. 2 (Spring 2006): 576.

106. Ibid.

107. During Braithwaite's tenure working at the Cornhill Company Press, in 1917 and 1918, the firm's publishing list included African American authors whose bound volumes of verse

ranged from almost entirely to virtually no use of racial dialect and at least one illustrated autobiography. These diverse works included James Weldon Johnson, *Fifty Years and Other Poems* (Boston: Cornhill Company, 1917); William Edwards, *Twenty-Five Years in the Black Belt* (Boston: Cornhill Company, 1918); Charles Bertram Johnson, *Songs of My People* (Boston: Cornhill Company, 1918); Johnson, *Heart of a Woman and Other Poems*; Waverley Turner Carmichael, *From the Heart of a Folk: A Book of Songs* (Boston: Cornhill Company, 1918); Joseph S. Cotter, *The Band of Gideon: And Other Lyrics* (Boston: Cornhill Company, 1918).

108. George Hutchinson, *The Harlem Renaissance in Black and White* (Cambridge, MA: Harvard University Press, 1995), 358–359.

109. Charles Chesnutt to Houghton Mifflin, October 8, 1921, Houghton bMS AM 1925 (366), Houghton Library, Harvard University.

110. Unnamed Houghton Mifflin employee to Charles Chesnutt, October 24, 1921, Houghton bMS AM 1925 (366), Houghton Library, Harvard University.

111. Fenton Johnson, *Tales of Darkest America* (Chicago: Favorite Magazine, 1920), 6–7. For scholarship on Johnson's career, see Lorenzo Thomas, "Fenton Johnson: The High Cost of Militance," in *Extraordinary Measures: Afrocentric Modernism and Twentieth-Century American Poetry* (Tuscaloosa: University of Alabama Press, 2000), 12–44; James P. Hutchinson, "Fenton Johnson: Pilgrim of the Dusk," *Studies in Black Literature* 7 (Autumn 1976): 14–15.

112. Clement Wood, "Nigger Hebb'n," "Debbil-Foot," and "De Glory Road," in *The Earth Turns South* (New York: E. P. Dutton, 1919), 17–23.

113. Untitled review, *The Brooklyn Daily Eagle*, May 24, 1919, 15.

114. W.H.C., "A Varying Muse: Clement Wood Pipes Well and Also Not So Well," *New-York Tribune*, July 5, 1919, 7.

115. "The Earth Turns South," *The Montgomery Advertiser*, July 14, 1919, 4.

116. Wood, "Nigger Hebb'n," 17–18.

117. Clement Wood, *Nigger: A Novel* (New York: E. P. Dutton, 1922).

118. William Thornton Whitsett, "Nigger," *The Charlotte Observer*, November 5, 1922, C4.

119. "Some Late Books," *The Montgomery Advertiser*, October 30, 1922, 4.

120. Brookes More to William Stanley Braithwaite, February 8, 1921, MS Am 1444 (809), WSB.

121. George Hutchinson has analyzed this letter and situated More's agitation with Wood in a broader discussion of conservative reactions against free verse. See Hutchinson, *Harlem Renaissance in Black and White*, 352–353.

122. More to Braithwaite, February 8, 1921.

123. Braithwaite, "Negro in American Literature," 35.

124. Clement Wood, "American Negro Poetry," *New York Evening Post*, June 10, 1922, 716.

125. Clement Wood, "A Man's Song," *New York Evening Post*, October 21, 1922, 127.

126. Clifford Gessler, "A Colored Nude Descends Stair amid Bouquets," *Honolulu Star-Bulletin*, September 6, 1924, 9.

127. John Weaver, "Personally Conducted," *Brooklyn Daily Eagle*, March 29, 1924, 4.

128. Fanny Butcher, "Dialect Hurdle Is High Hazard for New Firbank Yarn," *Chicago Daily Tribune*, March 22, 1924, 11.

129. In 1916, the essay Brander Matthews penned on this topic would be renamed when it was published as a book chapter, titled "The Decline and Fall of Negro-Minstrelsy," in *A Book*

about the Theater (New York: Charles Scribner's Sons, 1916), 217–234. Cultural historian Eric Lott also writes about this essay in *Love and Theft: Blackface Minstrelsy and the American Working Class* (New York: Oxford University Press, 1993), 34.

130. "A 'Prancing Nigger' among the New Books of Fiction," *New York Times Book Review*, March 23, 1924, 8, qtd. in Steven Moore, *Ronald Firbank: An Annotated Bibliography of Secondary Materials, 1905–1995* (Normal, IL: Dalkey Archive Press, 1996), 12.

131. Carl Van Vechten qtd. in Eric King Watts, *Hearing the Hurt: Rhetoric, Aesthetics, and Politics of the New Negro Movement* (Tuscaloosa: University of Alabama Press), 175.

132. Charles Chesnutt to W.E.B. Du Bois, October 27, 1926, WDP.

133. Charles Chesnutt to Oscar W. Baker, August 24, 1927, in Jesse S. Crisler, Robert C. Leitz III, and Joseph R. McElrath Jr., eds., *An Exemplary Citizen: Letters of Charles W. Chesnutt, 1906–1932* (Stanford, CA: Stanford University Press, 2002), 235.

134. "Dr. Du Bois Raps 'Nigger Heaven,'" *Pittsburgh Courier*, December 4, 1926, 11.

135. Charles Duane Van Vechten qtd. in Randall Kennedy, *Nigger: The Strange Career of a Troublesome Word* (New York: Knopf, 2008), 101.

136. Eric Walrond, "The Word 'Nigger,'" *Negro World*, February 4, 1922, reprinted in Tony Martin, ed., *African Fundamentalism: A Literary and Cultural Anthology of Garvey's Harlem* (Dover, DE: Majority Press), 100.

137. "Suggested that the Term 'Nigger' be Adopted," in Monroe Work, ed., *Negro Year Book: An Annual Encyclopedia of the Negro* (Tuskegee, AL: Negro Year Book Publishing Company, 1925), 82. Literary scholar Aldon Lynn Nielsen has suggested that for poets like "Carl Sandburg and Robert Frost, the vocabulary of white racism was one they spoke with fluency and with few signs of self-consciousness." This is true, to an extent. There were surprisingly few objections to white authors using the term *nigger* in their books during the 1910s. As Walrond's 1922 essay indicates, Black critics of the term were not silent. Nielsen, *Reading Race: White American Poets and the Racial Discourse in the Twentieth Century* (Athens: University of Georgia Press, 1988), 29. For other scholarship tracing how racism and segregation intersected with literary production in this period, see Nielsen, *Reading Race in American Poetry*; Andreas Müller-Hartmann, *The Discourse of Race and Southern Literature, 1890–1940* (Frankfurt: Peter Lang, 2000); Marx, *Idea of a Colony*; Frederik L. Rusch, ed., *A Jean Toomer Reader: Selected Unpublished Writings* (Oxford: Oxford University Press, 1993).

138. "Suggested that the Term 'Nigger' be Adopted," 82. See also Gwendolyn Bennett, "The Ebony Flute," *Opportunity*, October 1926, 356–358.

139. Carl Van Vechten, "Uncle Tom's Mansion," *New York Herald Tribune*, December 20, 1925, reprinted in Henry Louis Gates Jr. and Gene Andrew Jarrett, eds., *The New Negro: Readings on Race, Representation, and African American Culture, 1892–1938* (Princeton, NJ: Princeton University Press, 2008), 223–225.

140. Charles Chesnutt qtd. in Michael Nowlin, *Literary Ambition and the African American Novel* (Cambridge: Cambridge University Press, 2019), 36.

141. Heywood Broun, "It Seems to Me," *Buffalo Courier*, May 13, 1922, 6.

142. Carl Sandburg, *The Chicago Race Riots, July 1919* (New York: Harcourt, Brace and Howe, 1919), xx.

143. Jean Toomer to Waldo Frank, December 29, 1922, in Rusch, *Jean Toomer Reader*, 85. On Toomer's relationship with Anderson and Frank, see Mark Helbling, "Sherwood Anderson and

Jean Toomer," *Negro American Literature Forum* 9, no. 2 (1975): 35–39; Mark Helbling, "Jean Toomer and Waldo Frank: A Creative Friendship," *Phylon* 41 (1980): 167–178.

144. Sherwood Anderson, "The South," *Vanity Fair* 27 (September 1926): 49–50, 138, reprinted in Welford Dunaway Taylor and Charles E. Modlin, eds., *Southern Odyssey: Selected Writings by Sherwood Anderson* (Athens: University of Georgia Press, 1997), 33.

145. A few important studies on Toomer include Darwin T. Turner, ed., *The Wayward and the Seeking: A Collection of Writings by Jean Toomer* (Washington, DC: Howard University Press, 1980); George Hutchinson, "Jean Toomer and the 'New Negroes' of Washington," *American Literature* 63, no. 4 (1991): 683–692; Michael J. Krasny, "Jean Toomer's Life Prior to *Cane*: A Brief Sketch of the Emergence of a Black Writer," in Therman B. O'Daniel, ed., *Jean Toomer: A Critical Evaluation* (Washington, DC: Howard University Press, 1988), 41–45; William M. Ramsay, "Jean Toomer's Eternal South," *Southern Literary Journal*, Fall 2003, 74–89.

146. Herbert Gorman, "Tradition and Experiment in Modern Poetry," *New York Times Book Review*, March 27, 1927, 2.

147. George R. Stewart, "American Poetry," in Albert Bushnell Hart and William M. Schuyler, eds., *The American Year Book: A Record of Events and Progress* (Garden City, NY: Doubleday, Doran & Company Inc., 1928), 716.

148. Ibid.

149. Jean Toomer to Horace Liveright, September 5, 1923, in Rusch, *Jean Toomer Reader*, 94.

150. Jean Toomer to John McClure, June 30, 1922, excerpted in Cynthia Earl Kerman and Richard Eldridge, *The Lives of Jean Toomer: A Hunger for Wholeness* (Baton Rouge: Louisiana State University Press, 1987), 96.

151. Charles Egleston, ed., *Dictionary of Literary Biography: The House of Boni & Liveright, 1917–1933* (Detroit, MI: Thomson Gale, 2004), 307.

152. Herschel Brickell, "Two Books Deal with Negro at Opposite Poles," *Minneapolis Sunday Tribune*, April 20, 1924, 9.

153. R. P. Sims, "Music Festival at the Institute: Negro Art Will Hold Sway at Two-Day Festival Stages Tonight and Friday Night at Colored Institute," *Bluefield Daily Telegraph*, May 21, 1925, 11.

154. "Current Comment: A Negro Renaissance," *The Kingsport Times* [Kingsport, TN], May 8, 1925, 4.

155. Alexandre Dumas *père* qtd. in Eric Martone, *Finding Monte Cristo: Alexandre Dumas and the French Atlantic World* (Jefferson, NC: McFarland & Company, 2018), 41.

156. Alexander Pushkin to Peter Andreevich Vyazemsky, June 24 or 25, 1824, in J. Thomas Shaw, ed., *The Letters of Alexander Pushkin. Three Volumes in One* (Madison: University of Wisconsin Press, 1967), 161.

157. W. H. Ferris, "'Individuality' Is Race's Greatest Need," *Pittsburgh Courier*, November 27, 1926, 8.

158. McKay, *Long Way from Home*, 121.

159. Locke also claimed to be "dumb-struck by your attitude as you seem to be with mine. It is a simple enough proposition for the future—for I shall gladly respect your wishes to be left out [of subsequent revised editions of *The New Negro* (1925) anthology] and left alone." Alain Locke to Claude McKay, April 27, 1927, Box 5, Folder 138, Claude McKay Collection, James Weldon Johnson Manuscripts, Yale Collection of American Literature, Beinecke Rare Book and Manuscript Library, Yale University.

160. Alain Locke to Claude McKay, March 13, 1930, Box 5, Folder 138, Claude McKay Collection, James Weldon Johnson Manuscripts, Yale Collection of American Literature, Beinecke Rare Book and Manuscript Library, Yale University.

161. McKay, *Long Way from Home*, 208.

162. W. S. Braithwaite to Alain Locke, April 13, 1925, in Butcher, *William Stanley Braithwaite Reader*, 268.

163. Locke, "Negro Poets of the United States," 147.

164. Ferris, "'Individuality' Is Race's Greatest Need," 8.

165. Ezra Pound to Alice Corbin Henderson, October 14, 1916, in Ira Nadel, ed., *The Letters of Ezra Pound to Alice Corbin Henderson* (Austin: University of Texas Press, 1993), 170.

166. Mitchell Dawson, "Bring Out Your Dead: Braithwaite's Death-Cart," *The Little Review* 3, no. 4 (June–July 1916): 24.

167. Alice Corbin Henderson qtd. in Szefel, "Beauty and William Braithwaite," 576.

168. Newcomb, *How Did Poetry Survive?* 43.

169. Alice Corbin Henderson, "Poetry of the American Negro," *Poetry* 10, no. 3 (June 1917): 158.

170. Wood, "American Negro Poetry," 716.

171. Koritha Mitchell, "Identifying White Mediocrity and Know-Your-Place Aggression: A Form of Self-Care," *African American Review* 51, no. 4 (Winter 2018): 253.

172. Willard Wattles, "On Reading The Braithwaite Anthology for 1916," *Poetry* 10, no. 1 (April 1917): 52–54.

173. Consider, for example, Louis Untermeyer's claim that "Braithwaite's inclusiveness [in the 1915 anthology] makes all the more perplexing his omission of Carl Sandburg and Max Eastman. An anthology of the year's poetry with nothing from the pen of either of these poets is incredible." Untermeyer, "Poetry Comes Back," *The Masses* 8, no. 4 (February 1916): 6.

174. In 1916, Braithwaite declared: "Mr. Sandburg, a much-heralded innovator, has not lived up to prophecy." See W. S. Braithwaite, *Anthology of Magazine Verse for 1916 and Year Book of American Poetry* (New York: Laurence J. Gomme, 1916), xv.

175. Carl Sandburg to Alice Corbin Henderson, November 27, 1917, in Herbert Mitgang, ed., *The Letters of Carl Sandburg* (New York: Harcourt, Brace & World, 1968), 123–124.

176. John Gould Fletcher, *The Autobiography of John Gould Fletcher*, ed. Lucas Carpenter (Fayetteville: University of Arkansas Press, 1988), 229. This autobiography was originally published as Fletcher, *Life Is My Song: The Autobiography of John Gould Fletcher* (New York: Farrar & Rinehart, 1937).

177. H. L. Mencken to George Sterling, March 7, 1919, in S. T. Joshi, ed., *From Baltimore to Bohemia: The Letters of H. L. Mencken and George Sterling* (Madison, NJ: Fairleigh Dickinson University Press, 2001), 55.

178. Allen Tate qtd. in Müller-Hartmann, *Discourse of Race and Southern Literature, 1890–1940*, 136.

179. Ibid.

180. W. S. Braithwaite to Joel E. Spingarn, June 4, 1926, Box 1, Folder 1, Joel E. Spingarn Collection, Yale Collection of American Literature, Beinecke Rare Book and Manuscript Library, Yale University.

181. Twelve Southerners, *I'll Take My Stand; The South and the Agrarian Tradition* (New York: Harper, 1930).

182. Allen Tate, "The Fugitive 1922–1925: A Personal Recollection Twenty Years After," *The Princeton University Library Chronicle* 3, no. 3 (April 1942): 83.

183. Herman Clarence Nixon to W. T. Couch qtd. in Emily Bingham and Thomas A. Underwood, eds., *The Southern Agrarians and the New Deal: Essays after "I'll Take My Stand"* (Charlottesville: Published for the Southern Texts Society by the University Press of Virginia, 2001), 157–158.

184. Robert Penn Warren, "The Briar Patch," in Twelve Southerners, *I'll Take My Stand*, 251.

185. Anderson, "The South," 33.

186. For recent scholarship on this cultural epoch, see Sarah Gardner, *Reviewing the South: The Literary Marketplace and the Southern Renaissance, 1920–1941* (Cambridge: Cambridge University Press, 2017).

187. William Stanley Braithwaite, *Anthology of Magazine Verse for 1925 and Yearbook of American Poetry* (Boston: B. J. Brimmer and Company, 1925), xii.

188. Allen Tate's open letter to Tom Mabry is quoted in Thomas A. Underwood, *Allen Tate: Orphan of the South* (Princeton, NJ: Princeton University Press, 2000), 291.

189. Tom Mabry qtd. in George Hutchinson, *In Search of Nella Larsen: A Biography of the Color Line* (Cambridge, MA: Harvard University Press, 2006), 410.

190. Qtd. in Underwood, *Allen Tate*, 291.

191. James Smethurst, *African American Roots of Modernism: From Reconstruction to the Harlem Renaissance* (Chapel Hill: University of North Carolina Press, 2011), 153.

192. C. E. Bechhofer's excerpt of a lengthy passage from Sinclair Lewis's novel *Main Street* (New York: Harcourt, Brace, & Co., 1920) illustrated the former's candid interpretation of the American scene in the early twentieth century. "[Gopher Prairie, Minnesota] aspired to succeed Victorian England as the chief mediocrity of the world [. . .] seeking to dominate the earth, to drain the hills and seas of colour [. . .] and to dress the high gods in 'Klassy Kollege Klothes.'" According to Bechhofer, heightened demand for books like *Main Street* enabled the "willing self-analysis" that the fictive residents of Gopher Prairie lacked otherwise. Bechhofer, *Literary Renaissance in America*, 108–109.

193. Henderson qtd. in Szefel, "Beauty and William Braithwaite," 576.

194. H. B. Hunting to W.E.B. Du Bois, January 26, 1939, DBP.

195. Ezra Pound, "Small Magazines," *The English Journal* 19, no. 9 (November 1930): 689–704.

196. Moreover, as literary historian George Hutchinson has argued, the Harlem Renaissance was continuous with earlier interracial collaborations. See Hutchinson, *Harlem Renaissance in Black and White*, 19.

Chapter 2. Integration and Its Discontents

1. Langston Hughes's reflections on this new epoch illuminate this shift. In 1931, Hughes noted, "I have had the feeling for some time that the modern Negro Art Movement in America has been largely over the heads, and out of the reach, of the masses of the Negro people. Its appeal within the race has been mainly to a small group of 'intellectuals.'" Kelly Quinn, "Langston Hughes and Prentiss Taylor: The Golden Stair Press," *Archives of American Art Journal* 52, nos. 3/4 (Fall 2013): 18.

2. James Weldon Johnson, *Negro Americans, What Now?* (New York: Viking Press, 1934), 93.

3. Ibid., 17–18.

4. Ibid., 15.

5. For an overview of the rise of twentieth-century interracial publishing relationships supported by white Jewish and African American professional collaborations, see George Bornstein, *The Colors of Zion: Blacks, Jews, and Irish from 1845 to 1945* (Cambridge, MA: Harvard University Press, 2011), 164–166.

6. With positive continuities from the Harlem Renaissance in mind, George Hutchinson has observed: "Considerably more black fiction was published in the 1930s than in the 1920s, by a broader range of publishers and magazines, despite a shrinkage in fiction publication overall." Hutchinson's reflections suggest how little remembered this cultural epoch remains beyond literary scholars who focus on the period. Hutchinson, "Introduction," in Hutchinson, ed., *Cambridge Companion to the Harlem Renaissance* (Cambridge: Cambridge University Press, 2007), 8.

7. "Negro Hailed as New Writer," *The New York Sun*, March 4, 1940, reprinted in Keneth Kinnamon and Michel Fabre, eds., *Conversations with Richard Wright* (Jackson: University Press of Mississippi, 1993), 28–30.

8. Trudi McCullough, "'Strange Fruit,' Southern Woman's Novel, Plea against Segregation," *St. Louis Post-Dispatch*, April 9, 1944, 4D.

9. Langston Hughes, "Letters and Pictures to the Editor," *Ebony* 1, no. 2 (November 1945): 51.

10. Adam Green, *Selling the Race: Culture, Community, and Black Chicago, 1940–1955* (Chicago: University of Chicago Press, 2007), 160.

11. "Backstage," *Ebony*, August 1974, 26.

12. Cathryn Halverson, *Faraway Women and the "Atlantic Monthly"* (Amherst: University of Massachusetts Press, 2019), 164. Prior to Halverson's recent scholarship on Harrison's background and travelogue, many biographical details about this popular Black author were either unknown or inaccurate. See Cathryn Halverson, "My Great, Wide, Beautiful World," in *Playing House in the American West: Western Women's Life Narratives, 1839–1987* (Tuscaloosa: University of Alabama Press, 2013), 159–175; Halverson, "'Betwixt and Between': Dismantling Race in *My Great, Wide, Beautiful World*," *Journal X: a journal in culture & criticism* 4, no. 2 (Spring 2000): 133–157; and Halverson, "Juanita Harrison and *My Great, Wide, Beautiful World*," in *Faraway Women and the "Atlantic Monthly,"* 159–208.

13. For a concise overview of Harrison's book and career, see Adele Logan Alexander's introduction to a reprinted edition of *My Great, Wide, Beautiful World*, in *African American Women Writers, 1910–1940* (New York: G. K. Hall, 1996), xv–xxviii.

14. For examples of scholarship on Black authors and elites abroad, see Erica Griffin, "The 'Invisible Woman' Abroad: Jessie Fauset's New Horizon," in Dolan Hubbard, ed., *Recovered Writers/Recovered Texts* (Knoxville: University of Tennessee Press, 1997), 1–19; Corey D. B. Walker, "'Of the Coming of John [and Jane]': African American Intellectuals in Europe, 1888–1938," *Amerikastudien/American Studies* 47, no. 1 (2002): 7–22; Claire Garcia, "'For a Few Days We Would Be Residents in Africa': Jessie Redmon Fauset's 'Dark Algiers the White,'" *Ethnic Studies Review* 30, nos. 1–2 (2007): 103–114.

15. For an overview of this theme in twentieth-century African American writing, see Trudier Harris, *From Mammies to Militants: Domestics in Black American Literature* (Philadelphia: Temple University Press, 1982).

16. Macmillan advertisement, *New York Herald Tribune*, July 17, 1936, 13.

17. Halverson, *Faraway Women and the "Atlantic Monthly,"* 187, 195.

18. Ibid., 192.

19. Mildred Morris, "Preface," in Juanita Harrison, *My Great, Wide, Beautiful World* (New York: Macmillan, 1936), ix.

20. See, for example, Henry Bellamann, "The Literary Highway," *The Charlotte Observer*, April 19, 1936, 37; Polly Eggleston, "Book Reviews," *Battle Creek Enquirer*, May 24, 1936, 4.

21. Juanita Harrison qtd. in Halverson, *Faraway Women and the "Atlantic Monthly,"* 246 n. 42.

22. Juanita Harrison, "My Great, Wide, Beautiful World," serial, *Atlantic*, October 1935, 434–443; and November 1935, 601–612.

23. Printing estimate and *California Eagle* qtd. in Halverson, *Faraway Women and the "Atlantic Monthly,"* 161–162. "Miss Harrison's Book in Fifth Printing," *California Eagle*, August 14, 1936, 2.

24. Frank Marshall Davis, "World in Review: Another Year Passes," *Atlanta Daily World*, December 28, 1936, 2.

25. Ellery Sedgwick, *The Happy Profession* (Boston: Little, Brown, 1946), 210.

26. Juanita Harrison qtd. in Morris, "Preface," ix.

27. "She Is Number One U.S. Servant," *Afro-American*, March 19, 1938, 13.

28. Jean Toomer, "Blue Meridian," in Alfred Kreymborg, Lewis Mumford, and Paul Rosenfeld, eds., *The New Caravan* (New York: W. W. Norton, 1936), 645.

29. Peter Monro Jack, "The New Caravan's Wide Diversity," *The New York Times*, January 17, 1937, 2. See Richard Wright, "Big Boy Leaves Home," in Kreymborg, Mumford, and Rosenfeld, *New Caravan*, 124–158.

30. Isadore Cecilia Williams qtd. in H. L. Mencken, "Designations for Colored Folk," *American Speech* 19, no. 3 (October 1944): 165.

31. W.E.B. Du Bois, *Dusk of Dawn*, ed. Henry Louis Gates Jr. (Oxford: Oxford University Press, 2014 [1940]), 52–55.

32. Ralph Ellison to Stewart Lillard, August 28, 1973, in John F. Callahan and Marc C. Conner, eds., *The Selected Letters of Ralph Ellison* (New York: Random House, 2019), 711–712.

33. Frank Yerby qtd. in Veronica T. Watson, ed., *The Short Stories of Frank Yerby* (Jackson: University Press of Mississippi, 2020), xi.

34. Susan Linnee, "Frank Yerby May Be Impatient Man, but He's Prolific Writer," *The Atlanta Constitution*, October 16, 1983, 11H.

35. Langston Hughes, *The Big Sea: An Autobiography*, in Joseph McLaren, ed., *The Collected Works of Langston Hughes*, vol. 13 (Columbia: University of Missouri Press, 2001), 36.

36. Richard Wright, *Black Boy: A Record of Childhood and Youth* (New York: Harper, 1945), 3.

37. Ibid., 21.

38. Langston Hughes to Kyle Crichton, March 6, 1933, Box 93, Charles Scribner's Sons Archive, Scribner Room, Department of Rare Books and Special Collections, Firestone Library, Princeton University.

39. Kyle Crichton to Langston Hughes, March 24, 1933, Box 93, Charles Scribner's Sons Archive, Scribner Room, Department of Rare Books and Special Collections, Firestone Library, Princeton University.

40. Rebecca Chalmers Barton, ed., *Witnesses for Freedom: Negro Americans in Autobiography* (New York: Harper & Brothers, 1948), 91.

41. Ibid., 89.

42. Ibid., 87.

43. Alain Locke, "Foreword," in ibid., x.

44. Scholarly interpretations of "passing" are undoubtedly capacious, but various strategies of Black authors like Harrison arguably challenge how the term captures the dynamism of their ambitions. See, for example, Gayle Wald, *Crossing the Line: Racial Passing in Twentieth-Century U.S. Literature and Culture* (Durham, NC: Duke University Press, 2000).

45. Halverson, *Faraway Women and the "Atlantic Monthly,"* 38.

46. Carl Van Vechten to Langston Hughes, January 4, 1936, in Emily Bernard, ed., *Remember Me to Harlem: The Letters of Langston Hughes and Carl Van Vechten, 1925–1964* (New York: Random House, 2002), 135–136.

47. Carl Van Vechten to Gertrude Stein, January 9, 1936, in Edward Burns, ed., *The Letters of Gertrude Stein and Carl Van Vechten, 1913–1946* (New York: Columbia University Press, 1986), 470–471.

48. James Weldon Johnson, *Along This Way: The Autobiography of James Weldon Johnson* (New York: Viking, 1933), 383. See Laura Claridge, *The Lady with the Borzoi: Blanche Knopf, Literary Tastemaker Extraordinaire* (New York: Farrar, Straus and Giroux, 2016), 73.

49. Hughes, *Big Sea*, 196.

50. W.E.B. Du Bois, *Mansart Builds a School* (New York: Mainstream Publishers, 1959), 232.

51. Langston Hughes qtd. in Faith Berry, *Langston Hughes: Before and beyond Harlem* (Westport, CT: Lawrence Hill, 1983), 245.

52. W. S. Braithwaite to Nella Larsen, June 19, 1934, in Philip Butcher, ed., *The William Stanley Braithwaite Reader* (Ann Arbor: University of Michigan Press, 1972), 284.

53. For an important scholarly account connecting Yerby to his peers as well as to mentorship from James Weldon Johnson, see Gene Andrew Jarrett, "The Race Problem Was *Not* Theme for Me," in *Deans and Truants: Race and Realism in African American Literature* (Philadelphia: University of Pennsylvania Press, 2006), 143–166.

54. James Weldon Johnson to Frank Yerby, November 4, 1933, Box 25, Folder 568, James Weldon Johnson and Grace Nail Johnson Papers, Beinecke Rare Book and Manuscript Library, Collection of American Literature, Yale University (hereafter JWJ).

55. Frank Yerby to James Weldon Johnson, May 14, 1933, Box 25, Folder 568, JWJ.

56. Johnson to Yerby, November 4, 1933.

57. Frank Yerby to James Weldon Johnson, May 2, 1934, Box 25, Folder 568, JWJ.

58. Max Spindel, "Costume Tale Showing Evils of Slavery," *The Philadelphia Inquirer*, February 10, 1946, 15.

59. Dial announcement for *The Treasure of Pleasant Valley*, Box 1, Folder 4, Dial Press Records, Beinecke Rare Book and Manuscript Library, Collection of American Literature, Yale University.

60. See, for example, Sterling North, "A Legacy of Words Left by Gertrude Stein," *The Times Dispatch* [Richmond, VA], July 13, 1947, D-7.

61. Helen M. Strauss, *A Talent for Luck: An Autobiography* (New York: Random House, 1979), 72.

62. Grace Nail Johnson to Frank Yerby, February 1946, Box 38, Folder 269, JWJ.

63. Guirdex Massé, "Circling the Boundaries of the Tradition: The Strange Case of Frank G. Yerby," in Matthew Teutsch, ed., *Rediscovering Frank Yerby: Critical Essays* (Jackson: University Press of Mississippi, 2020), 37.

64. Harper & Brothers announcement for Richard Wright's *Native Son*, Box 46, Folder 573, Richard Wright Papers, Beinecke Rare Book and Manuscript Library, Collection of American Literature, Yale University.

65. Arna Bontemps, "Famous WPA Authors," *Negro Digest*, June 1950, 46.

66. See, for example, Robert Bone, "Richard Wright and the Chicago Renaissance," *Callaloo* 28 (1986): 446–468.

67. Anne Meis Knupfer, *The Chicago Black Renaissance and Women's Activism* (Urbana: University of Illinois Press, 2006), 52.

68. Robert Bone and Richard Courage, "Bronzeville's 'Writing Clan,'" in *The Muse in Bronzeville: African American Creative Expression in Chicago, 1932–1950* (New Brunswick, NJ: Rutgers University Press, 2011), 161–181.

69. Qtd. in ibid., 227.

70. Frank Yerby to John S. Cousins, May 14, 1944, qtd. in Jarrett, *Deans and Truants*, 149.

71. Harry Hansen, "Novel May Awaken Readers to Study of Negro Problem," *Chicago Sunday Tribune*, March 19, 1944, Box 14, Folder 13, Muriel Fuller Papers, Archives and Special Collections, Hunter College Libraries, Hunter College of the City University of New York, New York City (hereafter MFP).

72. Ibid.

73. In 1947, William York Tindall, a professor of English at Columbia, explained that novels like Smith's fit neatly into a genre he described as "sociological best-sellers." Tindall argued, "That these best-selling novels do not exaggerate more than is proper to humanitarian art can be seen by looking through the daily papers. Items of a single week provide abundant corroboration." A small sample of Tindall's examples included descriptions of conditions: "Down South [where] five or six Negroes are shot down. In England (with Palestine as an excuse) Jewish shops are stoned. [...] Although we keep ourselves from saying that some of our best friends are Jews, we sometimes think it." Tindall, "The Sociological Best-Seller," *College English* 9, no. 2 (November 1947): 55–56.

74. Imani Perry, *Looking for Lorraine: The Radiant and Radical Life of Lorraine Hansberry* (Boston: Beacon Press, 2018), 20.

75. Bernard DeVoto to Henry S. Canby, May 12, 1944, Box 2, Folder 58, Henry Seidel Canby Papers, Yale Collection of American Literature, Beinecke Rare Book and Manuscript Library, Yale University.

76. Ward Morehouse, "Lillian Smith Spent Seven Years on Novel," *Miami Daily News*, June 11, 1946, 7.

77. Frank Yerby, "Health Card," in Bruce A. Glasrud and Laurie Champion, eds., *The African American West: A Century of Short Stories* (Boulder: University of Colorado, 2000), 133.

78. John S. Cousins to Frank Yerby, May 14, 1944, Box 266, Folder 4304, Langston Hughes Papers, James Weldon Johnson Collection, Yale Collection of American Literature, Beinecke Rare Book and Manuscript Library, Yale University.

79. Frank Yerby to John S. Cousins, June 11, 1944, Box 266, Folder 4304, Langston Hughes Papers, James Weldon Johnson Collection, Yale Collection of American Literature, Beinecke Rare Book and Manuscript Library, Yale University.

80. Chester Himes qtd. in "Angry Author from Brooklyn," *Ebony* 1, no. 8 (July 1946): 48–49.

81. Qtd. in John Williams and Lori Williams, eds., *Dear Chester, Dear John: Letters between Chester Himes and John A. Williams* (Detroit, MI: Wayne State University Press, 2008), 200.

82. Northwestern University Radio Department, *Of Men and Books* (Evanston, IL: Northwestern University Radio Department, 1941), 55.

83. *Edward P. Morgan and the News* transcript, April 6, 1959, Box 63, Folder 10, Lorraine Hansberry Papers, Schomburg Center for Research in Black Culture, New York Public Library.

84. Qtd. in M. Lynn Weiss, *Gertrude Stein and Richard Wright: The Poetics and Politics of Modernism* (Jackson: University Press of Mississippi, 1998), 3.

85. Jarrett, *Deans and Truants*, 131.

86. Willard Motley, Notebook 1, May 22, 1947, Box 6, Folder 5, Willard Motley Papers, Rare Books and Special Collections, Northern Illinois University (hereafter WMP).

87. "Willard Motley: Ex-Tramp Writes 600,000-Word-Best Seller—All in Pencil," *Ebony* 2, no. 11 (September 1947): 47.

88. Theodore "Ted" Purdy to Willard Motley, January 30, 1948, Box 10, Folder 2, WMP.

89. Richard Wright, "Introduction," in St. Claire Drake and Horace Cayton, *Black Metropolis: A Study of Negro Life in a Northern City* (New York: Harcourt, Brace and Company, 1945), xxxi.

90. Willard Motley to Theodore "Ted" Purdy, March 21, 1947, Box 9, WMP.

91. Willard Motley, Diary, July 1, 1947, Box 6, Folder 12, WMP.

92. Willard Motley, *Knock on Any Door* (New York: Appleton-Century-Crofts, 1947), 182–183.

93. Alan Wald, "Willard Motley," in Steven C. Tracy, ed., *Writers of the Black Chicago Renaissance* (Urbana: University of Illinois Press, 2011), 263.

94. Bernie Lovely, "Review: 'It Takes a Large Cemetery to Bury All of Our Dreams' [reviewed work: Jerome Klinkowitz, ed., *The Diaries of Willard Motley* (Ames: Iowa State University Press, 1979)]," *Callaloo* 7 (October 1979): 114.

95. H. W. van Couenhoven to Dana Ferrin, ca. May 3, 1947, Box 9, WMP.

96. William Samilov to Willard Motley, July 24, 1948, Box 10, WMP.

97. William Samilov to Willard Motley, December 31, 1948, Box 10, WMP.

98. Willard Motley to William Samilov, January 5, 1949, Box 10, WMP.

99. William Samilov to Willard Motley, January 15, 1949, Box 10, WMP.

100. In the letter Samilov wrote Motley on December 31, 1948, he explained that he was having difficulty relaying messages through Rick's family. "The prison officials were always 100% against Rick and me, so perhaps they have scared his family also." In his January 15, 1949, letter to Motley, Samilov discussed how religion figured into his queer relationship. "Rick and I were never religious. Rick was born Catholic and actually seemed to resent the church. However, we would go to church on special holidays in prison like Xmas, etc. We kind of liked the Priest because he had gone to bat for us at times. [. . .] Nevertheless, after we left church Rick would say 'You are my Christ Billy. I don't need [any] other God with you.' Remarks like that used to shake me."

101. Sheldon Eckfeld to Willard Motley, July 12, 1947, Box 9, WMP.

102. Glenn Clawson to Willard Motley, January 31, 1948, Box 10, WMP.

103. See, for example, Blanche Wiesen Cook, *Eleanor Roosevelt, vol. 2: The Defining Years, 1933–1938* (New York: Penguin, 2000), 192–195; Marc Peyser and Timothy Dwyer, *Hissing Cousins: The Untold Story of Eleanor Roosevelt and Alice Longworth* (New York: Doubleday, 2016).

104. For a recent discussion of Eleanor Roosevelt's "intersectional" friendship with Pauli Murray, see Patricia Hill Collins, *Intersectionality as Critical Social Theory* (Durham, NC: Duke University Press, 2019).

105. Clawson to Motley, January 31, 1948.

106. Commentary on *Knock on Any Door* was published in Eleanor Roosevelt's syndicated newspaper column published daily. For just one example of how newspapers printed Roosevelt's endorsement of Motley's novel, see Roosevelt, "Finds Leisure to Review and Comment on Two New Books," *Des Moines Tribune*, April 29, 1947, 4.

107. Theodore Purdy to Willard Motley, March 16, 1948, Box 10, WMP.

108. Theodore Purdy to Willard Motley, March 22, 1948, Box 10, WMP.

109. Alma Booker to Willard Motley, ca. July 3, 1947, Box 9, WMP.

110. Willard Motley, Diary, July 6, 1947, Box 6, Folder 12, WMP.

111. Willard Motley to Virgil Scott, February 13, 1948, Box 10, WMP.

112. Theodore Purdy to Willard Motley, November 7, 1947, Box 9, WMP.

113. Theodore Purdy to Willard Motley, October 7, 1948, Box 10, WMP.

114. Jack Conroy to Willard Motley, October 20, 1948, Box 10, WMP.

115. Willard Motley to Ted Patrick, January 13, 1948, Box 10, WMP.

116. Ted Patrick to Willard Motley, February 16, 1948, Box 10, WMP.

117. The first articles *Holiday* published on racial discrimination in the domestic hospitality sector were penned by John A. Williams, an African American author who wrote a two-part essay series for the magazine entitled "This Is My Country, Too, Part I" and "This Is My Country, Too, Part II," which appeared in August and September 1964, respectively.

118. Henry Ehrlich to Willard Motley, August 15, 1947, Box 9, WMP.

119. In a 1963 essay, Fuller explained that Yerby's "wife told [her] that if the contest novel had come back with a rejection slip, he would not have written anything else." Muriel Fuller, "Authors I Have Known," *The Christian Herald*, November 1963, Box 9, Folder 1, MFP.

120. Cameron Shipp to Muriel Fuller, November 21, 1949, Folder 10, Box 19, MFP.

121. Frank Yerby to Helen Strauss, excerpted in Strauss, *Talent for Luck*, 71.

122. Fuller, "Authors I Have Known."

123. Strauss, *Talent for Luck*, 70.

124. See, for example, Thomas D. Jarrett's criticisms of Yerby in his essay "Recent Fiction by Negroes," *The English Journal* 43, no. 8 (November 1954): 424; Nick Aaron Ford, "Four Popular Negro Novelists," *Phylon* 15, no. 1 (1st Qtr., 1954): 37–38; Robert Scott, "Black Power, and Baldwin's 'Another Country,'" *Journal of Black Studies* 1, no. 1 (September 1970): 25.

125. "The Foxes of Harrow: New Movie Ducks Controversial Miscegenation Theme," *Ebony* 3, no. 2 (December 1947): 14.

126. Ibid., 15.

127. Ben Burns, *Nitty Gritty: A White Editor in Black Journalism* (Jackson: University Press of Mississippi, 1996), 49.

128. Frank Yerby to Helen Strauss, ca. April 1964, Box 53, Frank Yerby Collection, Howard Gotlieb Archival Research Center, Boston University.

129. Fuller's two novels were published under a pen name: Olive Beatrice Muir, *Thy Name is Woman: A Novel* (New York: G. W. Dillingham, 1894); Olive Beatrice Muir, *With Malice Toward None* (Chicago: Rand, McNally & Company, 1900).

130. Olive Fuller to Muriel Fuller, ca. January 22, 1939, Box 24, Folder 24, MFP.

131. Ibid.

132. Muriel Fuller to Olive Fuller, January 24, 1939, Box 24, Folder 24, MFP.

133. See, for example, Jacqueline Goldsby, *A Spectacular Secret: Lynching in American Life and Literature* (Chicago: University of Chicago Press, 2006); Koritha Mitchell, *Living with Lynching: African American Lynching Plays, Performance, and Citizenship, 1890–1930* (Urbana: University of Illinois Press, 2011).

134. Olive Fuller to Muriel Fuller, April 1, 1944, Box 6, Folder 7, MFP.

135. Olive Fuller to Muriel Fuller, November 27, 1943, Box 6, Folder 7, MFP.

136. Olive Fuller to Muriel Fuller, April 1, 1944.

137. Olive Fuller to Muriel Fuller, November 27, 1943.

138. Olive Fuller to Muriel Fuller, July 31, 1946, Box 6, Folder 7, MFP.

139. Ibid.

140. Stephanie Brown, *The Postwar African American Novel: Protest and Discontent, 1945–1950* (Jackson: University Press of Mississippi, 2011), 74.

141. Langston Hughes, ed., *The Best Short Stories by Negro Writers: Anthology from 1899 to the Present* (Boston: Little, Brown and Company, 1967), x.

142. Strauss, *Talent for Luck*, 71.

143. Ellen Tarry, *The Third Door: The Autobiography of an American Negro Woman* (Tuscaloosa: University of Alabama Press, 1992 [1955]), 150.

Chapter 3. Challenging Little Black Sambo

1. Muriel Fuller, "For Every Land, for Every Taste, for Every Age, a Book," *News of Books and Authors*, September 1939, Box 10, Folder 4, Muriel Fuller Papers, Archives and Special Collections, Hunter College Libraries, Hunter College of the City University of New York, New York City (hereafter MFP). See Eleanore Hubbard Wilson, *Magical Jumping Beans* (New York: E. P. Dutton, 1939).

2. Fuller, "For Every Land, for Every Taste, for Every Age, a Book."

3. For a small but representative sample of contemporary discussions on perceptions of the utility and shortcomings of children's literature, including assessments that explicitly or implicitly argued that national and international interracial and interethnic social tensions were interrelated, see Charlemae Rollins, "Children's Books on the Negro: To Help Build a Better World," *Elementary English Review* 20, no. 6 (October 1943): 219–223; Dorothy Shepard Manley, "Improving Racial Attitudes through Children's Books," *The Elementary English Review* 21, no. 7 (November 1944): 267–269; Genevieve H. Haight, "Broadening the Child's Understanding of Human Relationships through Books," *Elementary English* 27, no. 5 (May 1950): 330–332; David K. Gast, "Minority Americans in Children's Literature," *Elementary English* 44, no. 1 (January 1967): 12–23; Charlemae Rollins, "Promoting Racial Understanding through Books," *Negro American Literature Forum* 2 (1968): 71–76.

4. Mary Dudziak, *Cold War, Civil Rights: Race and the Image of American Democracy* (Princeton, NJ: Princeton University Press, 2000), 9.

5. For an overview of reforms after the Great Depression, see Julia Mickenberg, "Civil Rights, History, and the Left: Inventing the Juvenile Black Biography," *MELUS* 27, no. 2 (2002): 65–93.

6. As Muriel Fuller noted in a 1947 speech to the Women's Press Club, she was remarkably confident in "this brave new world of publishing," which was "going to need women as never before" in key roles. "Surely the world revolution in progress today must also reach the greatest medium of all—the printed page. It is a thrilling and exciting era which is just ahead, and I'm glad I'm going to be part of it." Fuller, speech to the Women's Press Club, 1947, Box 10, Folder 13, MFP.

7. Historian Julia Mickenberg's scholarship has stressed deep interconnections between progressive ideals in the juvenile publishing industry, stretching from the 1930s, into World War II, and continuing during the Cold War. While Mickenberg points to the considerable freedoms the juvenile publishing sector enjoyed during the McCarthy era—most notably, the avoidance of scrutiny that plagued other media sectors—many of these men and women remained fair-weather friends of racial progressivism. See Mickenberg, *Learning from the Left: Children's Literature, the Cold War, and Radical Politics in the United States* (Oxford: Oxford University Press, 2006), 12.

8. Between 1935 and 1955 alone, Fuller authored thirty-nine "sketches" of children's book editors, publishers, and authors for *Publishers' Weekly*. Notable as well is the fact that many of these men and women did professional work in the publishing field that extended beyond the juvenile trade.

9. For just one of innumerable summaries of *The Story of Little Black Sambo*, see Lauren B. Hewes and Kayla Haveles Hopper, eds., *Radiant with Color and Art: McLoughlin Brothers and the Business of Pictures Books, 1858–1920* (Worchester, MA: American Antiquary Society, 2018), 140.

10. Alice Dalgliesh, "To Light a Candle," *Publishers' Weekly* 147, no. 17 (April 28, 1945): 1738.

11. Frederic Melcher, "Editorial: Possibilities for 1947," *Publishers' Weekly* 151, no. 1 (January 4, 1947): 41.

12. For a sample of recent scholarship on Black children's literature, and related thematic studies, see Katharine Capshaw Smith, *Children's Literature of the Harlem Renaissance* (Bloomington: Indiana University Press, 2006); Mickenberg, *Learning from the Left*; Julia Mickenberg and Philip Nel, eds., *Tales for Little Rebels: A Collection of Radical Children's Literature* (New York: New York University Press, 2008); Katharine Capshaw Smith, *Civil Rights Childhood: Picturing Liberation in African American Photobooks* (Minneapolis: University of Minnesota Press, 2014); Barbara Thrash Murphy and Deborah L. Murphy, *Black Authors and Illustrators of Books for Children and Young Adults: A Biographical Dictionary* (New York: Garland, 1999); Michelle Martin, *Brown Gold: Milestones of African American Children's Picture Books, 1845–2002* (New York: Routledge, 2004); Robin Bernstein, *Racial Innocence: Performing American Childhood from Slavery to Civil Rights* (New York: New York University Press, 2011); Moira Hinderer, "Talking to Children about Race: Children's Literature in a Segregated Era, 1930–1945," in Claudia Mills, ed., *Ethics and Children's Literature* (New York: Routledge, 2016), 41–55. For a recent state of the field, see Wanda Brooks and Jonda C. McNair, "'But This Story of Mine Is Not Unique': A Review of Research on African American Children's Literature," *Review of Educational Research* 79, no. 1 (March 2009): 125–163. For scholarship on Black children's literature prior to the twentieth century, see Chanta Haywood, "Constructing Childhood: The *Christian Recorder* and

Literature for Black Children, 1854–1865," *African American Review* 36, no. 3 (2002): 417–428; Katharine Capshaw and Anna Mae Duane, eds., *Who Writes for Black Children? African American Children's Literature before 1900* (Minneapolis: University of Minnesota Press, 2017); Donnarae MacCann, *White Supremacy in Children's Literature: Characterizations of African Americans, 1830–1900* (New York: Routledge, 2001).

13. There were multiple iterations of the publishing houses that John A. Hertel led or was a leading investor in. Though Hertel was the president of J. L. Nichols, *Floyd's Flowers* was published by Hertel, Jenkins & Co., the firm he cofounded with A. N. Jenkins in 1904.

14. In the mid-1960s and 1970s, writers, editors, and activists associated with the Council on Interracial Books for Children advocated for white capital to ensure that African Americans could publish Black and interracial books. See, for example, "Currents: The Need for Interracial Children's Books," *Publishers' Weekly* 194, no. 1 (July 1, 1968): 17.

15. Louis R. Harlan, "Booker T. Washington and the *Voice of the Negro*, 1904–1907," *The Journal of Southern History* 45, no. 1 (February 1979): 46.

16. Ibid., 47.

17. Ibid., 55.

18. John Giggie, *After Redemption: Jim Crow and the Transformation of African American Religion in the Delta, 1875–1915* (Oxford: Oxford University Press, 2007), 123.

19. John A. Hertel to Emmett Jay Scott, June 1, 1907, in Louis Harlan, ed., *The Booker T. Washington Papers, vol. 9: 1906–1908* (Urbana: University of Illinois Press, 1980), 295–296.

20. Katharine Capshaw Smith, "Childhood, the Body, and Race Performance: Early 20th-Century Etiquette Books for Black Children," *African American Review* 40, no. 4 (Winter 2006): 808 n. 4. See also Katherine Capshaw Smith, "The Legacy of Paul Laurence Dunbar: Dialect and Racial Configuration in the Works of Silas X. Floyd and Christina Moody," *Midwestern Miscellany* 34 (Spring/Fall 2006): 36–52.

21. J. E. Knox, the president of Brinkley Academy, qtd. in "Negro Leaders Speaking Out: Strong Expressions at Negro Baptist Convention," *Daily Arkansas Gazette*, October 8, 1905, 2.

22. "Books and Their Makers," *The New York Age*, October 5, 1905, 3.

23. *Floyd's Flower*'s advertisement in Alabama, seeking sales agents, published in *The Montgomery Times*, November 23, 1905, 8.

24. Between 1898 and the 1920s, the firm reprinted and updated Black scholar W. H. Crogman's edited volume *Progress of a Race, or, The Remarkable Advancement of the Afro-American Negro* (Atlanta: J. L. Nichols, 1898). Moreover, spinoffs of J. L. Nichols continued publishing, reprinting, and updating Black juvenile texts over the first quarter of the twentieth century. See, for example, Silas X. Floyd, *Charming Stories for Young and Old* (Washington, DC: Austin Jenkins, 1925).

25. Advertisement seeking sales agents for *The Dunbar Speaker* and "Crogman's New Progress," a new edition of that scholar's *Progress of a Race*, in *The Negro Star* [Wichita, KS], December 24, 1920, 4.

26. "Mrs. Nelson, Teacher, Is 'Locked Out': Suspended after Trip to See Harding by Howard School Principal," *The Evening Journal* [Wilmington, DE], October 5, 1920, 10.

27. "Praise for Mrs. Nelson," *The Evening Journal* [Wilmington, DE], August 17, 1920, 12.

28. Dunbar-Nelson included five of Pushkin's poems, in two different sections of her anthology for young readers. See Alice Moore Dunbar-Nelson, ed., *The Dunbar Speaker and*

Entertainer: Containing the Best Prose and Poetic Selections By and About the Negro Race (Naperville, IL: J. L. Nichols & Co., 1920), 17, 182–184.

29. Leslie Pinckney Hill, foreword to ibid., 9–10.

30. Carter G. Woodson, *The Mis-education of the Negro* (Washington, DC: Associated Press, 1933), 24.

31. Ibid., 103.

32. Muriel Fuller, "Three Little Pigs," *Publishers' Weekly* 124, no. 17 (October 21, 1933): 1431.

33. Advertisement for Ellis Credle's *Across the Cotton Patch*, in *The Horn Book Magazine* 11 (July–August 1935): 374.

34. See, for example, the Kirkus review for Credle's *Across the Cotton Patch* and *Little Jeemes Henry*.

35. Dalgliesh, "To Light a Candle," 1738.

36. Smith, *Civil Rights Childhood*, 27–28.

37. Beatrice Murphy, "The Book Worm," *Afro-American*, November 12, 1938, 15.

38. Louise Bechtel, "Reading as Experience," draft of speech given to the Child Study Association of New York, 11, December 3, 1936, Box 3, Folder 3, Papers of Louise Seaman Bechtel, George A. Smathers Libraries, University of Florida, Gainesville.

39. Trysh Travis, "The Women in Print Movement: History and Implications," *Book History* 11 (2008): 276.

40. Virginia Kirkus, "The Women Back of Books," in Ann Stoddard, ed., *Discovering My Job* (New York: T. Nelson and Sons, 1936), Box 10, Folder 13, MFP.

41. M. Tyler Sasser, "*The Snowy Day* in the Civil Rights Era: Peter's Political Innocence and Unpublished Letters from Langston Hughes, Ellen Tarry, Grace Nail Johnson, and Charlemae Hill Rollins," *Children's Literature Association Quarterly* 39, no. 3 (Fall 2014): 373.

42. Katharine Capshaw Smith, "From Bank Street to Harlem: A Conversation with Ellen Tarry," *The Lion and the Unicorn* 23, no. 2 (1999): 280–281.

43. In her interview with Smith, Tarry explained that this was especially important in her collaboration with Marie Hall Ets (and the book's photographers, Alexander Alland and Alexandra Alland) on *My Dog Rinty* in the mid-1940s: "Black people were reluctant to allow anybody white to come into their homes. I had to convince them. We had a story—the story was real to me by that time. And after all these years of working in Harlem, how could they not trust me?" Ibid., 280.

44. Sasser, "*The Snowy Day* in the Civil Rights Era," 373.

45. Tarry's title broke commercial records for Black-authored children's books. A decade after *My Dog Rinty* was published, *Jet* magazine described her as the "most successful" Black children's book author, noting that this book had "sold more than 23,500 copies, netting [Tarry] about 19 cents in royalties for each book sold." "How Successful Are Lady Authors?" *Jet*, October 13, 1955, 47.

46. Ellen Tarry, *The Third Door: The Autobiography of an American Negro Woman* (Tuscaloosa: University of Alabama Press, 1992 [1955]), 182.

47. Muriel Fuller, "May Massee of Viking Press," *Publishers' Weekly* 157, no. 10 (March 11, 1950): 1340.

48. Tarry also credited Massee's for being one of the first white editors in New York's corporate publishing business—in her case, Viking—to hire a Black assistant.

49. Crone's letter also stated that the slogan was intended to "convince members of the community that children's books are an important investment for homes, schools and libraries." Albert Crone to "Program Chairman," letter announcement, June 3, 1943, Box 6, Folder: Children's Book Committee—Minutes, Lists, etc., 1943, Council on Books in Wartime Collection, Seely G. Mudd Manuscript Library, Princeton University.

50. Ibid.

51. Muriel Fuller, meeting minutes, Children's Book Council, January 21, 1946, Box 1, Folder 2, MFP.

52. Ibid.

53. On the American government's effort to circumvent a direct role in "propaganda" campaigns during World War II via the Writers' War Board, which was not an official federal organization, see, for example, Thomas Howell, "The Writers' War Board: U.S. Domestic Propaganda in World War II," *The Historian* 59, no. 4 (Summer 1997): 795–813.

54. "Best Child's Book to Be Selected," *Brooklyn Daily Eagle*, September 16, 1943, 4.

55. Excerpt from the *American Library Association Bulletin* reprinted as "Honorary Award," *Wilson Library Bulletin* 39–40 (June 1944): 79.

56. For a recent selection of scholarly essays offering an overview of related transformations, see Kenneth B. Kidd and Joseph T. Thomas Jr., eds., *Prizing Children's Literature: The Cultural Politics of Children's Book Awards* (New York: Routledge, 2016).

57. Mickenberg, *Learning from the Left*, 108.

58. Nan Taylor, radio director, special Book Week broadcast, 1943, Box 6, Folder: Children's Book Committee—Minutes, Lists, etc., 1943, Council on Books in Wartime Collection, Seely G. Mudd Manuscript Library, Princeton University.

59. Langston Hughes to Alan Green, July 1, 1944, in Arnold Rampersad and David Roessel, with Christa Fratantoro, eds., *Selected Letters of Langston Hughes* (New York: Knopf, 2015), 258–259. Hughes closed his letter by noting that he had no intention whatsoever of reading Darby's book. He recommended that Green consider getting in touch with Arna Bontemps, whom he credited as the leading Black author of children's books in the United States, if he wanted "much more comprehensive criticism" of *Jump Lively Jeff*.

60. Adelaide C. Rowell qtd. in "Negro Dialect in Children's Books," *Publishers' Weekly* 140, no. 16 (October 18, 1941): 1557.

61. Georgia Cowen Poole, Charlemae Rollins, N. P. Tillman, Hallie Beachem Brooks, Eliza Atkins, Virginia Lacy Jones, and Wallace Van Jackson, "A Further Statement on Negro Dialect in Children's Books," *Publishers' Weekly* 141, no. 2 (January 10, 1942): 105.

62. *Library Journal*, undated, Box 9, Folder 6, MFP.

63. Fuller, meeting minutes, Children's Book Council, January 21, 1946.

64. "Currents in the Trade," *Publishers' Weekly* 146, no. 9 (August 26, 1944): 696.

65. "Special Displays to Feature Week: Plans for Books Week Observance Completed at Library," *The Morning Herald* [Hagerstown, MD], November 7, 1944, 3.

66. For an overview of this transformation in aspirational reading habits, see Amy Blair, *Reading Up: Middle-Class Readers and the Culture of Success in the Early Twentieth-Century United States* (Philadelphia: Temple University Press, 2011).

67. Mickenberg, *Learning from the Left*, 29.

68. Editor, "Children's Book Council Established as a Year-Round Agency to Promote Children's Books," *Publishers' Weekly* 147 (March 3, 1945): 1006–1007, Box 9, Folder 6, MFP.

69. A *Publishers' Weekly* editorial praising the CBC toward the beginning of 1945 verifies how popular these women had become within the otherwise male-dominated trade: "The time to take this step [organizing] is certainly now, when the demand for children's books is at an all-time high and when it is especially desirable to weld into cooperation all the groups which are creating this great demand." Assessments and recommendations like these supported the distinctive Black and interracial texts that corporate firms were publishing in greater numbers than ever before. Ibid.

70. Muriel Fuller, meeting minutes, Children's Book Council, December 10, 1945, Box 1, Folder 2, MFP.

71. Ibid.

72. See, for example, "Frontispiece—Native American Chiefs—From a Drawing by Cyrus Leroy Baldridge," *Opportunity: Journal of Negro Life* 8, no. 5 (May 1930): 134.

73. Muriel Fuller, "Vernon Ives of Holiday House," *Publishers' Weekly*, April 26, 1947, Box 9, Folder 4, MFP; Ruth Tooze, "Vernon Ives," November 1949, Box 9, Folder 4, MFP. It appears that Fuller saved Tooze's profile of Ives published two years later because of how much of the text was copied from her own profile two years earlier.

74. See, for example, Ann Mulloy Ashmore, "From *Elizabite* to *Spotty*: The Reys, Race, and Consciousness Raising," *Children's Literature Association Quarterly* 35, no. 4 (Winter 2010): 357–372; Sasser, "*The Snowy Day* in the Civil Rights Era," 362.

75. Robert Williams, "Book Lore," *The Morning Call* [Patterson, NJ], February 8, 1947, 14.

76. Jodi Melamed, *Represent and Destroy: Rationalizing Violence in the New Racial Capitalism* (Minneapolis: University of Minnesota Press, 2011), 54.

77. "Alabama Klan Assails a Second Children's Book," *Publishers' Weekly* 176, no. 19 (November 9, 1959): 20–21.

78. Ashmore, "From *Elizabite* to *Spotty*," 363.

79. Ibid., 358.

80. Ursula Nordstrom also corresponded with the Reys (in confidence) about Jackson's early work. A letter to Margret Rey from Nordstrom in 1944 notes: "Maggie, sending you this is against all the rules and regulations of this (or any other publishing house). Don't tell J.J. [Jesse Jackson] I sent it to you. I can't stress too much that I am doing a terrible thing in letting you see this." Qtd. in ibid., 364.

81. Muriel Fuller, "Ursula Nordstrom of Harper," *Publishers' Weekly*, October 25, 1947, Box 9, Folder 5, MFP.

82. Fuller, speech to Women's Press Club, 1947. Several years later, a throwaway comment by Vernon Ives, who had published *Boomba Lives in Africa* back in 1935, offers a sense of how these ideals were conveyed to white educators and publishers. In a comprehensive report on teenage reading published in 1953, Ives recommended that libraries, editors, and booksellers minimize their coverage of and concern with race and racial injustice within the United States: "When dealing with [domestic] racial problems, the informal approach is preferred, but there is a smaller need for serious treatment, too. In either case, the simpler the better." Poignantly, this advice in an otherwise meticulously researched essay on young adult reading made no other mention of the nation's racial minorities. Ives, "Teen-Age Reading: A Report Based on a Survey Made by the Publishers' Liaison Committee," reprinted from the *ALA Bulletin*, October 1953, and distributed by the Children's Book Council, Box 9, Folder 4, MFP.

83. Mickenberg, *Learning from the Left*, 8.

84. Muriel Fuller to Isabel Paterson, September 16, 1943, Box 17, Folder 1, MFP.

85. Letter to Harry Hansen, forwarded to Muriel Fuller, January 22, 1945, Box 15, Folder 6, MFP. The name of the editor who wrote this letter seems to be withheld, but this is difficult to know for certain.

86. Ibid.

87. Dalgliesh, "To Light a Candle," 1738.

88. Fuller, meeting minutes, Children's Book Council, December 10, 1945.

89. For an overview of the history of researchers and institutions associated with twentieth-century intercultural education, see Lauri D. Johnson and Yoon K. Pak, "Teaching for Diversity: Intercultural and Intergroup Education in the Public Schools, 1920s to 1970s," *Review of Research in Education* 43 (March 2019): 1–31.

90. See, for example, Helen Trager and Marian Radke Yarrow, *They Learn What They Live: Prejudice in Young Children* (New York: Harper, 1952).

91. Helen Trager, "Concerning the Juvenile Market," *Publishers' Weekly* 140, no. 16 (October 18, 1941): 1559.

92. Fuller, meeting minutes, Children's Book Council, December 10, 1945.

93. Ibid. Fuller's meeting notes on this topic went on at length. "It is very complicated; books were censored for the most trivial things. It boils down to the fact that no opinions can be expressed. To be valid, a book must have opinions."

94. Fuller, meeting minutes, Children's Book Council, January 21, 1946.

95. Ibid.

96. For examples of contemporaries describing the fall of "Little Sambo," "Uncle Remus," and similar racist depictions of African Americans, see Carol A. Parks, "Goodbye Black Sambo; Black Writers Forge New Images in Children's Literature," *Ebony*, November 1972, 60–70; Arna Bontemps, "Uncle Remus, Farewell," theme issue "Fall Children's Issue," *Book Week*, October 31, 1965, 3; Augusta Baker, "The Changing Image of the Black in Children's Literature," *Horn Book* 51 (February 1975): 79–88; Phyllis J. Yuill, *Little Black Sambo: A Closer Look* (New York: Racism and Sexism Resource Center for Educators, 1976). For a slightly later account, see Opal Moore and Donnarae MacCann, "The Uncle Remus Travesty, Part II: Julius Lester and Virginia Hamilton," *Children's Literature Association Quarterly* 11, no. 4 (Winter 1986–1987): 205–209.

97. Ursula Nordstrom's December 6, 1963, letter responding to an unidentified query was reprinted in Leonard S. Marcus, ed., *Dear Genius: The Letters of Ursula Nordstrom* (New York: HarperCollins, 1998), 168–169.

98. Muriel Fuller, "Literature, Children's," entry in the "1966 Int'l Yearbook," preserved in Box 9, Folder 1, MFP.

99. Courtney B. Cazden qtd. in "Children's Book Needs in a Changing Society," *Publishers' Weekly* 190, no. 4 (July 25, 1966): 36.

100. Judith Thompson and Gloria Woodard, "Black Perspective in Books for Children," in Donnarae MacCann and Gloria Woodard, eds., *The Black American in Books for Children: Readings in Racism* (Metuchen, NJ: Scarecrow Press, 1972), 16.

101. George Manuel Fenollosa qtd. in United States Congress, House Committee on Education and Labor, Ad Hoc Subcommittee on De Facto School Segregation, *Books for Schools and the Treatment of Minorities* (Washington, DC: Government Printing Office, 1966), 131–132.

102. Inez Hogan qtd. in Muriel Fuller, *More Junior Authors* (New York: H. W. Wilson, 1963), 111. Hogan started her prolific literary career as a children's book illustrator. Before selling

distorted images of Black children under her own name, she illustrated texts such as M. Genevieve Silvester's adaptation of *Little Black Sambo, and the Tar Baby* (Chicago: Mentzer, Bush and Co., 1930). Silvester advertised her professional work as a first-grade teacher to sell (and justify) the infamously racist depictions associated with this story.

103. Joseph Boskin, *Sambo: The Rise and Demise of an American Jester* (New York: Oxford University Press, 1986), 109.

104. Christine Noble Govan excerpted in "Negro Dialect in Children's Books," 1557.

105. "Tips for the Bookseller," *Publishers' Weekly* 173, no. 8 (February 24, 1958): 42.

106. Augusta Baker, "Significant Factors in Selecting and Rejecting Materials," in Annette Phinazee, ed., *Conference on the Georgia Child's Access to Materials Pertaining to American Negroes* (Atlanta: Atlanta University, 1968), 53.

107. Ibid.

108. "NYPL Issues Reading List for Children about Negroes," *Publishers' Weekly* 145, no. 3 (January 15, 1944): 206.

109. See the dedication page to Inez Hogan's *Mule Twins* (New York: E. P. Dutton, 1939).

110. Velma Varner qtd. in Muriel Fuller, "Velma Varner of World Publishing Company," *Publishers' Weekly*, July 27, 1959, preserved in Box 9, Folder 5, MFP.

111. Velma Varner, "Publishing for Children and Young Adults in the 1970s," draft of speech given at the State University of New York at Albany, no date [ca. "the first quarter of the second year of the seventies," according to the opening paragraph of Varner's talk], 10, Box 24, Folder 22, MFP. For an overview of the CIBC, see Beryle Banfield, "Commitment to Change: The Council on Interracial Books for Children and the World of Children's Books," *African American Review* 32, no. 1 (Spring 1998): 17–22.

112. For a recent study that has considered the "intersectional" history of twentieth-century children's book publishing, see Jodi Eichler-Levine, *Suffer the Little Children: Uses of the Past in Jewish and African American Children's Literature* (New York: New York University Press, 2013). Literary scholar Katharine Capshaw Smith has been prolific in moving stories related to this racial and ethnic cultural "revolution" beyond venues devoted to the study of children's literature. In that work and elsewhere, Smith has been an important advocate for building conversations between work on children's literature and racial and ethnic studies. Katharine Capshaw Smith, "Introduction: The Landscape of Ethnic American Children's Literature," theme issue "Multi-ethnic Children's Literature," *MELUS* 27, no. 2 (Summer 2002): 3–8; Katharine Capshaw Smith, "Ethnic Studies and Children's Literature: A Conversation between Fields," *The Lion and the Unicorn* 38, no. 3 (September 2014): 237–257. For an example of a recent scholarly essay bringing related Black literary histories to audiences beyond the children's literature field, see Nick Batho, "Black Power Children's Literature: Julius Lester and Black Power," *Journal of American Studies* 55, no. 1 (February 2021): 1–23.

113. Anne Beneduce qtd. in Sandra Roberts, "Books for Black Children by Black Writers: A Passing Fantasy?" *Publishers' Weekly* 222, no. 4 (July 23, 1982): 83.

114. Varner, "Publishing for Children and Young Adults in the 1970s," 3.

115. Ibid., 5.

116. Ibid., 4.

117. For scholarship in this area, see Nancy Tolson, "Making Books Available: The Role of Early Libraries, Librarians, and Booksellers in the Promotion of African American Children's Literature," theme issue "Children's and Young-Adult Literature Issue," *African American Review*

32, no. 1 (Spring 1998): 9–16; Laura Burt, "Vivian Harsh, Adult Education, and the Library's Role as Community Center," *Libraries and the Cultural Record* 44, no. 2 (2009): 234–244; LaGarrett King, "'A Narrative to the Colored Children in America': Leila Amos Pendleton, African American History Textbooks, and Challenging Personhood," *Journal of Negro Education* 84, no. 4 (2015): 519–533.

118. For an overview of this history from the beginning of the twentieth century, see Joel Taxel, "Children's Literature at the Turn of the Century: Toward a Political Economy of the Publishing Industry," *Research in the Teaching of English* 37, no. 2 (2002): 146–198; Leonard Marcus, *Golden Legacy: How Golden Books Won Children's Hearts, Changed Publishing Forever, and Became an American Icon along the Way* (New York: Random House, 2007); Leonard Marcus, *Minders of Make-Believe: Idealists, Entrepreneurs, and the Shaping of American Children's Literature* (Boston: Houghton-Mifflin, 2008). For an account of related corporate dominance in the production of children's books more recently, see Joel Taxel, "The Economics of Children's Book Publishing in the 21st Century," in S. Wolf, K. Coats, P. Enciso, and C. Jenkins, eds., *Handbook of Research on Children's and Young Adult Literature* (New York: Routledge, 2010), 479–494.

119. Kristin Hunter qtd. in "Currents," 17.

120. See Hinderer, "Talking to Children about Race."

Chapter 4. What Was Postwar American Culture?

1. Almost every critically and commercially successful Black author during this period was personally acquainted with related horrors and brutal injustices fueled by anti-Communism. Literary scholar William Maxwell has recently obtained FBI files for fifty-one Black authors from this period. Of those, twelve of these files, or 23 percent, were "devoted to women." Maxwell, *F.B. Eyes: How J. Edgar Hoover's Ghostreaders Framed African American Literature* (Princeton, NJ: Princeton University Press, 2015), 11–14.

2. For a recent collection of essays revisiting understudied literary output by marginalized groups in this decade, see Josh Lukin, ed., *Invisible Suburbs: Recovering Protest Fiction in the 1950s United States* (Jackson: University of Mississippi Press, 2008).

3. Bayard Rustin qtd. in Elton Fax, *Contemporary Black Leaders* (New York: Dodd, Mead & Company, 1970), 21.

4. For recent scholarship tracing changes in the categorization of African American writing, including the uptick in "white-life" novels after World War II, see Gene Andrew Jarrett, *Representing the Race: A New Political History of African American Literature* (New York: New York University Press, 2011); Gene Andrew Jarrett, *Deans and Truants: Race and Realism in African American Literature* (Philadelphia: University of Pennsylvania Press, 2008); John C. Charles, *Abandoning the Black Hero: Sympathy and Privacy in the Postwar African American White-Life Novel* (New Brunswick, NJ: Rutgers University Press, 2013); Stephanie Li, *Playing in the White: Black Writers, White Subjects* (Oxford: Oxford University Press, 2013).

5. Blyden Jackson's reflections on this turn to penning children's books is noteworthy for its equivocation on how important this work was. "Langston Hughes and Arna Bontemps have contented themselves, it is true, with juveniles, Hughes producing two within the year, but both of them are writing respectable juveniles. Frank Yerby has written a juvenile also, along with his

ninth novel." Jackson, "The Blithe Newcomers, Resume of Negro Literature in 1954: Part I," *Phylon* 16, no. 1 (1955): 8.

6. "The New Look in Paperback Covers," *Publishers' Weekly* 168, no. 13 (September 24, 1955): 1493.

7. John Oliver Killens qtd. in Keith Gilyard, *John Oliver Killens: A Life of Black Literary Activism* (Athens: University of Georgia Press, 2010), 149.

8. Gilyard, *John Oliver Killens*, 149.

9. Ibid. Other writers Gilyard cites as examples of Black authors Killens had in mind include Loften Mitchell, William Branch, Paule Marshall, Pauli Murray, Lorenz Graham, Frank London Brown, and Louis Peterson.

10. Ralph Ellison's *Invisible Man* (New York: Random House, 1952) may be an outlier in this respect. See Arnold Rampersad, *Ralph Ellison: A Biography* (New York: Knopf, 2007); Lawrence P. Jackson, *Ralph Ellison: Emergence of Genius* (New York: Wiley, 2002). Lawrence P. Jackson's other scholarship on this period is widely recognized for offering an expansive sense of Black literary output prior to the 1960s. See Jackson, *The Indignant Generation: A Narrative History of African American Writers and Critics, 1934–1960* (Princeton, NJ: Princeton University Press, 2011).

11. Designs by the acclaimed Black architect Paul Williams reflect similar racial ambiguities. See Karen E. Hudson, *Paul R. Williams, Architect: A Legacy of Style* (New York: Rizzoli, 1994).

12. As contemporary discourse and debates over several Black-authored books published after World War II suggest, American writers defied popular conceptions of what constituted "Negro literature" in a quantity that had not been seen since the 1910s. The books that follow represent just a sample of fictional and nonfictional works challenging contemporaries who categorized "Negro literature" as distinct, or separate, from "American" literature: Margaret Halsey, *Color Blind: A White Woman Looks at the Negro* (New York: Simon and Schuster, 1946), a book banned by the Georgia Board of Education in 1955 for not being "in accord with the Southern way of life"; Willard Motley, *We Fished All Night* (New York: Appleton, 1951) and *Let No Man Write My Epitaph* (New York: Random House, 1958); Ann Petry, *Country Place* (Boston: Houghton, 1947); Dorothy West, *The Living Is Easy* (Boston: Houghton, 1948); Zora Neale Hurston, *Seraph on the Suwanee* (New York: Charles Scribner's Sons, 1948); Chester Himes, *Cast the First Stone* (New York: Coward-McCann, 1952); Richard Wright, *Savage Holiday* (New York: Avon, 1954); James Baldwin, *Giovanni's Room* (New York: Dial, 1956); and Frank Yerby's third and fourth novels, *Golden Hawk* (New York: Dial, 1948) and *Pride's Castle* (New York: Dial, 1949). In a famous essay, Nick Aaron Ford described these two novels as Yerby's first books to "completely ignore the racial angle." Ford, "A Blueprint for Negro Authors," *Phylon* 11, no. 4 (1950): 375.

13. "The Negro in American Culture," WBAI radio panel, 1961, moderated by Nat Hentoff; other participants included Langston Hughes, Emile Capouya, Lorraine Hansberry, Alfred Kazin, and James Baldwin.

14. For an important study of how formidable African American contributions were in this period, see Waldo Martin, *No Coward Soldiers: Black Cultural Politics and Postwar America* (Cambridge, MA: Harvard University Press, 2005).

15. In recent years, scholarship on this period has tended to emphasize either the comparative or the international experiences and influence of canonical Black authors and cultural

professionals. See, for example, Gerald Horne, *Black and Red: W.E.B. Du Bois and the Afro-American. Response to the Cold War, 1944–1963* (Albany: State University of New York Press, 1986); Penny Von Eschen, *Race against Empire: Black Americans and Anticolonialism, 1937–1957* (Ithaca, NY: Cornell University Press, 1997); Mary Dudziak, *Cold War, Civil Rights: Race and the Image of American Democracy* (Princeton, NJ: Princeton University Press, 2000); Howard Winant, *The World Is a Ghetto: Race and Democracy since World War II* (New York: Basic Books, 2001); Thomas Borstelmann, *The Cold War and the Color Line: American Race Relations in the Global Arena* (Cambridge: Cambridge University Press, 2001); Carol Anderson, *Eyes Off the Prize: The United Nations and the African American Struggle for Human Rights, 1944–1955* (New York: Cambridge University Press, 2003); Penny Von Eschen, *Satchmo Blows Up the World: Jazz Ambassadors Play the Cold War* (Cambridge, MA: Harvard University Press, 2004); Greg Barnhisel, *Cold War Modernists: Art, Literature, and American Cultural Diplomacy* (New York: Columbia University Press, 2015).

16. "Let's Look and Listen," *Atlanta Daily World*, November 20, 1952, 3.

17. Malcolm Nash, "Our Authors Surmounting Barriers, Yerby in Lead: Negro Authors First Critics of Bigotry," *New York Amsterdam News*, July 3, 1954, 16.

18. Thomas D. Jarrett, "Recent Fiction by Negroes," *The English Journal* 43, no. 8 (November 1954): 425.

19. As a result, white collaborators and interlocutors were often crucial in brokering professional connections and relationships beyond African American communities. Haywood Patterson and Earl Conrad's *Scottsboro Boy* (New York: Bantam Books, 1951 [1950]) is just one of countless variations on progressive interracial initiatives in this era.

20. For investigation of the possibilities and constraints imposed on Black authors and other intellectuals in the early Cold War years, see Ross Posnock, *Color and Culture: Black Writers and the Making of the Modern Intellectual* (Cambridge, MA: Harvard University Press, 2000); Richard King, *Race, Culture, and the Intellectuals, 1940–1970* (Baltimore, MD: Johns Hopkins University Press, 2004).

21. Langston Hughes, ed., *The Best Short Stories by Negro Writers* (Boston: Little, Brown and Company, 1967), xiii.

22. "One for the Books," *Ebony* 1, no. 7 (May 1946): 47.

23. Laura Hobson, "Trade Winds," *Saturday Review*, August 15, 1953, 6.

24. "How Successful Are Lady Authors?" *Jet*, October 13, 1955, 46.

25. Paula Rabinowitz, *American Pulp: How Paperbacks Brought Modernism to Main Street* (Princeton, NJ: Princeton University Press, 2014), 37.

26. David Dempsey, "In and Out of Books," *New York Times*, January 20, 1952, BR8.

27. Frank L. Schick, *The Paperbound Book in America: The History of Paperbacks and Their European Backgrounds* (New York: R. R. Bowker, 1958), 77.

28. Thomas L. Bonn, "Elements of Success," *Paperback Quarterly* 4, no. 4 (Winter 1981): 37.

29. "You Meet Such Interesting People," *Publishers' Weekly* 153, no. 21 (May 22, 1948): 2169.

30. Martin listed several cities where "VendAvon" book dispensers were available, including New York, Boston, Washington, D.C., and Tucson. The machines held somewhere between four and six hundred books and approximately twenty-four different titles. Martin also noted that VendAvon was "installed on ferryboats, airports, super markets, motion picture lounges,

hospitals, luncheonettes, and military posts." Gertrude Martin, "Book Reviews," *The Chicago Defender*, March 17, 1951, 7.

31. Ibid. Martin also announced that a number of Black authors had recently been published in cheap paperback edition, and not just by Avon. "Three of Mr. Yerby's four novels are now in 25c editions and currently available which is certainly unusual. Another author with three works being displayed in the cheaper editions is Richard Wright who is represented by 'Native Son,' 'Black Boy,' and 'Uncle Tom's Children.'"

32. The functionality and progress this heralded arguably correspond with the vitality of American cities historian Michael Johns has outlined in a revisionist assessment of the 1950s. Johns, *Moment of Grace: The American City in the 1950s* (Berkeley: University of California Press, 2003).

33. "Shop Talk," *Publishers' Weekly* 156, no. 19 (November 5, 1949): 1997.

34. Ibid.

35. Pettis Perry qtd. in "Hugh Gordon Book Shop Opening Celebrated," *The California Eagle* [Los Angeles, CA], July 8, 1948, 6.

36. Adele Young qtd. in "Favorite Sayings," *The Pittsburgh Courier*, December 4, 1954, 15.

37. Matthew Delmont's study of Philadelphia in the 1950s offers a sense of how formative local situations are for understanding intersections between culture and civil rights. Delmont, *The Nicest Kids in Town: American Bandstand, Rock 'n' Roll, and the Struggle for Civil Rights in 1950s Philadelphia* (Berkeley: University of California Press, 2012).

38. "New Shop," *Publishers' Weekly* 154, no. 3 (July 17, 1948): 224.

39. Deaderick Jenkins, *It Was Not My World: A Novel to End All Novels* (Los Angeles: self-published, 1942); Paul Williams, *The Small Home of Tomorrow* (Hollywood, CA: Murray & Gee, 1945); Paul Williams, *New Homes for Today* (Hollywood, CA: Murray & Gee, 1946); Deaderick Jenkins, *Letters to My Son* (Los Angeles: Deaderick F. Jenkins Publishing, 1947); Buddy Green and Steve Murdock, *The Jerry Newson Story* (Berkeley, CA: East Bay Civil Rights Congress, 1950). Suggesting how nationally prominent these California titles once were, the cover of James Baldwin's *Notes of a Native Son* (Boston: Beacon Press, 1955) is surely a copy of the template popularized years earlier by Green and Murdock's pamphlet, *The Jerry Newsom Story*. James Baldwin's "Letter to My Nephew," published in *The Fire Next Time* (New York: Dial Press, 1963), may also be a reference to Jenkins's *Letters to My Son*.

40. For a sense of how prominent they were as "Freedom of the Press" activists in the Bay Area in the early 1950s, see "Daily Knave," *Oakland Tribune*, August 11, 1952, 1. For a summary of Newsom's legal problems, see "Parole Denied Jerry Newsom," *The San Francisco Examiner*, December 4, 1952, 49.

41. "Doomed Prisoner: 3 Authors Write [Wesley Robert] Wells' Life Story," *Pittsburg Courier*, January 13, 1951, 10.

42. The Children's Book Council had agreed "to co-sponsor the fair by supplying an exhibit of 1,000 books for children." Also supportive of Bowles's endeavor were seventeen out of twenty-four publishers "of adult books" she had contacted, who sent books based on her requests for representation from a mix of publishing houses. Bowles argued that all families needed the intellectual, cultural, and social support fairs could provide. She offered Hampton's telephone directory as proof of the insufficiency in regional literary resources: There were "only two book dealers," and "both specializ[ed] in religious books." Minnie Redmond Bowles,

"A College-Community Book Fair and a Resulting Proposal," *Publisher's Weekly*, July 30, 1956, 466–469, preserved in Box 9, Folder 6, Muriel Fuller Papers, Archives and Special Collections, Hunter College Libraries, Hunter College of the City University of New York, New York City.

43. Ibid.

44. "Wide Publicity, Sales Rise Resulted from Book Week," *Publishers' Weekly* 169, no. 1 (January 7, 1956): 29.

45. A small representative sample of titles from different literary genres published by regional publishing houses includes Mae Gleaton Shokunbi, *Songs of the Soul* (Philadelphia: Dorrance & Co., 1945); Mae Gleaton Shokunbi, *Mother Nature Wins: An Operetta for Children in Two Acts* (Philadelphia: Theodore Presser Co., 1946); Harry Washington Greene, *Holders of Doctorates among American Negroes: An Educational and Social Study of Negroes Who Have Earned Doctoral Degrees in Course, 1876–1943* (Boston: Meador, 1946); Arthur Furr, *Democracy's Negroes: A Books of Facts Concerning the Activities of Negroes in World War II* (Boston: House of Edinboro, 1947); Idabelle Yeiser, *Lyric and Legend* (Boston: Christopher Publishing House, 1947); Edwin Bancroft Henderson, *The Negro in Sports* (Washington, DC: Associated Publishers, 1949); John Sinclair Perry, *Voice of Humanity: Song of the New World* (Boston: Christopher Publishing House, 1952); John Wesley Groves, *Pyrrhic Victory, a Collection of Short Stories* (Philadelphia: United, 1953); Florenz Hough, *Black Paradise* (Philadelphia: Dorrance, 1953); Anne Scott, *Case 999—A Christmas Story* (Boston: Meador, 1953); Herman Dreer, *The Tie that Binds: A Novel of a Youth Who Seeks to Understand Life* (Boston: Meador, 1958); Jack Calvert Walls, *Out of the Deep* (Boston: Christopher Publishing House, 1958); Estelle Atley Eaton, *Out of My Dreams and Other Verses* (Boston: Christopher Publishing House, 1959).

46. Several publishers in New York published Black-authored books between World War II and 1960, including Ace, Beacon, Universal, New Voices, Wendell Malliet & Company, Coward-McCann, Franklin Watts, William-Frederick Press, A. A. Wyn, Exposition Press, Great-Concord, Pageant Press, Burdge, Comet Press, Troubador, Vantage Press, Rinehart & Company, Mainstream, Lion, Schulte Company, Vanguard, and Ziff Davis Publishing Company.

47. Edward Uhlan, *The Rogue of Publisher's Row: Confessions of a Publisher* (New York: Exposition Press, 1956), 205.

48. "Good Books," *The Pittsburgh Courier*, June 9, 1956, 8.

49. Uhlan, *Rogue of Publisher's Row*, 76.

50. John W. Parker, "The Adventures of an Easy-Going Black Woman," *The Journal of Negro Education* 24, no. 4 (Autumn 1955): 456.

51. Noting that "big" and "really popular novelists" such as Hemingway, Faulkner, and Yerby had escaped the acuity of the industry's consolidation because of their ability to keep publishing hardback fiction, one publisher, Simon Michael Bessie, cautioned in 1958 that he was much less optimistic for "middling novelists." Bessie, "American Writing Today: A Publisher's Viewpoint," *The Virginia Quarterly Review* 34, no. 1 (Winter 1958): 16–17.

52. "Frank Yerby Named Most Noted Author," *Atlanta Daily World*, August 1, 1952, 1.

53. Frank Yerby qtd. in Dempsey, "In and Out of Books," BR8.

54. Frank Yerby qtd. in "The Week's Census: World Mourns Death of Richard Wright," *Jet* 19, no. 8 (December 15, 1960): 18.

55. Chester Himes qtd. in Michel Fabre and Robert Skinner, eds., *Conversations with Chester Himes* (Jackson: University Press of Mississippi, 1995), 21.

56. "Notes about Writers and Writing," *Negro Digest* 13, no. 8 (June 1964): 50.

57. Chester Himes to Marcel Duhamel, July 19, 1955, Box 1, Chester Himes Papers, Amistad Research Center, Tulane University, New Orleans.

58. Lisa Rosset, *James Baldwin* (New York: Chelsea House, 1989), 78–79.

59. James H. Silberman, "Dial to Publish New James Baldwin Novel," September 20, 1956, Box 1, Folder 5, Dial Press Records, Beinecke Rare Book and Manuscript Library, Collection of American Literature, Yale University.

60. Trudier Harris, ed., *New Essays on "Go Tell It on the Mountain"* (Cambridge: Cambridge University Press, 1996), 9.

61. Paul S. Nathan, "Books into Films," *Publishers' Weekly* 161, no. 18 (May 3, 1952): 1867.

62. In 1966, Fern Marja Eckman described Baldwin as being "hurled" into a depression by warnings from American publishers that *Giovanni's Room*'s queer theme would ruin his reputation. After it was rejected by multiple publishers because of the novel's explicit queer plot, Dial accepted *Giovanni's Room* and offered Baldwin a contract for *Another Country* (1962) at the same time. Baldwin was particularly irked by the fact that his agent, Helen Strauss, only secured a $2,000 advance from Dial for these two books. Eight years later, when Dial offered Norman Mailer a $125,000 advance, Baldwin fumed: "Don't talk to me about it! That's *my* money!" Eckman, *The Furious Passage of James Baldwin* (New York: M. Evans & Company, 1966), 138.

63. James Baldwin qtd. in Marlon Ross, "White Fantasies of Desire: Baldwin and Racial Identities of Sexuality," in Dwight McBride, ed., *James Baldwin Now* (New York: New York University Press, 1999), 15.

64. L. D. Reddick, "No Kafka in the South," *Phylon* 11, no. 4 (1950): 383.

65. Joseph Henry, "Trends of Negro Thought" (Ph.D. dissertation, Allen University, 1952), 2.

66. For a discussion of Ellison's *Invisible Man* as a contribution to a longer corpus of social thought outlining social alienation, universalism, and the "prospects for social cohesion" and "the possibilities of freedom," see Randal Doane, "Ralph Ellison's Sociological Imagination," *The Sociological Quarterly* 45, no. 1 (Winter 2004): 161–184.

67. Ralph Ellison to Albert Murray, April 9, 1953, in John F. Callahan and Marc C. Conner, eds., *The Selected Letters of Ralph Ellison* (New York: Random House, 2019), 322.

68. Extracts from Ralph Ellison's National Book Award acceptance speech on January 27, 1953, were published in *The Crisis* as "Light on 'Invisible Man,'" *Crisis* 60, no. 3 (March 1953): 157–158.

69. It is also notable how neatly Ellison's slightly veiled references to the African American literary field in this speech align with James Baldwin's infamous attack on "protest" novels in the late 1940s. Baldwin, "Everybody's Protest Novel," *Zero*, Spring 1949, 54–58.

70. Alfred Chester and Vilma Howard, "The Art of Fiction: An Interview," *Paris Review*, Spring 1955, reprinted in Maryemma Graham and Amritjit Singh, eds., *Conversations with Ralph Ellison* (Jackson: University Press of Mississippi, 1995), 11.

71. Ralph Ellison to Stanley Hyman, May 29, 1970, in Callahan and Conner, *Selected Letters of Ralph Ellison*, 681.

72. Harvest Breit, "Talk with Frank Yerby," *New York Times*, May 13, 1951, BR11.

73. Elizabeth Lawrence to Gwendolyn Brooks, March 15, 1946, Container 1, Folder 34, Gwendolyn Brooks Papers, Bancroft Library, University of California, Berkeley (hereafter GBP).

74. Elizabeth Lawrence to Gwendolyn Brooks, January 5, 1953, Container 1, Folder 34, GBP.

75. Gwendolyn Brooks qtd. in George Kent, *A Life of Gwendolyn Brooks* (Lexington: University Press of Kentucky, 1990), 176.

76. Jacqueline Goldsby, "'Something Is Said in the Silences': Gwendolyn Brooks's Years at Harper's," *American Literary History* 33, no. 2 (Summer 2021): 245.

77. Brooks's professional trajectory here and in later years was somewhat typical for the cohort of leading Black authors of this generation. Brooks's first position as a professional writer was as a book reviewer for *Negro Digest*. By the end of the 1940s, she became a regular contributor to the *Chicago Daily News* and the *Chicago Sun-Times* since 1948. Demand for her professional contributions increased exponentially over the 1950s and 1960s.

78. Nora Brooks Blakely, "Annie and Gwen's Pulitzer," *Ebony Jr.*, May 1983, 43.

79. Arthur Youngberg to Gwendolyn Brooks, June 12, 1958, Container 1, Folder 24, GBP.

80. Amy Absher, *The Black Musician and the White City: Race and Music in Chicago, 1900–1967* (Ann Arbor: University of Michigan Press, 2014), 140.

81. Scholarship regularly posits that "conservatism" constrained Brooks and other modernist authors who found space in the mainstream in the 1950s. See, for example, Alan Filreis, *Counterrevolution of the Word: The Conservative Attack on Modern Poetry, 1945–1960* (Durham: University of North Carolina Press, 2007).

82. John S. Lash, "What Is 'Negro Literature'?" *College English* 9, no. 1 (October 1947): 42.

83. "Negro Novelist to Talk at University," *Chicago Tribune*, May 16, 1948, 14.

84. Chester Himes qtd. in James Sallis, *Chester Himes: A Life* (Edinburgh: Payback Press, 2000), 152.

85. For a concise overview of this history, see LeRoy Ashby, "Building a Wartime Consensus in the 1940s and 1950s," in *With Amusement for All: A History of American Popular Culture since 1830* (Lexington: University Press of Kentucky, 2006), 265–301.

86. Henry F. Winslow, "Church Sermon," *The Crisis* 60, no. 10 (December 1953): 637–638.

87. "Book of the Week," *Jet*, May 21, 1953, 50.

88. Qtd. in Thadious M. Davis, *Southscapes: Geographies of Race, Region, and Literature* (Chapel Hill: University of North Carolina Press, 2011), 52.

89. Davis, *Southscapes*, 52.

90. Muriel Fuller to Florence, November 25, 1954, Box 17, Folder 13, Muriel Fuller Papers, Archives and Special Collections, Hunter College Libraries, Hunter College of the City University of New York, New York City.

91. Alain Locke, "The High Price of Integration: A Review of the Literature of the Negro for 1951," *Phylon* 13, no. 1 (1952): 7–18.

92. Alain Locke, "From *Native Son* to *Invisible Man*: A Review of the Literature of the Negro for 1952," *Phylon* 14, no. 1 (1953): 35.

93. Ibid., 39.

94. "Alain Locke Books Set for Publication in '56," *Jet*, August 4, 1955, 49.

95. This address was published two years later as William Stanley Braithwaite, "Alain Locke's Relationship to the Negro in American Literature," *Phylon Quarterly* 18, no. 2 (1957): 166.

96. Ibid., 168.

97. Ibid., 173.

98. After the war, multiple generations of professional African Americans that might otherwise have been subjected to either Jim Crow or Cold War politics stayed abroad as long as they

could. See Arthur Redding, "What's Black and White and Red All Over? The Cold War and the Geopolitics of Race," in *Turncoats, Traitors, and Fellow Travelers: Culture and Politics of the Early Cold War* (Jackson: University of Mississippi Press, 2012), 57–78.

99. See, for example, Oliver Harrington and M. Thomas Inge, *Why I Left America, and Other Essays* (Jackson: University Press of Mississippi, 1993). For a discussion of a cohort of Black artists and intellectuals who strategically engaged the U.S. government in this era, see Tony Perucci, *Paul Robeson and the Cold War Performance Complex: Race, Madness, Activism* (Ann Arbor: University of Michigan Press, 2012), 41–45.

100. The most developed body of scholarship on this history has focused primarily on France. For important examples of this scholarship, see Michel Fabre, *Black American Writers in France, 1840–1980* (Champaign: University of Illinois Press, 1993); James Campbell, *Exiled in Paris: Richard Wright, James Baldwin, Samuel Beckett, and Others on the Left* (Berkeley: University of California Press, 1995); Tyler Stovall, *Paris Noir, African Americans in the City of Light* (Boston: Houghton Mifflin, 1996).

101. Gibson's insistence that several leading Black authors were resident in Europe "mainly because of the social and political [problems] which everyone knows" is an important reminder of the unequal access to professional opportunities for Black intellectuals due to a mix of racial prejudices, Jim Crow, and Cold War hysteria, which were by no stretch insignificant factors for those who expatriated in this era. Richard Gibson qtd. in Jackson, *Indignant Generation*, 471. Gibson's critique of this "white-collar" employment corresponds with Andrew Hoberek's analysis of Ralph Ellison's *Invisible Man* as a critique of these enterprises. See Hoberek, "Race Man, Organization Man, *Invisible Man*," in *The Twilight of the Middle Class: Post–World War II American Fiction and White-Collar Work* (Princeton, NJ: Princeton University Press, 2005), 53–69.

102. George Lipsitz argues that "the racialized nature of social democratic policies in the United States since the Great Depression has, in my judgement, actually increased the possessive investment in whiteness among European Americans among European Americans over the past half-century." Lipsitz, "The Possessive Investment in Whiteness: Racialized Social Democracy and the 'White' Problem in American Studies," *American Quarterly* 47, no. 3 (September 1995): 372. For a monograph-length survey of this topic, see Lipsitz, *The Possessive Investment in Whiteness: How White People Profit from Identity Politics* (Philadelphia: Temple University Press, 1998).

103. Brenda Gayle Plummer, *Rising Wind: Black Americans and U.S. Foreign Affairs, 1935–1960* (Chapel Hill: University of North Carolina Press, 1996); Michael Krenn, *Black Diplomacy: African Americans and the State Department, 1945–1969* (Armonk, NY: M. E. Sharpe, 1998).

104. Jonathan Shandell, *The American Negro Theatre and the Long Civil Rights Era* (Iowa City: University of Iowa Press, 2018); Julie Burrell, *The Civil Rights Theatre Movement in New York, 1939–1966* (New York: Palgrave, 2019).

105. For a broader overview of Black activism in the theatrical field, see Glenda Eloise Gill, *No Surrender! No Retreat! African-American Pioneer Performers of Twentieth-Century American Theater* (New York: St. Martin's Press, 2000).

106. Related accusations were by no means limited to African Americans. For studies tracing how progressive American authors from a variety of backgrounds were ensnared by surveillance directed by the federal government in this period, see Herbert Mitgang, *Dangerous Dossiers: Exposing the Secret War against America's Greatest Authors* (New York: D. I. Fine, 1988); Natalie

Robins, *Alien Ink: The FBI's War on Freedom of Expression* (New Brunswick, NJ: Rutgers University Press, 1993); David Johnson, *The Lavender Scare: The Cold War Persecution of Gays and Lesbians in the Federal Government* (Chicago: University of Chicago Press, 2004); Claire A. Culleton and Karen Leick, eds., *Modernism on File: Writers, Artists, and the FBI, 1920–1950* (New York: Palgrave, 2008); Frances Stonor Saunders, *The Cultural Cold War: The CIA and the World of Arts and Letters* (New York: The New Press, 2013).

107. Ernest Crichlow to W.E.B. Du Bois, October 10, 1952, W.E.B. Du Bois Papers (MS 312), Special Collections and University Archives, University of Massachusetts Amherst Libraries.

108. Slogan printed on an invitation to a benefit gala hosted by the Round-Up Committee and the American Negro Theatre, to be held on April 22, 1945, preserved in Box 2, Folder 27, James Baldwin Early Manuscripts and Papers, James Weldon Johnson Collection in the Yale Collection of American Literature, Beinecke Rare Book and Manuscript Library, Yale University.

109. Gladys P. Graham, "It Happened in New York," *Alabama Tribune*, January 30, 1948, 4.

110. See Frederick Woltman, "Here's Complete List of 97 Communist Fronts," *The Pittsburgh Press*, February 1, 1948, 13.

111. "Circular Letter from Committee for the Negro in the Arts," June 17, 1949, W.E.B. Du Bois Papers (MS 312), Special Collections and University Archives, University of Massachusetts Amherst Libraries.

112. At the time, the group's interracialism and attempts to encourage integration were not entirely ignored. In 1949, one CNA-sponsored conference was described by New York's *Daily News* as an "interracial conference on 'Radio, Television and the Negro People.'" The CNA was reported to have revealed "that there are only six Negro engineers in all radio; six Negro writers and only one full time; six Negro announcers and a few Negro actors." Sid Shalit, "Looking and Listening," *Daily News* [New York], July 5, 1949, 43.

113. "Young Concert Artists on History Week Show," *Pittsburgh Courier*, February 14, 1948, 15.

114. In 1951 the *Pittsburgh Courier* reported that the CNA's initial plan to sponsor a workshop was intended as a corrective to racial prejudices and biases in corporate publishing: "The committee feels that there are many young Negro writers whose material may better express the life of the Negro in America which has heretofore [been] written mostly by whites." "Scribblers' Workshop Set," *Pittsburgh Courier*, October 27, 1951, 16.

115. Ruth Jett qtd. in "Literary Chapter Newest on Agenda," *New York Age*, June 17, 1950, 5.

116. Mary Helen Washington, *The Other Black List: The African American Literary and Cultural Left of the 1950s* (New York: Columbia University Press, 2014), 90.

117. John O. Killens, "Who Needs It: The Black Culture Generation Gap," *Black World* 22, no. 10 (August 1973): 33.

118. Because the CNA functioned as an umbrella organization, each field was organized further under its own group, or "workshop." The "Harlem Writers' Workshop" of the YMCA and the CNA first joined forces at the end of 1948. The former group started advertising its programming at the beginning of 1949. At the end of 1950, the *New York Age* announced that the group had changed its name to "Scriven Echo" and was meeting at the YMCA on Wednesdays. By early 1955, the group was known as the Harlem Writers' Workshop once again. "Johnny Gotham's New York Beat," *New York Age*, December 9, 1950, 10.

119. William Maxwell has discussed how Hansberry, Alice Childress, and Julian Mayfield were monitored by the federal government, independent of their connections to the CNA. See

Maxwell, "Total Literary Awareness: Why Cold War Hooverism Pre-read Afro-Modernist Writing," in Steven Belletto and Daniel Grausam, eds., *American Literature and Culture in an Age of Cold War: A Critical Reassessment* (Iowa City: Iowa University Press, 2012), 24–28.

120. Walter Forsberg, "Red Star/Black Star: The Early Career of Film Editor Hortense 'Tee' Beveridge, 1948–1968," in Allyson Nadia Field and Marsha Gordon, eds., *Screening Race in American Nontheatrical Film* (Durham, NC: Duke University Press, 2019), 116.

121. Julian Mayfield offered the following description of the CNA in the early 1950s. Mayfield described the group's members as having "social and political responsibilities" to one another, as "honorable men and women who [had] banded together in a common struggle." Julian Mayfield to Louis, November 17, 1953, Box 7, Folder 1, Julian Mayfield Papers, Schomburg Center for Research in Black Culture, New York Public Library (hereafter JMP).

122. Julian Mayfield to John Farrar, June 10, 1954, Box 7, Folder 1, JMP.

123. Three years earlier, Owen Dodson's *Boy at the Window* (1951) was published as a hardcover with Farrar. The same year this now-venerable firm published Dodson's hardcover book, his novel was also published as a Popular Library paperback under a new title, *When Trees Were Green* (1951).

124. Julian Mayfield, "A Challenge to a Bestseller: Crisis or Crusade," *Negro Digest* 17, no. 8 (June 1968): 19.

125. Julian Mayfield to Charlie, July 28, 1953, Box 7, Folder 1, JMP.

126. Jackson, *Indignant Generation*, 311.

127. Brian Dolinar, *The Black Cultural Front: Black Writers and Artists of the Depression Generation* (Jackson: University Press of Mississippi, 2012), 66–67.

128. Mayfield, "Challenge to a Bestseller," 18.

129. William Branch summarized and provided excerpts of the letter he received from this white woman in a letter to Hansberry. William Branch to Lorraine Hansberry, January 16, 1952, Box 63, Folder 15, Lorraine Hansberry Papers, Schomburg Center for Research in Black Culture, New York Public Library (hereafter LHP).

130. Poking fun at the New York publishing house Scribner in what was likely a reference to white patrons and patronage, a letter to the *New York Age* from "Charles Scribner" decried the fact that white attendees outnumbered Blacks at the CNA-sponsored event this Black theater patron had recently attended. Charles Scribner, "Asks Support," *New York Age*, February 9, 1952, 11.

131. Edward Murrain, "Front and Center," *New York Age*, January 30, 1954, 9.

132. For an overview of Childress's legacy and an important sample of these texts, see Kathy Perkins's "Introduction," in Perkins, ed., *Selected Plays: Alice Childress* (Evanston, IL: Northwestern University Press, 2011), ix–xxxv.

133. John G. Rideout to Alice Childress, November 17, 1955, Box 10, Folder 1, Alice Childress Papers, Schomburg Center for Research in Black Culture, New York Public Library (hereafter ACP).

134. James O. Hopson to Alice Childress, February 17, 1956, Box 10, Folder 1, ACP.

135. Alice Childress qtd. in "A Survey: Black Writers' Views on Literary Lions and Values," *Negro Digest* 17, no. 3 (January 1968): 86.

136. Marcia Stephen to Alice Childress, September 13, 1956, Box 10, Folder 1, ACP.

137. Indeed, rather than perceiving their mastery of classics as an elite exercise, members of Negro Actors Associated performed these works virtually anywhere in their efforts to reach new audiences. "We began by playing in Parks, Halls, lawns, or in any place that would provide

us with the space because we were interested in 'bringing theatre to the people.'" Mae Henderson to Alice Childress, May 2, 1956, Box 10, Folder 1, ACP.

138. While Henderson's group wanted to "do a play about Negro life" such as Childress's *Trouble in Mind*, up to that point its members had little choice but to perform texts such as Sophocles's *Oedipus Rex* (429 B.C.) and Shakespeare's *Macbeth* (1606). While canonical Western texts like these had affirmed the "merit [of the NAA] as an outstanding theatre group," the "great dearth of scripts, and very few [Black] writers at this time" made it difficult to perform anything else. Ibid.

139. George Platt to Lorraine Hansberry, March 23, 1961, Box 63, Folder 1, LHP.

140. See, for example, Imani Perry, *Looking for Lorraine: The Radiant and Radical Life of Lorraine Hansberry* (Boston: Beacon Press, 2018); Soyica Diggs Colbert, *Radical Vision: A Biography of Lorraine Hansberry* (New Haven, CT: Yale University Press, 2021); Charles J. Shields, *Lorraine Hansberry: The Life behind "A Raisin in the Sun"* (New York: Henry Holt, 2022).

141. "Blind Players to Do 'Raisin in the Sun,'" *New York Amsterdam News*, April 13, 1963, 21, preserved in Box 63, Folder 12, LHP.

142. William Reuben to Lorraine Hansberry, March 20, 1959, Box 63, Folder 3, LHP.

143. Barbara Smith to Lorraine Hansberry, April 28, 1959, Box 64, Folder 5, LHP.

144. Lonnie Coleman to Lorraine Hansberry, no date, Box 63, Folder 15, LHP.

145. Maxwell, *F.B. Eyes*, 9–12.

146. Scholarly references to Moore are remarkably limited, but he was published in a collection of Black poetry in the early 1960s edited by Paul Breman. See Breman, ed., *Sixes and Sevens: An Anthology of New Poetry* (London: Paul Breman, 1962), 71. Also see Paul Breman and Lauri Ramey, eds., *The Heritage Series of Black Poetry, 1962–1975* (Farnham, UK: Ashgate, 2008), 1–17.

147. Willard Moore, "Seeing Me," no date, Box 63, Folder 15, LHP.

148. Julian Mayfield to Lorraine Hansberry, April 7, 1959, Box 63, Folder 15, LHP.

149. Charles H. Nichols Jr., "The Forties: A Decade of Growth," *Phylon* 11, no. 4 (1950): 379–380.

Chapter 5. Toward Disunion

1. Julian Mayfield, "Challenge to Negro Leadership: The Case of Robert F. Williams," *Commentary*, April 1961, 297–305, Box 62, Folder 3, Lorraine Hansberry Papers, Schomburg Center for Research in Black Culture, New York Public Library (hereafter LHP).

2. In the twenty-first century, *Commentary* describes (or advertises) itself "as the flagship of neoconservatism in the 1970's." Qtd. in Sigrid Weigel, *"Escape to Life": German Intellectuals in New York. A Compendium on Exile after 1933* (Berlin: De Gruyter, 2012), 91.

3. John Ehrman, "*Commentary*, the *Public Interest*, and the Problem of Jewish Conservatism," theme issue "American Jewish Conservatism," *American Jewish History* 87, nos. 2/3 (June/September 1999): 161. Also see Jim Willis, *The Mind of a Journalist: How Reporters View Themselves, Their World, and Their Craft* (Thousand Oaks, CA: SAGE Publishing, 2009), 100.

4. For decades, scholarship on *Commentary*'s editors, who are closely associated with the "New York Intellectuals," has tended to emphasize generational rather than interracial tensions in examinations of these men. See, for example, Richard Pells, *The Liberal Mind in a Conservative Age: American Intellectuals in the 1940s and 1950s* (New York: Harper and Row, 1985); Alan Wald,

The New York Intellectuals: The Rise and Decline of the Anti-Stalinist Left from the 1930s to the 1980s (Chapel Hill: University of North Carolina Press, 1987); David Laskin, *Partisans: Marriage, Politics, and Betrayal among the New York Intellectuals* (New York: Simon and Schuster, 2000).

5. For an overview of civil rights coverage in the mainstream press in this period, see Gene Roberts and Hank Klibanoff, *The Race Beat: The Press, the Civil Rights Struggle* (New York: Knopf, 2006).

6. Mayfield, "Challenge to Negro Leadership," 298.

7. Nancy K. Bristow, *Steeped in the Blood of Racism: Black Power, Law and Order, and the 1970 Shootings at Jackson State College* (Oxford: Oxford University Press, 2020), 10.

8. Stokely Carmichael qtd. in Peniel E. Joseph, *Stokely: A Life* (New York: Basic Civitas, 2014), 167.

9. Paul R. Reynolds to Frank S. MacGregor, April 21, 1954, Box 34, Folder: "Wright, Richard April–June 1954," Charles Scribner's Sons Archive, Scribner Room, Department of Rare Books and Special Collections, Firestone Library, Princeton University (hereafter CSS).

10. Paul R. Reynolds to Frank S. MacGregor, April 19, 1954, Box 34, Folder: "Wright, Richard April–June 1954," CSS.

11. Frank MacGregor to Richard Wright, April 23, 1954, Box 34, Folder: "Wright, Richard April–June 1954," CSS.

12. Richard Wright to Frank MacGregor, April 27, 1954, Box 34, Folder: "Wright, Richard April–June 1954," CSS.

13. See, for example, David Chappell, *Inside Agitators: White Southerners in the Civil Rights Movement* (Baltimore, MD: Johns Hopkins University Press, 1994); Tracy Elaine K'Meyer, *Interracialism and Christian Community in the Postwar South: The Story of Koinonia Farm* (Charlottesville: University Press of Virginia, 1997).

14. Jean-Paul Sartre, "For Whom Does One Write?" in *What Is Literature?* trans. Bernard Frechtman (New York: Harper and Row, 1965), 71–74.

15. For a well-known discussion of Jean-Paul Sartre's essay on Richard Wright, within a broader discussion on critical theory and Black texts, see Henry Louis Gates Jr., *Figures in Black: Words, Signs, and the "Racial" Self* (New York: Oxford University Press, 1989), 55–56.

16. For an overview of how Lillian Smith contributed to Southern and national discourses on desegregation, see Ted Ownby, *Hurtin' Words: Debating Family Problems in the Twentieth-Century South* (Chapel Hill: University of North Carolina Press, 2018), 92–103.

17. W. J. Howland, "The South Sees Her Own—Lillian Smith's Contribution," *Vassar Chronicle* 13, no. 3 (October 8, 1955): 3.

18. Charlotte Beck, *Robert Penn Warren, Critic* (Knoxville: University of Tennessee Press, 2006), 100.

19. Robert Penn Warren, "Divided South Searches Its Soul," *Life*, July 9, 1956, 98–114.

20. Letter to Robert Penn Warren, July 10, 1956, Box 22, Folder 425, Robert Penn Warren Papers, Yale Collection of American Literature, Beinecke Rare Book and Manuscript Library, Yale University.

21. Robert Penn Warren to Leonard Casper, September 1, 1958, in Randy Hendricks, James A. Perkins, and William Bedford Clark, eds., *Selected Letters of Robert Penn Warren, vol. 4: New Beginnings and New Directions, 1953–1968* (Baton Rouge: Louisiana State University Press, 2008), 235.

22. See, for example, Aniko Bodroghkozy, "Fighting for Equal Time: Segregationists vs. Integrationists," in *Equal Time: Television and the Civil Rights Movement* (Urbana: University of Illinois Press, 2012), 61–88. For a discussion of Black-led initiatives to desegregate America's culture industry, see Daniel Widener, *Black Arts West: Culture and Struggle in Postwar Los Angeles* (Durham, NC: Duke University Press, 2010).

23. Cross-racial collaborations were by no means always harmonious, but neither were they always negative. See, for example, Nathan Podhoretz, "Liberalism and the Negro: A Round-Table Discussion," *Commentary* 37 (March 1964): 25–42.

24. For recent scholarship on television and the Civil Rights Movement, see Sasha Torres, *Black, White, and in Color: Television and Black Civil Rights* (Princeton, NJ: Princeton University Press, 2003); Bodroghkozy, *Equal Time*.

25. Dennis Powers, "Lorraine Hansberry on 'the Movement,'" *Oakland Tribune*, October 30, 1964, 27.

26. Leonard Lyons, "Best of Broadway," *Philadelphia Inquirer*, March 11, 1964, 32.

27. Richard Avedon qtd. in Joshua L. Miller, "A Striking Addiction to Irreality: *Nothing Personal* and the Legacy of the Photo-Text Genre," in D. Quentin Miller, ed., *Re-viewing James Baldwin: Things Not Seen* (Philadelphia: Temple University Press, 2000), 174.

28. "London Letter: James Baldwin's New Book," *The Guardian* [Manchester, UK], September 4, 1964, 12.

29. Julian Mayfield qtd. in John O'Brien, ed., *Interviews with Black Writers* (New York: Liveright, 1973), 145.

30. Don Edwards, "Propagandist Voices," *Sydney Morning Herald*, June 2, 1962, 15.

31. Calvin C. Hernton, "Blood of the Lamb: The Ordeal of James Baldwin," in John A. Williams and Charles F. Harris, eds., *Amistad 1: Writings on Black History and Culture* (New York: Vintage Books, 1970), 193.

32. For a recent overview of the historical tensions surrounding this "dialogue," see Michael Eric Dyson, *What Truth Sounds Like: Robert F. Kennedy, James Baldwin, and Our Unfinished Conversation about Race in America* (New York: Macmillan, 2018).

33. "Negro Group Claims North Has Problem," *Chattanooga Daily Times*, May 25, 1963, 7.

34. James Baldwin, *The Cross of Redemption: Uncollected Writings*, ed. Randall Kenan (New York: Vintage, 2011), 136.

35. Evan Thomas, one of Robert Kennedy's biographers, explains that in the week after his meetings with Baldwin, Kennedy's Justice Department estimated that more than 750 demonstrations had taken place between May 10, 1963, and the end of July that same year. Thomas, *Robert Kennedy: His Life* (New York: Simon and Schuster, 2000), 243.

36. See, for example, Brittney C. Cooper, "Queering Jane Crow: Pauli Murray's Quest for an Unhyphenated Identity," in *Beyond Respectability: The Intellectual Thought of Race Women* (Urbana: University of Illinois Press, 2017), 87–114; David W. Southern, *John Lafarge and the Limits of Catholic Interracialism, 1911–1963* (Baton Rouge: Louisiana State University Press, 1996).

37. Julius Lester, ed., *The Thought and Writings of W.E.B. Du Bois*, vol. 1 (New York: Random House, 1971), 65.

38. The furor Roosevelt's dinner caused has been documented in a book-length investigation. See Deborah Davis, *Guest of Honor: Booker T. Washington, Theodore Roosevelt, and the White House Dinner that Shocked a Nation* (New York: Atria, 2012).

39. James Baldwin, "Letter from a Region in My Mind," *The New Yorker*, November 17, 1962, 59–144.

40. While Baldwin's novel was framed as a "surrealistically chaotic story of race," this reviewer still maintained that every literate American should read *The Fire Next Time*: "Because of its deadly calm, this book is more eloquent than anything else Baldwin has written. It is not a pleasant thing to read. But by its very candor, it is a book that scarcely can be ignored. Anyone who wants, or tries, to understand our American heritage had better read what Baldwin has to say." Miles A. Smith, "Baldwin at His Most Eloquent," *The Evening Sun* [Hanover, PA], January 31, 1963, 18.

41. Eleanor Roosevelt, "Some of My Best Friends Are Negro," in Era Bell Thompson and Herbert Nipson, eds., *White on Black: The Views of Twenty-Two White Americans on the Negro* (Chicago: Johnson Publishing Company, Inc., 1963), 3–17.

42. For an overview of how the Kennedy family's enormous wealth enabled John F. Kennedy's social habits, see Fredrik Logevall, *JFK: Coming of Age in the American Century, 1917–1956* (New York: Penguin, 2020).

43. James Baldwin, "Lorraine Hansberry at the Summit," *Freedomways* 19, no. 49 (1979): 269.

44. "Robert Kennedy Naïve on Race Question, Negro Writer Says," *St. Louis Post-Dispatch*, May 26, 1963, 2A.

45. In an editorial titled "Naive Attorney General?" the Minneapolis *Star Tribune* rhetorically questioned, "[W]e wonder how much good it does for Negro novelist James Baldwin to label Atty. Gen. Robert F. Kennedy's efforts on the Negroes' behalf naive." "Naive Attorney General?" *Minneapolis Morning Tribune*, May 29, 1963, 4.

46. Arthur M. Schlesinger Jr., *Robert Kennedy and His Times* (Boston: Houghton Mifflin, 1978), 330.

47. Wallace Putnam to Lorraine Hansberry, October 5, 1963, Box 63, Folder 4, LHP.

48. Baldwin, *Cross of Redemption*, 136.

49. Schlesinger, *Robert Kennedy and His Times*, 330–335.

50. Lena Horne, with Richard Schickel, *Lena* (Garden City, NY: Doubleday, 1965), 277.

51. Ibid., 280.

52. Hernton, "Blood of the Lamb," 196.

53. For an overview of these organizations, and recent debates surrounding the parameters of the Civil Rights Movement, see Richard K. Scher, "Unfinished Business: Writing the Civil Rights Movement," in Robert P. Steed and Laurence W. Moreland, eds., *Writing Southern Politics: Contemporary Interpretations and Future Directions* (Lexington: University Press of Kentucky, 2006), 65–90.

54. Chris Matthews, *Bobby Kennedy: A Raging Spirit* (New York: Simon & Schuster, 2017), 242–243.

55. Robert F. Kennedy qtd. in Nicholas Buccola, *The Fire Is upon Us: James Baldwin, William F. Buckley Jr., and the Debate over Race in America* (Princeton, NJ: Princeton University Press, 2019), 184.

56. Lorraine Hansberry qtd. in ibid.

57. Buccola, *Fire Is upon Us*, 184.

58. Robert F. Kennedy qtd. in Baldwin, "Lorraine Hansberry at the Summit," 271.

59. Horne, *Lena*, 278.

60. James Baldwin, "Many Thousands Gone," *Partisan Review* 18 (November–December 1951), reprinted in Baldwin, *Notes of a Native Son* (Boston: Beacon Press, 1955), 28.

61. As Michael Nowlin has recently argued, Richard Wright was Baldwin's forebear among leading Black authors in both admiring and referencing Henry James's work. Nowlin, "Henry James and the Making of Modern African American Literature," *Henry James Review* 39, no. 3 (Fall 2018): 282–292.

62. Çiğdem Üsekes, "James Baldwin and Lorraine Hansberry: Two Revolutionaries, One Heart, One Mind," *Obsidian* 9, no. 2 (Fall/Winter 2008): 13.

63. Lorraine Hansberry, "Life in America: Conversations on a Train," draft, no date, Box 63, Folder 4, LHP.

64. Baldwin, "Lorraine Hansberry at the Summit," 272.

65. Julian Mayfield, "*Lorraine Hansberry*: A Woman for All Seasons," *Freedomways* 19, no. 49 (1979): 267.

66. For a discussion of more than thirty thousand African Americans moving to several white suburbs in the 1960s that were already marked by economic precarity, in a broader study of race and suburbanization, see Andrew Wiese, *Places of Their Own: African American Suburbanization in the Twentieth Century* (Chicago: University of Chicago Press, 2009), 249–254.

67. See, for example, Rachael A. Woldoff, *White Flight/Black Flight: The Dynamics of Racial Change in an American Neighborhood* (Ithaca, NY: Cornell University Press, 2011); Kevin M. Kruse, *White Flight: Atlanta and the Making of Modern Conservatism* (Princeton, NJ: Princeton University Press, 2005).

68. Mayfield, "*Lorraine Hansberry*," 267.

69. Julius Lester, *Look Out Whitey! Black Power's Gon' Get Your Mama!* (New York: Dial, 1968); Leslie Alexander Lacy, *The Rise and Fall of a Proper Negro: An Autobiography* (New York: Macmillan, 1970); Calvin Hernton, *Coming Together: Black Power, White Hatred, and Sexual Hang-Ups* (New York: Random House, 1971).

70. Review: Julius Lester, *Look Out Whitey! Black Power's Gon' Get Your Mama! Publishers' Weekly* 193, no. 20 (May 13, 1968): 55.

71. Paul Reynolds to Jack Fischer, April 30, 1953, Box 34, Folder: "Wright, Richard April–December 1953," CSS.

72. The other manuscript Reynolds and Fischer were referring to was John Gunther's *Inside Africa* (New York: Harper & Brothers, 1955).

73. Editor to Frank Yerby [ca. 1959], Box 53, Frank Yerby Collection, Howard Gotlieb Archival Research Center, Boston University (hereafter FYC).

74. Frank Yerby to Editor [ca. 1959], Box 53, FYC.

75. "Fairoaks Is Typical of Yerby," *The Birmingham News*, September 8, 1957, E7.

76. For discussions of Mailer's essay and its adaptation, see Andrea Levine, "'The (Jewish) White Negro': Norman Mailer's Racial Bodies," *MELUS* 28, no. 2 (Summer 2003): 59–81; Steve Shoemaker, "Norman Mailer's 'White Negro': Historical Myth or Mythical History?" *Twentieth Century Literature* 37, no. 3 (Autumn 1991): 343–360.

77. LeRoi Jones to Lorraine Hansberry, June 23, 1961, Box 63, Folder 15, LHP.

78. Norman Mailer, *The White Negro: Superficial Reflections on the Hipster* (San Francisco: City Lights Books, 1957), unpaginated, sec. IV. Mailer's essay was originally published as "The White Negro," *Dissent*, Summer 1957, 276–293.

79. Mailer, *White Negro*, sec. II.

80. Loraine Hansberry, "The Negro Writer and His Roots: Toward a New Romanticism," *The Black Scholar* 12, no. 2 (March/April 1981): 7.

81. "Explosive Youth: Introduction to a Sit-In," *Look*, January 3, 1961, 36b–36d, preserved in Box 62, Folder 3, LHP.

82. Glenford E. Mitchell and William H. Peace III, eds., *The Angry Black South: Southern Negroes Tell Their Own Story* (New York: Corinth Books, 1962).

83. Theodore Wilentz to Lorraine Hansberry, October 23, 1961, Box 63, Folder 3, LHP.

84. Kenneth Tynan to Lorraine Hansberry, January 18, 1960, Box 63, Folder 4, LHP.

85. Hugh Hefner to Lorraine Hansberry, October 12, 1962, Box 63, Folder 7, LHP.

86. Jane McManus to Lorraine Hansberry, January 28, 1963, Box 63, Folder 8, LHP.

87. Norman Podhoretz, "My Negro Problem—and Ours," *Commentary* 35 (1963): 101, preserved in Box 63, Folder 16, LHP.

88. Norman Podhoretz, "'My Negro Problem—and Ours' at 50," *Commentary*, May 2013, 11.

89. Lorraine Hansberry, "'My Negro Problem'—II," draft, Box 63, Folder 16, LHP.

90. For the most part, Anderson found that *Time* "seemed to be on the side of the angels in most matters that are important to me—race, education, theatre, music, art, medicine, science—and gives marvelous coverage to them." John L. Anderson to Lorraine Hansberry, Letter 1, no date, Box 64, Folder 6, LHP; John L. Anderson to Lorraine Hansberry, Letter 2, February 29, 1964, Box 64, Folder 6, LHP.

91. Helen Strauss to Frank Yerby, April 1964, Box 53, FYC.

92. Frank Yerby to Helen Strauss, ca. April 1964, Box 53, FYC.

93. Blanche Dorsky to Lorraine Hansberry, June 25, 1964, Box 63, Folder 10, LHP.

94. Amiri Baraka qtd. in Mollie Godfrey, ed., *Conversations with Lorraine Hansberry* (Jackson: University Press of Mississippi, 2020), 176–177.

95. Larry Neal, "The Black Arts Movement," *The Drama Review* 12, no. 4 (Summer 1968): 29.

96. LeRoi Jones to Lorraine Hansberry, June 13, 1961, Box 63, Folder 15, LHP.

97. Hettie Jones qtd. in Deborah Thompson, "Keeping Up with the Joneses: The Naming of Racial Identities in the Autobiographical Writings of LeRoi Jones/Amiri Baraka, Hettie Jones, and Lisa Jones," *College Literature* 29, no. 1 (Winter 2002): 83.

98. Jones to Hansberry, June 23, 1961.

99. Ted Wilentz and Bill Zavatsky, "Ahead of the Reader: A Short History of Corinth Books," *TriQuarterly* 43 (Fall 1978): 606–608.

100. Amiri Baraka, "black writing," in *Home: Social Essays* (New York: William Morrow, 1966), 163.

101. James Hill, "Anti-heroic Perspectives: The Life and Works of Frank Yerby" (Ph.D. dissertation, University of Iowa, 1976), 35.

102. Frank Yerby, "Note to the Reader," draft [ca. 1969], Box 53, FYC.

103. Letter to the Editor, *Ebony*, September 1966, 14.

104. For a discussion of the African American critiques of leading Black authors during the Black Power era, see John S. Wright, *Shadowing Ralph Ellison* (Jackson: University of Mississippi Press, 2006), 4–13.

105. Ralph Ellison to Harold Calicutt, February 3, 1971, in John F. Callahan and Marc C. Conner, eds., *The Selected Letters of Ralph Ellison* (New York: Random House, 2019), 690.

106. Qtd. in David Remnick, "Visible Man," *The New Yorker*, March 7, 1994, 36.

107. Gwendolyn Brooks, "And a Gentle Man," *Chicago Daily News*, June 3, 1967, preserved in Oversized Box 3, Gwendolyn Brooks Papers, Bancroft Library, University of California, Berkeley.

108. Frances Ward and Val Gray Ward, "The Black Artist—His Role in the Struggle," *The Black Scholar* 2, no. 5 (January 1971): 26–27, Oversized Box 3, Gwendolyn Brooks Papers, Bancroft Library, University of California, Berkeley.

109. Julian Mayfield to Sandra Drake, October 3, 1971, Box 4, Folder 14, Julian Mayfield Papers, Schomburg Center for Research in Black Culture, New York Public Library (hereafter JMP). If you were "single, [and] young," according to a letter Mayfield sent to another Black academic, John Henrik Clarke, by 1968, Cornell was offering "scholars in African and Afro-American history" residency positions that came with a $10,000 salary. Julian Mayfield to John Henrik Clarke, May 23, 1968, Box 4, Folder 10, JMP.

110. Martha Biondi, *The Black Revolution on Campus* (Berkeley: University of California Press, 2012), 5.

111. Mayfield to Drake, October 3, 1971.

112. Sandra Drake to Julian Mayfield, September 28, 1969, Box 4, Folder 14, JMP.

113. Julian Mayfield to Sandra Drake, no date, Box 4, Folder 14, JMP.

114. John Oliver Killens qtd. in Keith Gilyard, *John Oliver Killens: A Life of Black Literary Activism* (Athens: University of Georgia Press, 2010), 297–298.

115. Julian Mayfield to David Du Bois, August 26, 1970, Box 4, Folder 15, JMP.

116. Ibid.

117. Stokely Carmichael, "The Failure of White Activism," in William S. McConnell, ed., *The 1960s: Great Speeches in History* (San Diego: Greenhaven Press, 2003), 111.

118. "Ginny" to Muriel Fuller, April 26, 1970, Box 20, Folder 7, Muriel Fuller Papers, Archives and Special Collections, Hunter College Libraries, Hunter College of the City University of New York. Ginny's letter also lamented that Yale's "kewpie of a president" and his "sinister trouble-making far-left" chaplain were "doing all they can to help stir up the student body. When do they get an education, I wonder?"

Coda

1. Qtd. in "Dr. Mary McLeod Bethune Was Famous as an Educator and Public Servant," *The Morning Call* [Allentown, PA], February 14, 1964, 15.

2. Kathleen Belew, *Bring the War Home: The White Power Movement and Paramilitary America* (Cambridge, MA: Harvard University Press, 2019).

3. Daniel T. Rodgers, *Age of Fracture* (Cambridge, MA: Harvard University Press, 2011).

4. Julian Mayfield qtd. in John O'Brien, ed., *Interviews with Black Writers* (New York: Liveright, 1973), 146.

5. Toni Cade, ed., *The Black Woman: An Anthology* (New York: New American Library, 1970); Pat Crutchfield Exum, *Keeping the Faith: Writings by Contemporary Black American Women* (New York: Fawcett, 1974); Akasha Gloria Hull, Patricia Bell-Scott, and Barbara Smith, eds., *All the Women Are White, All the Blacks Are Men, but Some of Us Are Brave* (New York: Feminist Press, 1982); Erlene Stetson, ed., *Black Sister: Poetry by American Black Women,*

1746–1980 (Bloomington: Indiana University Press, 1981); Claudia Tate, ed., *Black Women Writers at Work* (New York: Continuum, 1984); Nikki Giovanni and Margaret Walker, *A Poetic Equation: Conversations between Nikki Giovanni and Margaret Walker* (Washington, DC: Howard University Press, 1974); Joanne M. Braxton and Andrée Nicola McLaughlin, eds., *Wild Women in the Whirlwind: Afra-American Culture and the Contemporary Literary Renaissance* (New Brunswick, NJ: Rutgers University Press, 1990).

6. Mary Helen Washington, ed., *Midnight Birds: Stories of Contemporary Black Women Writers* (New York: Anchor Books, 1980), xiii.

7. Ibid., xv.

8. For representative examples of related texts, see, for example, Darwin Turner, *Afro-American Writers* (New York: Appleton-Century-Crofts, 1970); Mel Watkins, ed., *Black Review No. 1* (New York: William Morrow & Company, 1971); Julian Mayfield, ed., *Ten Times Black: Stories from the Black Experience* (New York: Bantam, 1972).

9. Henry Louis Gates Jr. to Chester Himes, 1976, Box 1, Chester Himes Papers, Amistad Research Center, Tulane University, New Orleans.

10. Mary Helen Washington, review: John Hicks, *The Long Whip, Negro Digest* 19, no. 2 (December 1969): 90.

11. Malcolm Nash, "Negro Writers Prove Themselves to Be Outstanding American Novelists," *The Lincoln Clarion*, December 16, 1955, 7.

12. Dial announcement for Frank Yerby's *Jarrett's Jade*, Box 1, Folder 8, Dial Press Records, Beinecke Rare Book and Manuscript Library, Collection of American Literature, Yale University.

13. "The Departed," *Negro Digest* 11, no. 11 (September 1962): 50.

14. Prince E. Wilson, "Great Negroes History Forgot," *Dayton Daily News*, September 2, 1968, 24.

15. Helen M. Strauss, *A Talent for Luck: An Autobiography* (New York: Random House, 1979), 9.

16. Ibid., 72.

17. Jesse McCarthy, "Language and the Black Intellectual Tradition," in *Who Will Pay Reparations on My Soul? Essays* (New York: Liveright, 2021), 146–147.

INDEX

A NOTE ON THE TYPE

This book has been composed in Arno, an Old-style serif typeface in the
classic Venetian tradition, designed by Robert Slimbach at Adobe.